ON PURPOSE

PRACTICAL WISDOM FOR DESIGNING A LIFE OF PURPOSE
INSPIRED BY THE LIFE AND TEACHINGS
OF THE LUBAVITCHER REBBE

MENDEL KALMENSON

&Chabad.ORG

718-735-2000
editor@chabad.org

Published by
EZRA PRESS
770 Eastern Parkway, Brooklyn, New York 11213
718-774-4000 / Fax 718-774-2718
editor@kehot.com

Order Department:
291 Kingston Avenue, Brooklyn, New York 11213
718-778-0226 / Fax 718-778-4148
www.kehot.com

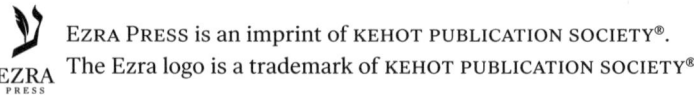

EZRA PRESS is an imprint of KEHOT PUBLICATION SOCIETY®.
The Ezra logo is a trademark of KEHOT PUBLICATION SOCIETY®.

3 5 7 9 11 12 10 8 6 4

ISBN: 978-0-8266-9015-9

Printed in China

A woman of valour who can find!
Her worth is beyond that of pearls.
Proverbs 31:10

———

This book is dedicated
to my dear wife

TANYA

and to the wisdom and care
she surrounds me with

———

Sacha

Dedicated to our dear daughter

CHANA BRACHA

on the occasion of her Bas Mitzvah

———

and to the merit of

MENACHEM
UZIEL
YEHUDAH

———

Lovingly sponsored by

**Yekusiel and Hinda
Kalmenson**

Table of Contents

About The Rebbe

THE REBBE, Rabbi Menachem Mendel Schneerson (1902–1994), of righteous memory, is widely regarded as one of the most influential religious personalities of modern times.

Seventh in the dynastic lineage of Chabad-Lubavitch leaders, leadership was thrust upon the reluctant Rebbe 70 years ago, catalyzing a post-holocaust spiritual revival whose effects are felt ever more widely and deeply with the passage of time.

The Rebbe's ubiquitous mitzvah campaigns catapulted Jewish learning and practice to the very center of Jewish life, and his holistic Torah prescription for personal fulfillment and global harmony uplifts and empowers from the halls of power to the forgotten and downtrodden. People of all faiths, nationalities and backgrounds travel from across the globe to pray at his resting place for blessing and inspiration.

Foreword

THE ADVENT OF ARTIFICIAL intelligence has given machines an ever-increasing ability to perform many of the tasks to which people have devoted their lives. Skills once deemed crucial and positions once seen as indispensable seem to be disappearing, leaving some wondering what purpose they have in a world where so much can be done for us, often better than we could on our own.

"If no one needs me," one may wonder, "what purpose do I serve?" Is there meaning to our presence on earth? Why are we here in the first place, and what are we to do about it?

To address these pressing questions, Rabbi Mendel Kalmenson has dug deep into the well of the teachings of the Rebbe, Rabbi Menachem M. Schneerson, of righteous memory, to present a breathtakingly clear and prescient worldview.

The Torah, illuminated by the teachings of the Rebbe, demonstrate how every moment, every interaction, and every thing has infinite purpose, invested into it by the Creator of all. It is up to us to unpack that meaning and bring it to fruition. This purpose exists not just on a micro level, but also on the cosmic plane, as each of us contributes to the ultimate human endeavor, of creating for G-d a "home here on earth."

As deftly demonstrated in this new work, the Rebbe's writings and teachings continue to be as relevant as ever, providing a living and inspired path for all to follow.

This book joins the growing library of publications from Chabad.org who all share the aim of making Torah and its timeless wisdom ever more accessible.

We pray that this book, and the timeless wisdom it shares, provides one more step toward steering the universe toward its ultimate purpose. May it happen soon!

Chabad.org
Rosh Chodesh Kislev 5785
Brooklyn, NY

Introduction

W HEN THE *ON* BUTTON of a computer is pressed, an arrangement of plastic, glass, metal, and silicon is suddenly transformed into one of the most sophisticated machines ever invented, capable of instantly transmitting the near-sum of human knowledge, connecting billions of people in real time, and managing spacecraft on their voyages to the furthest reaches of our solar system.

What the *on* button does for computers, a clear and activated sense of purpose does for human beings, elevating us to become much more than a collection of genes, cells, tissue, instincts, and inclinations.

Once we discover and actuate our unique purpose, all of our disparate parts and potentials coalesce, transforming us into the most powerful force in creation—an unstoppable engine of creativity, connection, and possibility that is immeasurably more alive and potent than the sum of our individual parts.

Without purpose, we merely exist—like an instrument sitting on a shelf.

But once our Divine purpose is switched on, we become truly and magnificently alive in the fullest sense.

Indeed, a clear sense of purpose dramatically elevates our well-being in every way. Emerging research shows that having purpose in life increases life satisfaction, improves mental and physical health,[1] lowers the risk of cognitive decline,[2] betters sleep,[3] enhances resilience and self-esteem, and decreases chances of anxiety and depression.[4, 5, 6]

In fact, a sense of purpose increases the longevity, not just the quality, of our lives.

For example, a meta-analysis of ten studies involving more than 136,000 people found that people with the highest sense of purpose displayed the lowest risk of death (15.2%), while those with the lowest observed sense of purpose died at more than twice the rate of their purpose-driven counterparts (36.5%).[7]

This might explain why, according to Neil Pasricha, bestselling author of *The Happiness Equation*: "The two most dangerous years in your life are the year you're born (because of infant mortality) *and the year you retire.*"[8]

The connection between purpose and life expectancy is seen in the pioneering work of Dan Buettner, a National

Geographic fellow and longevity researcher who studied regions around the world known as blue zones—unique communities defined by high concentrations of people who have lived for more than one hundred years.

Buettner's research revealed that a strong sense of purpose was a defining characteristic among those who had lived for more than a century.

The connection between purpose and longevity is not just found in blue zones. A number of additional studies have demonstrated that people with a clear sense of purpose live longer, regardless of where they may live. Incredibly, those who embrace purpose and meaning as a driving force in their daily lives added an average of seven years to their life expectancy.[9] That makes living with purpose an even greater contributor to longevity than regular physical exercise, which at best contributes 6.9 years![10]

Of course, the benefits of living a life of purpose extend well beyond the confines of self-interest and personal well-being. By actualizing our Divinely endowed purpose, we take our place at the epicenter of a radiating chain of blessings that we were uniquely designed to bestow upon the world.

But finding our unique purpose is a difficult and overwhelming affair in today's ever-expanding, hyper-connected reality, with mobile technologies putting the world, with all of its problems and possibilities, into our hands at every moment.

As a point of contrast, a weekday edition of *The New York Times* contains more information about the world than the average person was likely to come across during an entire lifetime in seventeenth-century England.[11]

The dizzying, exponential proliferation of information and opportunities makes choosing *any* direction in life daunting, let alone one that is uniquely ours. As our awareness of the world dilates faster than most can keep up with, the question of our individual purpose and contribution can become paralyzing.

The disheartening result of these difficulties can be seen in statistics that show only about a quarter of American adults say they have a clear sense of what makes their lives meaningful, while forty percent say they don't have a sense of purpose at all.[12]

The potential consequences of living without a clear sense of purpose are that the person remains aimless and adrift, burdened with numbness, emptiness, regret, and unfulfilled potential.

This brings us to the most critical question of our time: In a world beset by distraction and inundated with countless causes, how do we discover our own unique purpose?

Helping you find answers to that question is the objective of this book, which draws on the living wisdom, teachings, and example of one of the greatest spiritual leaders and teachers of our time.

R. Menachem Mendel Schneerson, of righteous memory (1902-1994), known universally as the Rebbe, spent a lifetime guiding countless people toward their purpose in life, mobilizing everyone he encountered to share their unique light with the world. He saw every human being as a soul on a mission from on high to bring hope and healing to the world, and he helped all he met see themselves as such.

The Rebbe's philosophy on purpose is predicated upon several core spiritual principles from Jewish tradition that compose the basis of our search for purpose, summarized in the foundational axiom:

The day you were born is the day G-d decided that the world cannot exist without *you*.

Indeed, Jewish mysticism teaches[13] that before your soul descended to earth, you were appointed to cultivate, elevate, illuminate, and transform a specific portion of this world into a welcoming home for the Divine. Your part of this precious mission is one of a kind, crafted by G-d for you—and you alone—to contribute to history, humanity, and the world.

As pioneering Austrian psychiatrist Viktor Frankl summarized in Man's Search for Meaning:

"Everyone has his own specific vocation or mission in

life. Therein he cannot be replaced, nor can his life be repeated."[14]

This perspective, in turn, imparts every life with monumental significance, and can be summarized in the Rebbe's life-changing teaching that birth is G-d's way of saying *you matter.*[15]

Put simply: You don't matter because you exist. You exist because *you matter.*

Drawing from hundreds of the Rebbe's letters, talks, lessons, and encounters with people from all walks of life, this book was crafted with the aim of helping you discover why and how you matter, and what to do about it.

The first section, Perspectives on Purpose, addresses some of life's most urgent, essential, and existential questions:

Do I have an essence? Does my life have intrinsic value and meaning?

In a vast world made up of billions of people, do I truly matter?

Am I here for a reason?

If so, how do I discover my purpose in life?

The second section, Purpose in Practice, offers practical wisdom and a set of empowering tips, tools, and guidelines to help you discover where your unique purpose lies.

Based on the premise that every element in your life is Divinely appointed and orchestrated, from your inner makeup to the people, places, circumstances, and events you encounter in life—this section offers a bespoke toolkit for the monumental task of discerning and activating your unique Divine design and purpose in creation.

The third section, Reflections on Purpose, aims to help you crystallize and concretize the focus and locus of your journey toward personal meaning and purpose.

This section offers profound spiritual and psychological insights into the benefits of living with purpose, coupled with a variety of time-tested practices to help you design a life of intentionality and purpose.

Ultimately, it is our hope that the wisdom presented in this book helps you ignite, internalize, and actualize your blessed mission in life so you can reap the ever-unfolding joy and benefits of living with and on purpose.

Mendel Kalmenson
Rosh Chodesh Kislev I 5785
London

PART I

Perspectives
on Purpose

CHAPTER 1

Who Am I?

I N EARLY 1984, R. Moshe Kotlarsky, one of the Rebbe's emissaries and future vice-chairman of Merkos L'Inyonei Chinuch, received an urgent phone call from the Rebbe's secretary with a mission. The Rebbe wanted him to travel immediately to the island of Curaçao, though he wasn't told why.

R. Kotlarsky departed for Curaçao together with R. Levi Yitzchak Krinsky, who was then a *yeshivah* student. Upon landing, they took a taxi to the local synagogue and encountered a man who was leaving the building. They approached him and told him that they were sent by the Lubavitcher Rebbe.

The man appeared stunned, his eyes widening. "Then you must have come for me."

After regaining his composure, he introduced himself as Chaim Groisman, a non-observant Jew whose son attended the local public school. After a period of peaceful attendance, changes had occurred within the school's administration, and they began requiring Jewish students to participate in Catholic worship services on Sundays. He shared that his young son Eli had been expelled from the school after a confrontation with its headmaster over his refusal to attend those services.

The series of events affected their social connections with the other residents of the island, leaving them feeling isolated and helpless.

"I had just come to the synagogue to pray for guidance!" the man exclaimed.

After a lengthy and heartfelt conversation, R. Kotlarsky encouraged Chaim to send his son abroad to receive a Jewish education, and he invited Chaim to come to Chabad Lubavitch headquarters in Brooklyn for a visit. While there, Chaim decided to enroll his son Eli in the Lubavitcher *yeshivah*.

After their stay in Crown Heights, Chaim wrote a two-page letter to R. Kotlarsky. The letter was filled with gratitude for the help provided, as well as the privilege of spending time in the Rebbe's uplifting presence.

He concluded his letter with these earnest words:

> "I would like you to extend to the Rebbe my most sincere appreciation and other good feelings, but for lack of good English I do not

know what words to use. Just tell the Rebbe that a small Jew from Curaçao felt that the Rebbe touched my soul; thank you for doing it."

R. Kotlarsky passed this letter on to the Rebbe, who sent the following poignant response to Chaim:

"I was pleased to receive your regards through our esteemed mutual friends.

I must, however, take exception to your referring to yourself as: "a small Jew from Curacao." There is surely no need to emphasize to you at length that every Jew, man or woman, has a *Nefesh Elokis* [Divine soul], which is a "part of G-dliness above," as explained in the *Tanya*, beginning of chapter two. Thus, there is no such thing as "a small Jew," and a Jew must never underestimate his or her tremendous potential."[16]

The Rebbe's insistence that there is no such thing as a small Jew represents a bold response to one of the great challenges of our times. Namely, that despite living in an era defined by unprecedented achievement, many of us still somehow struggle with feelings of insignificance, inadequacy, aimlessness, and lack of purpose.

Born into a world that so often denies any inherent significance or meaning to our existence, we clamor to craft a satisfying sense of self as we struggle through life, building our personal worth from a host of external validations—accomplishments, accolades, success, and status.

But even if we succeed in these gratifying pursuits, many of us still struggle with a lingering doubt about our personal value and purpose.

This conundrum was highlighted by the Rebbe shortly after he assumed the mantle of Chabad leadership, when he observed: "The great challenge of today's youth is the sense of inadequacy they carry: *'Mi ani u'mah ani*—Who am I, and what am I?'"[17]

So often this crucial existential question is accompanied by a despondent, whispered insistence: "I am small. I am nobody."

Origin of the Species

This endemic sense of smallness is no accident. Indeed, the notion that we are born void of intrinsic value results primarily from a fundamental shift in the way we understand the source of our selfhood, and what lies beneath the vast complexities forming our identities.

Today, due to the entrenchment of dominant theories regarding human origin and development, our identity is perceived as something we must struggle to construct during the course of our lives.

This vacuous approach to identity formation was championed by framers of our depersonalized sense of self, including Aristotle, Charles Darwin, and Sigmund Freud.

Tracing back as far as ancient Alexandria and built through centuries of theoretical inquiry, these men ultimately crystallized a narrative that says we are merely the product of accidental intersections between biological, evolutionary, and psychological imperatives. This view has manifested more recently in the popular notions that we are a random dance of particles, probabilities, and genetic expressions.

Together, these men birthed a paradigm that ceaselessly hammers home the notion that we come into this world bereft of any true value or intrinsic nobility. Even as scientific theories behind this dour sentiment have evolved and shifted over the years, the resulting view that we are fundamentally insignificant continues to be reinforced.

Steven Hawking, one of the great scientific celebrities of our time, summarized it thusly,

"The human race is just a chemical scum on a moderate-sized planet, orbiting around a very average star in the outer suburb of one among a hundred billion galaxies. We are so insignificant that I cannot believe the whole universe exists for our benefit."[18]

Based on this cynical worldview, we are told that if we want to be somebody, that somebody must be crafted, curated, and cobbled together. All of this intrapersonal effort amounts to an impossible attempt to become through our own efforts what the Rebbe insists we already are at birth—inherently, infinitely, and irrevocably valuable, worthy of love, and Divine by design.

In the Rebbe's own words:

> Our Sages said that "Each and every soul was in the presence of His Divine Majesty before coming down to this earth," and that "The souls are hewn from under the seat of glory." These sayings emphasize the essential nature of the soul, its holiness and purity...[19]

In but a few concise words, the Rebbe deconstructs the prevailing materialist mindset and reveals our spiritual foundation and fundamental composition.

For each of us, this G-dly essence—eternal and pure—represents a sacred inheritance, which includes our unique purpose, as well as all the tools required to live up to it.

Moreover, though each of us is made, like Adam, in the image of our creator, each inherited spark of the Divine and the purpose it imparts is entirely unique—a distinct, holographic reflection of G-d's perfect wholeness.

As the Mishnah teaches:

"Adam was created singly [rather than in pairs like the other living creations]... to proclaim the greatness of the Holy One, Blessed Be He, for a human being casts many coins with one die and they are all alike, each one the same as the other, but the King of kings, the Holy One, Blessed

Be He, has cast all of humanity with the die of the first man, and yet not one of them is like his fellow."[20]

This Divine spark at the root of our being imprints each of us as utterly unique, endows us with our own distinct purpose, imparts more significance to our lives than could ever be accumulated or earned, and is, in the Rebbe's view, who we truly are and always will remain in essence.

Put simply: You don't *have* a soul; you *are* a soul.

Rather than seeing ourselves as small and insignificant, the Rebbe urges us to internalize the fact that our intrinsic identity and essence is an embodied piece of the Divine. This empowering perspectival shift positions us to proactively answer the crucial questions of life—who am I, why am I here, and what is my purpose on earth?

CHAPTER 2

Why Am I Here?

O N THE EVENING OF Simchat Torah 5719 (1958),[21] the central study hall of 770 Eastern Parkway was alive with revelry and song. Following the traditional *hakafot* [dancing with the Torah scrolls] and a festive meal, the Rebbe returned to the main sanctuary of 770 in the early morning hours to teach a Chasidic tune from days past, as he had for the previous several years.

Taking the center of the room, the Rebbe began to sing a haunting tune that rose and fell dramatically in melody, pitch, and emotional tone—from heartbroken longing to uplifting notes of fierce hope. The distinctive tune kindled the souls of the men who had gathered. After the song faded, leaving the crowd in almost tangible silence, the Rebbe told the story of the song's origins.

There was once a Sufi Muslim warlord, tribal leader,

and imam named Shamil, who had valiantly fended off Russian invaders from his stronghold in the Caucasus Mountains during successive incursions in the 1800s. Time and again, the mountain-dwelling rebels and their leader kept the Russian soldiers at bay thanks to the remoteness and fortitude of their mountain fortress. The Russians, repeatedly defeated but determined, drew Shamil out of hiding by offering a farcical truce. Shamil was ambushed and then exiled to the heart of Russia, where he mourned and yearned to return to his mountain home.

During the Simchat Torah *farbrengen* the next day, the Rebbe repeated the backstory to the song he had shared the previous evening:

> "When he was in exile, he would occasionally remember the high mountains where he was free of the bonds of government, without the restrictions of the jail, and even without the restraints of a settled city of residence and the limitations and constraints of culture, and [how] now he was enslaved…and a great yearning for those high mountains, where he was as free as an eagle in the heavens, would awaken in him, and he would sing this song, which begins with yearning and ends with hope that he would eventually return home."[22]

The story embodied in Shamil's song, the Rebbe continued, served as a sublime, wordless metaphor that uniquely expresses the dramatic journey of each soul. The soul, which is inherently holy and in effortless alignment with G-d, descends from the perfect, undifferentiated elation of the heavens into the physical world, where it is clothed in the body of a human being. The physical body, with its base needs, compulsions, and desires, restricts the soul, engendering a state of spiritual exile from the perfect oneness it had enjoyed prior to incarnation. The stirring song of Shamil, the Rebbe concluded, mirrors the intense pathos of the soul in exile, and its hope to one day return to dwell in the infinite light of its Creator and source.

With this simple song and story, the Rebbe addresses a critical and inevitable question regarding the soul's relationship with the broken world into which it is born. If, as the Rebbe reinforced time and again, our truest self is part of G-d's essence, why rip us from a state of perfection and clarity and send us into a conflicted reality dominated by the agonizing illusion of separation?

The answer, according to the Rebbe, lies in the deep, essential connection between the story and purpose of creation, and the starring role assigned to humans within that Divine drama.

Descent for the Sake of Ascent

To understand the purpose of the soul's descent into the world, we must first step back and take a brief look at the purpose of creation itself.

According to Kabbalah, our understanding of the true nature of reality is inherently limited. What we perceive to be a dead dance of forces, functions, and mute matter is actually a living, unified field of Divine energy that animates and orchestrates every aspect and iota of our universe. Mystical sources describe the process of creation as involving a series of obfuscations that hide Divinity behind an elaborate and thoroughly convincing illusion of fragmentation. Blinded to the infinite light that binds everything together, we instead see a simulation of disconnected forces and phenomena, seemingly devoid of meaning or purpose.

The appearance of fragmentation, as with all things, serves a distinct purpose in the story of creation. As philosopher Bertrand Russell summarized, "When creating the universe, G-d wrote a good detective story with all of the clues pointing in the wrong direction."

Similarly, Kabbalistic tradition tells us that sparks of G-d's essence were scattered and hidden throughout our world so they could be sought out and reunited by humankind. In this way, we become G-d's collaborative partners in the sacred work of unveiling the true, underlying oneness behind the facade of multiplicity, and revealing His infinite, illuminating presence on earth.

Each of us inherits an essential part in this great cosmic drama and is given a blessed corner of this world to redeem and elevate. The coordinates of our personal lives, in turn, become the constellation of our unique purpose.

Like Adam, the first human, who was empowered to *replenish the earth and steward it*[23] by virtue of his inborn Divinity, we are each tasked with revealing the intimate link between creation and its Creator.

As the Rebbe writes in a communal letter issued in the days preceding Rosh Hashanah 5720 (1959):

"When G-d created Adam, his soul—his Divine image—permeated and irradiated his whole being, by virtue of which he became the ruler over the entire Creation. All the creatures gathered to serve him and to crown him as their creator. But Adam, pointing out their error, said to them: "Let us all come and worship G-d, our Maker!" The world conquest which was given to man as his task and mission in life, is to elevate the whole of Nature, including the beasts and animals...so that the whole of Creation will realize that G-d is our Maker."[24]

This short teaching helps frame the purpose of the soul's disruptive descent, exile, and embodiment. Prior to incarnation, the soul exists in a state of utter awe and alignment with the Creator, experiencing no sense of self or separation—much like a child in the womb. From this perfect, spiritually amniotic existence, the soul is plucked and enclothed within a body, for whom G-d or spirit doesn't feel nearly as immediate or real as hunger and cold. But in so doing, the soul gains access to a vessel that allows it to inhabit and impact the physical world—the crown of G-d's creation. The soul *must* incarnate, because the physical world can't be completed from the heavenly realms. It must be worked on from within.

This is why our souls are sent from on high to act as ambassadors of Divine consciousness and light to influence and illuminate the physical world. Ignited by the power of our purpose, we are each tasked with doing our part to reveal the seeds of Divinity planted throughout the events, circumstances, and trajectories of our lives. As we do, step by step, choice by choice, we move creation toward its ultimate redemption.

We are here on a mission, and we all arrive uniquely empowered to bring Divine light into the world. The soul's descent represents a precious opportunity to participate in the ongoing process of creation. By definition, our physical existence is a purpose driven phenomenon laden with incredible spiritual significance. This purpose—to elevate and unify the world—is why we are here, and why each of us, body and soul, matters more than we can ever truly fathom.

CHAPTER 3

A Divine Roadmap

R ABBI DOVID OF LELOV once told a young man who witnessed him studying the Talmudic Tractate of Bava Kama:

"Know, my son, that just as you are now studying the Tractate of *Bava Kama*, so in the future, when Mashiach comes, there will be a tractate of Dovid of Lelov—a tractate in its own right."[25]

This poetic teaching reveals a radical perspective on Torah and its role in our lives. The Torah we study in the World to Come will include a "personal" Torah, compiled from the lessons we learned by applying the word of G-d to the unique circumstances and story of our lives.

* * *

In order to succeed in our mission to reveal the Divine essence within all, G-d provided an operating manual for life on earth called the Torah, which was given to help us decipher our place in the world and identify our unique contribution to its sanctification and betterment.[26]

The Rebbe referenced this point in a letter written to a prominent doctor who questioned the intelligent design of the universe, saying:

> "[Anyone] who contemplates the solar system, for example, or the complexities of an atom, must come to the conclusion and conviction that our universe did not come about by some "freak accident." Wherever you turn, you see design and purpose.
>
> Since the Creator created the world with a purpose, it is also logical to assume that He wished the purpose to be realized, and therefore, would reveal to...humankind, what this purpose is, and how to go about realizing it."[27]

And how did G-d reveal this purpose and the potential paths to its fulfillment? By bestowing the Torah to humankind.

The word Torah, the Rebbe stressed repeatedly, stems from the Hebrew root *horaah*,[28] which means instruction. It is the roadmap given to help each of us align with our unique role in unveiling the Divinity within all things.

Within the Torah there are 613 *mitzvot*. The simple meaning of the word mitzvah is command, referring to the 613 Divine commandments given to the Jewish people, along with seven commandments given to all humankind, defining specific actions that we should or shouldn't take.

A few examples among the Torah's many *mitzvot* include such diverse activities as wrapping *tefillin*, declaring G-d's Oneness, observing Shabbat, eating kosher, and helping the poor and needy.

There are also *mitzvot* that include prohibitions against slander, gossip, and theft, for example.

In Chasidic thought, however, the word mitzvah is correlated with the Aramaic word *tzavta*[29]—to connect or attach—shedding light on the fact that these practices empower us to progressively reorient and reunite our inner and outer realities to align and harmonize with the obscured omnipresence of G-d.

This perspective—that Torah and *mitzvot* are the manual and tools for clarifying and sanctifying everyday life—transforms everything we do into an opportunity to repair the world. Blessings before and after eating, for example, become powerful intention setting practices. We get to choose whether to engage with the act of eating in a manner that is hedonistic or holy, indulgent or illuminating, healthy or harmful, energizing or enervating.

Here is a great secret: Why did G-d create various types of food and drink that human beings desire? Because they, too, contain Divine sparks that long to be returned to holiness.[30] Commenting on the verse, *Hungry and also thirsty, their souls* enwrapped *in them*,[31] the Baal Shem Tov taught that, in fact, it is the soul that makes us hungry and thirsty. Our desire for food is a response to a sort of spiritual magnetism, leveraging our physical appetite to draw us toward the spiritual work of elevating Divine sparks hidden within the most basic elements of the material world. We are thus invited to find G-d everywhere, even in a glass of water.

Mitzvot governing our social interactions—giving charity or acting with care and generosity—reveal and ground us in the essential interconnectedness of all human life. A simple nod and smile to someone on the street subtly repairs the fraying edges of our social fabric. A moment of expressed kindness to someone who is suffering does the same. Reaching out to an estranged family member becomes a spiritual act of cosmic repair. We are sent to find G-d within the lives of our friends, our family, and the strangers that cross our paths.

Every mitzvah, no matter how seemingly insignificant, brings us closer to fulfilling our ultimate purpose—the revelation and reunification of the Infinite One. We don't need to achieve greatness, earn status, or accomplish extravagant feats to repair the world. Even the least of us can contribute profoundly to the purpose of creation by following the slightest of commandments given to us by G-d.

The Inner Dimension

However true and beautiful the above paradigm, it left

little room for the individual to apply the wisdom of Torah to the specific nuances of their lives.

For much of the previous 3,200 years, it was traditionally understood that when individuals engaged with the Torah, its various texts and traditions largely focused on external actions (behavioral or ritual) and spoke to the Jewish people as members of a collective, but not necessarily in a holistic or personal sense.[32] In short, the Torah was largely perceived to address the average person as a member of a broader community bound by a shared set of laws, teachings, traditions, and practices.

However, our understanding of the Torah's power to address and illuminate our individual trajectory and purpose in life began to shift radically in the eighteenth century with the advent of the Chasidic movement, founded by the Baal Shem Tov. This perspectival evolution reached a further momentous breakthrough and poetic crystallization with the founding of the Chabad Chasidic movement by R. Schneur Zalman of Liadi, known as the Alter Rebbe.

The proverbial upwelling of Chasidism sparked a profound paradigm shift in the hearts of the masses and the minds of scholars, wherein the Torah was revealed to address not only the external practices of Judaism but also the inner life of each individual soul.

Chasidism helped elucidate and illuminate the radical idea that there is an inner dimension to the Torah—an intimate, Divine manual that addresses the depths and destinies of each unique soul. Through this lens, every facet of one's internal life can be connected to their ultimate purpose, evoking the sparks of Divine potential within each and every encounter, experience, and aspect of their life story.

This revelation was revolutionary in its simplicity, courageously acknowledging the inescapable reality that everyone grapples with internal challenges and emotions for which there are no Biblical commandments or explicit guidance. The Baal Shem Tov, and his many disciples after him, went to great pains to validate the fact that these personal struggles are an essential part of every person's daily life and must therefore be written into their sacred story. Overcoming them, in turn, constitutes a powerful and personal spiritual triumph. The Alter Rebbe, in particular, declared that these acts of internal redemption—of connecting our inner world to G-d at all times—are essential components in our service of G-d. This internal space represented the last frontier of spiritual pursuit, the last unclaimed aspect of each person's quest for spiritual growth and redemption.

Through this transformative new lens, the Torah was now seen as a source of wisdom and a bespoke beacon to illuminate the particular path of each person, including the specific conditions of their individual lives and purpose.

Furthermore, this holistic approach to the role of Torah in our lives was conceived in such a way that nothing was lost. Rather, the new Chasidic approach *added* depth and dimension to existing lenses. Additionally, it invited every single person to become a contributing participant and integral part of the living tradition.

Where Are You?

A profound and paradigmatic example of this individually focused approach to Torah occurred in 1798, when the Alter Rebbe was imprisoned on false charges that his teachings undermined the imperial authority of the czar of Russia.[33]

He was held in the Peter-Paul Fortress in Petersburg for fifty-three days. Given the severity of the charges, the unforgiving political climate of the time, and the dehumanized status endured by Jews throughout Russia, the Alter Rebbe had resigned himself to the inevitability of his execution and began to prepare himself for martyrdom via prayer and deep contemplation.

Meanwhile, among the Rebbe's interrogators was a government minister who happened to possess a broad knowledge of the Torah and its commentaries. During one interrogation, the minister posed a question to the Alter Rebbe that had perplexed many scholars and sages regarding the exchange between G-d and Adam after the latter ate from the forbidden tree.

The Torah says, *And G-d called to the man and said to him: "Where are you?"*[34]

"Did G-d not know where Adam was?" the minister asked.

The Alter Rebbe quoted the traditional answer attributed to R. Shlomo Yitzchaki, the revered French scholar and commentator, known widely as Rashi.

"*Where are you?*" he explained, "was G-d's gentle way of approaching Adam, preparing for a delicate conversation about the consequences of eating from the Tree of Knowledge."

"I already know what Rashi says," the minister replied. "I wish to hear how the Rebbe understands the verse."

The Alter Rebbe asked, "Do you believe that the Torah is eternal? That its every word applies to every individual, under all conditions and at all times?"

"Yes," said the minister.

R. Schneur Zalman was gratified to hear this affirmation of the Torah's eternal and individual applicability—one of the core teachings for which he was now standing trial.

"*Where are you*," explained the Rebbe, "is G-d's perpetual call to every human being. Where are *you* in the world? What have you accomplished? You have been allotted a certain number of days, hours, and minutes in which to fulfill your mission in life. You have lived [so many] years and [so many] days"—here the Alter Rebbe mentioned the exact age of the minister, to the day. "Where are you along your life's journey? What have you achieved so far [in your mission in life]?"

Upon inquiring of Adam, *"Where are you?"* G-d was not only addressing a particular person who lived at a particular time, but He was also addressing each of us at every moment of our lives!

At that very moment, the Alter Rebbe made a monumental turnabout. Only moments earlier, he had been ready to step out of the stream of his life's journey. But the interrogator's question—which the Alter Rebbe interpreted as a direct message from above to remind him of the importance of his own earthly mission—inspired him anew and encouraged him to channel his spiritual yearnings into even more intensified dedication to his life's purpose in this world.

The auspiciousness and deep synchronicity of the unexpected encounter were taken as a sign by the Alter Rebbe that it was time to redouble his efforts to spread the spiritual doctrine he had just shared: Every individual has a unique purpose to fulfill in this world, and the Torah is the manual by which each of us can decipher and align with our sacred purpose and find real-life, real-time guidance toward it's fulfillment.[35]

Where are *you* on the path of your Divine purpose? For those seeking guidance, there is a multidimensional map given to us by G-d called the Torah, which is waiting for you to traverse its many paths and drink from its endless wellsprings of wisdom. The invaluable lessons it contains for those who choose to both follow in its path while blazing their own trail will undoubtedly help clarify, guide, and inspire you to become who you were meant to be.

CHAPTER 4

Do I Really Matter?

I F YOU REALLY WANT to know someone well—what captures their interest, imagination, and passion—study the passages highlighted in the books on their nightstand.

In this spirit, it is deeply telling that amid the vast body of Jewish literature and wisdom, the Rebbe repeatedly underscored the following three teachings:

1. "Whoever saves a single life is considered as though he saved an entire world."[36]

2. "Therefore [since all humanity descended from one person], each and every person is obligated to say: 'The world was created for me.'"[37]

3. "One should see the world and himself as being perched upon a scale with an equal balance of good and evil. When he does one good deed, the

scale is tipped to the good, and he brings salvation to himself and the entire world."[38]

Together, these three maxims help form the bedrock of the Rebbe's purpose-driven philosophy, which cast each and every individual as invaluable and indispensable contributors to creation as a whole.

This was the dignifying truth provided by the Rebbe to an individual who was dealing with a demoralizing personal crisis. He confided that his communal work had suffered so many disappointments that he felt unimportant to the point of despair. The Rebbe replied:

> I must make special reference to your remark about your personal feeling that there is "no further use for me," etc. Needless to say, there is no room or justification for such a feeling, G-d forbid, for this would be counter to one of the basics of *Yiddishkeit* [Judaism] in general, and of Chabad in particular, which declares that every Jew is like a complete world...[39]

The Rebbe's life-affirming perspective emerges from the Kabbalistic notion that, from the very first moment, G-d has prepared the way and arranged the right circumstances to bring life to you as part of a story that spans the entirety of creation. Literally and figuratively, G-d crafted the cosmos to make your existence possible. Why? Because you are loved that much, always and in all ways, and because you are essential to the world in a way that is irreducible, irreplaceable, and inimitable.

Although it seems hard to fathom, G-d's plan doesn't work without you. This sublime understanding represents the deeper meaning of the Mishnaic teaching quoted earlier: "The world was created for me."

Far from a new age platitude or a narcissistic mantra, "the world was created for me" conveys the radical truth that you are essential to the goal of creation, and the world's ultimate purpose would remain unfulfilled without you.

As the Rebbe wrote inspiringly in a calendar compendium of wisdom for youth:

> "Let no one say, 'What can I do to help in this lofty task?' For this world is a great royal palace, the palace of G-d, King of the Universe, erected out of numerous component parts, big and small. Even the smallest particle of the great edifice would leave a gap if it were missing. Each one of us must, therefore, do his share."[40]

First Man of Action

The Rebbe expounded on this theme in a letter written in 1964 during the days leading up to Rosh Hashanah. The essential event celebrated by the Jewish new year is the creation of Adam, the first human, who initiated the purpose of creation by acknowledging the power of its

Creator, thereby establishing G-d's rule over the cosmos and setting in motion the cosmic drama in which we all play a pivotal role.

The Rebbe elaborates:

> "One of the main distinguishing features in the creation of Man is that Man was created single, unlike other species, which were created in large populations. This indicates emphatically that *one single individual has the capacity to bring the whole of Creation to fulfillment,* as was the case with the first Man, Adam..."[41]

The Rebbe concludes the letter by saying that the same is true for each of us:

> "Every Jew, regardless of time and place and personal status, has the fullest capacity (hence also duty) to rise and attain the highest degree of fulfillment, and accomplish the same for the Creation as a whole."

Contrary to pessimistic views that say we are powerless in our attempts to change the world, the Rebbe taught repeatedly that each of us is uniquely imbued with the indwelling spirit of the infinite, including the Divine purpose it imparts and the sacred power to illuminate and uplift creation as a whole. This awareness leaves little room for the modern, prevailing worldview that we are forlorn, insignificant, and disempowered, living in a broken world too large for us to influence at all.

> "Rosh Hashanah disproves the contentions of those who do not fulfill their duty with the excuse that it is impossible to change the world...that the world is so huge and one is so puny—how can one hope to accomplish anything?
>
> "...There were times when the said idea— namely, the ability of a single individual to 'transform' the world—met with skepticism, and demanded proof, etc.
>
> "However...[in our time], we have seen how one individual brought the world to the brink of destruction, but for the mercies of the King of the Universe, Who ordained that 'the earth shall stand firm; shall not fall.'"

This is a truly extraordinary example of the Rebbe's ability to find something positive and redemptive, even in the seemingly irredeemable realm of evil. Taking a positive example from the architect of the indescribable horrors of the Holocaust, the Rebbe transmutes one man's terrible abuse of power into a life-altering message for each of us:

If this one person had the power to shift the course of history, so does each of us! This awareness infuses every action we take with tremendous import. If I matter, my actions matter, in no small terms.

The Rebbe concludes with an axiomatic truth upon which he called often:

> "If such is the case in the realm of evil, surely one's potential is much greater in the realm of good. For, in truth, Creation is essentially good and therefore more inclined toward the good than the opposite."

Great Expectations

This radical teaching lay at the heart of the Rebbe's response to R. Yitzchok Meir Gurary, when he asked the Rebbe for guidance in 1970.

Although he was well equipped with stories and lessons from the great sages and Chasidim of old, Gurary explained that he believed his students were in need of a powerful, all-encapsulating truth that would inspire them to remain deeply committed to a life of piety and faith while living in the modern world. The Rebbe replied:

> "Your message should continuously reaffirm the teaching of Maimonides that every person should consider themselves, and the world, on an even scale. Impress upon them that every action they take, no matter how small or seemingly insignificant, holds great potential, and it could be that these seemingly small actions are the ones that will bring about the true and complete redemption."[42]

This was the Rebbe's spiritual antidote to what he viewed as the primary challenge of our time. As mentioned in Chapter 1, the Rebbe diagnosed modern youth as suffering from a deep sense of personal insignificance, represented by the question: *Mi ani, u'mah ani?* Who am I, and what am I? This can be further distilled to the self-deprecating existential equation:

If I don't matter, what I do doesn't matter!

The Rebbe taught the opposite: Not only do you matter, but your every action, large or small, has the power to shape creation and history as a whole.

No Small Deed

Time and again, the Rebbe insisted that we weren't just given *the power* to elevate creation, but we were entrusted with the *sacred duty and responsibility* to do so.

In the Rebbe's words:

"Herein lies the profound, yet clear, directive, namely, that one man—each and every man—is potentially capable of 'conquering the world.' ...If a person does not fulfill his task and does not utilize his inestimable Divine powers—it is not merely a personal loss and failure, but it is something that affects the destiny of the whole world."[43, 44, 45]

This powerful truth is illustrated in the story of a man who was called to the beach to paint a boat. While he painted, the man discovered that the boat had sprung a leak, so he decided to mend it before finishing his appointed task, collecting payment, and heading home. The following day, the owner of the boat came to the painter and presented him with an additional, large sum.

Surprised, the painter reminded the boat's owner that he had already been paid.

"This is not for the paint job; it is for mending the leak in the boat," the man replied.

"That was such a small thing that I didn't even want to charge you for it. Surely you are not paying me this huge amount for so small a thing?"

"My dear friend, you do not understand," the man said. "Let me tell you what happened..."

"When I asked you to paint the boat, I had forgotten to mention the leak to you. When the boat was nice and dry, my children took the boat out and went fishing. When I found that they had gone out in the boat, I was frantic because I remembered that the boat had a leak! Imagine my relief and happiness when I saw them coming back safe and sound. I examined the boat and saw that you had repaired the leak. Do you now see why I am so grateful? You saved the lives of my children! I don't have enough money to repay you for your 'small' good deed..."[46]

Every action shapes events in ways we can never imagine or foresee, even if it seems small or insubstantial at the time. Even the smallest kindness or act of charity has the potential to result in tremendous good as it reverberates throughout the world. And the same is true of the converse. As our Sages teach, "*mitzvah goreret mitzvah, aveirah goreret aveirah*—one good deed brings another good deed, one transgression brings another transgression."[47] Each act, each choice, amplifies and propagates, creating more of its kind. In this way, every one of our actions becomes an axis from which a world of possibilities can unfurl.

The Rebbe illustrated this crucial truth on the afternoon of a summer Shabbat in 1969, coinciding with the historic launch of the Apollo 11 spacecraft. During the *farbrengen*, he proceeded to use the lunar mission as a real-time parable to illustrate the holy significance of a single person's actions, and the power of just one person to shape the course of history, saying:

> "The Baal Shem Tov taught us that 'from everything a person sees or hears, he must derive a lesson in the service of his Creator.' Indeed, this event, and its every aspect and detail, is full of instructive insights into our mission in life."[48]

The Rebbe then referenced the delicately balanced constellation of factors at play every moment throughout the historic journey. The Apollo 11 mission was the product of decades of work by an estimated four hundred thousand people working across dozens of scientific, engineering, and technological disciplines. He told how every person was given a role with meticulously orchestrated, elaborate parameters and procedures. Every movement within the cockpit, every switch flipped, every nap, every gesture, and every act was governed by an exquisitely arranged plan upon which the success of a billion-dollar project[49] and the achievement of humanity's highest aspirations all depended. Within this delicate arrangement, each act had the potential to save or sabotage the mission.[50]

The Rebbe concluded that if this is the case with a billion-dollar scientific project, how much more so when applied to the cosmic drama and Divine dance of creation itself?

Joseph's About Face

To the Rebbe, there was nothing figurative or poetic about this idea. Indeed, he believed that each deed matters to all of creation in the most literal sense, emphatically extolling the transformational power of a single action to shape history.

The Rebbe vividly illustrated this understanding during a talk given on 19 Kislev 5721 (1960), in which he drew on the example of the great Biblical Joseph and his struggle to deny the temptation presented by his master's wife.

As told in the Torah, Joseph steadfastly denied her advances until one day when he broke down and entered her home, intent on fulfilling his desire. The Talmud tells us that moments before succumbing to her embrace, Joseph was seized by a vision of his father, which impelled him to break from temptation and flee.[51]

Upon deeper inspection,[52] this story becomes emblematic of the world-shaping power of each individual and their choices.

As recounted in Genesis, Joseph's life as a young man had been violently disrupted. Ambushed and sold into slavery by his own envious brothers, Joseph was taken by slave traders to Egypt, where he was purchased by Potiphar, one of Pharaoh's senior ministers. Over time, Potiphar became so impressed by the young man's intelligence that he appointed Joseph to manage his entire estate. Described in the Torah as uniquely handsome, Joseph had also captured the attention of Potiphar's wife, who tormented Joseph by insistently and relentlessly inviting him to her bed.

As the Talmud describes:

"Each day, Potiphar's wife would attempt to seduce him. Clothes she wore for him in the morning she would not wear for him in the evening...

"She said, 'Surrender yourself to me.'

"'No,' he said.

"She threatened him, 'I shall confine you in prison...I shall subdue your proud stature...I will blind your eyes.'

"Joseph refused, nonetheless, saying, '...How then can I do this great wickedness and sin against G-d?'

"Despite her threats, Joseph reminded her: 'I am afraid of the Holy One, Blessed Be He.'

"To which she replied, 'But He is not here.'"

Imagine the weight, the temptation to despair, represented by those ominous words. Undoubtedly, there must have been days in Joseph's grueling, lonely existence when he felt truly forsaken. He was little more than an adolescent, with no friends or relatives nearby, no meaningful connections from which to draw hope, support, or comfort. His mother had passed when he was just eight years old, and his beloved father Jacob believed him dead. His jealous, hateful brothers had sold him into bondage, utterly extinguishing his youth. A slave in an alien land and culture, Joseph had been stripped of his very selfhood, forced to withstand a never-ending series of degradations. And though he may have secured favor and status in the eyes of his master, all his true sources of meaning—what made him matter—were gone. His mother, father, family, home, community, sovereignty, and safety had all been taken from him. And just as he had begun to receive dignified status from his master as overseer of his estate, Joseph's refusal of his master's wife threatened to rob him of everything else.

Why, then, would a desolate, lonely slave risk what was left of his life in response to the vision of his father's visage? How, in a world that was cruelly indifferent to his suffering, could the mere image of his father encourage Joseph to deny himself a moment of pleasure, comfort, and safety from the constant threats of his master's wife?

The answer emerges from a Talmudic passage, which says, "The beauty of Jacob reflected the beauty of Adam."[53]

According to the Rebbe's rendering, when Joseph saw the visage of Jacob, he saw the face of Adam as well, which reminded him of Adam's cataclysmic act of eating from the forbidden tree. Joseph recalled how one person, in one moment, with a single, seemingly inconsequential decision to eat from the Tree of Knowledge, forever changed the history of all humankind because, as the Rebbe observed, "...Every single human being is part of the knot in which heaven and earth are interlaced."

Standing in this holy recognition—shocked into the rhythm of his true, universal importance—Joseph was reinvigorated by a sudden, unassailable nobility and strength. He was lifted from the mire of his own powerlessness the moment he reclaimed the conviction that, like Adam, he played a crucial role in the redemption of humanity and the evolving history of the world at large.

This seemingly insignificant choice set off a series of events by which Joseph would become viceroy of Egypt, save the ancient world from famine, and leverage his new status to relocate and reunite his family in a bountiful settlement in Egypt. This series of events, in turn, served as the backdrop for the birth of the people of Israel and their great Exodus from Egypt to the Promised Land.

Like Joseph, we each experience periods of life when we feel alone, betrayed, belittled, powerless, and separated from our support systems. We may have experienced great loss, been rendered hopeless, and perhaps tempted to think, "But He is not here!" In those moments when we feel like we don't matter, and hence our actions don't matter—precisely in those moments—we *must* remember that every action, whether we realize it or not, has the power to shape the great wholeness of which we are always a part.

PART II

Purpose
in Practice

CHAPTER 5

The Book of Your Life

W HEN SEEKING TO DISCOVER our life's purpose, it is common to look for direction outside of ourselves.

Whether it be from teachers, gurus, therapists, life coaches, educational institutions, or wisdom traditions, most people seek external guidance hoping to make sense of the presumably random circumstances of their lives so they can actualize their dormant potential.

And while various forms of external guidance do indeed have a role to play in the story of our lives, the principle of specific Divine Providence, as elucidated by the Baal Shem Tov, teaches that the greatest indicators of our life's purpose are embedded and can be found in our inner world, composition, and makeup. Hence, the greatest guide to seeking and finding our purpose in life is our own Divine design.

This was the fundamental philosophy set out by the sixth Lubavitcher Rebbe, R. Yosef Yitzchak Schneersohn, in a letter to young Eliyahu Tzvi Einbinder as he set out in search of his purpose in life:

> "The Torah states: *These are the offspring of Adam.* [The Hebrew term for] *toldot Adam*, offspring, can also be read as *life story*—the life story of a person is a book that he must study. That book must be a guide for the person's life.
>
> "*Toldot adam* can also be translated as a person's birth. Here it means:
>
> 1. The purpose for which this person was born into this world;
> 2. to whom this person was born;
> 3. in which place this person was born;
> 4. in what time this person was born;
> 5. what kind of training (upbringing) and education this person had;
> 6. the kind of environment in which this person grew up;
> 7. which talents this person has;
> 8. what kind of natural character traits one has;
> 9. what kind of hobbies and interests one has;
> 10. what kind of Divine Providence guided the

person until he became self-directed and took a stand in life.

"Taken together, these ten things compose the life of a person. They form a book that the person must study and then choose to follow in all of their affairs, both in their relationship with G-d and in their relationship with other people."[54]

This ten-point guide provides a comprehensive framework for discerning how each part of your inner world and personal circumstances are Divinely imparted to help you identify and fulfill your mission in life.

The Golden Rule

According to the mystics, every single aspect of creation is crafted and guided by the hand of G-d for a reason. This monumental notion is a cornerstone of Chasidic thought, as introduced and elucidated by the Baal Shem Tov, who sparked a revolution in thinking about G-d's immanent involvement in creation. This foundational principle is what we might refer to as the "Golden Rule" of spiritual perception and consciousness—in Hebrew *Hashgachah Pratit*, which translates as Specific Divine Providence or synchronicity.

The Torah teaches that G-d not only created the world but that He continues to direct it throughout all time. G-d is therefore referred to both as "the Creator" and "the

Director" of the world. In the Book of Ezekiel, for example, the prophet passionately decries those who think that G-d has left the world to its own devices and is no longer intimately involved in its everyday unfolding.[55]

Maintaining this interconnected, big picture view of life is an *avodah*, spiritual labor, in and of itself. Indeed, we find numerous times throughout the ages when this perspective is submerged beneath other philosophical streams that seek to limit the scope of the Creator's involvement with creation. In dialectical fashion, such periods of *hester panim*, occlusion of G-d's presence, are inevitably rebalanced by an eruption of mystical consciousness and spiritual renaissance—revealing G-d's Face and Hand where it had been previously imperceivable.

In the case of the Chasidic revolution, beginning in the eighteenth century, it was the Baal Shem Tov who insisted that G-d's Providence guides every single detail of creation, not just human life. In the illuminated eyes of the Baal Shem Tov, even a single drop of rain is part of the master plan of creation.

As elucidated by the sixth Lubavitcher Rebbe, R. Yosef Yitzchak: "The Baal Shem Tov taught us the [deeper] meaning of *Hashgachah Pratit*: Not only are all the detailed movements of each creation governed by G-d's Providence, and this [*Hashgachah Pratit*] is actually their very source of life, but every move of each individual creation *has a place in the larger story of the entire creation...*"[56]

The delicate specificity of G-d's involvement in creation is highlighted in a moving story of the Baal Shem Tov. As he walked through the forest with some of his students, he drew the attention of his students to a single leaf that had blown off a tree and floated down to rest in front of them on the pathway. He related that this particular leaf had fallen from that exact tree, precisely at that moment, because it had been so orchestrated by G-d.

He then asked one of one of his students to lift the leaf, which he did, discovering a worm that had lain suffering in the summer sun, praying to G-d for respite. The fallen leaf was the answer to the worm's prayers, providing it shade from the sun.[57]

Here, the Baal Shem Tov connects the seemingly random, unrelated dots of circumstance to reveal a stunning constellation of Divine Providence encompassing every aspect of creation—the path of a falling leaf, the wind that loosed it from its branch, the worm that it fell to protect, and the journey of the students, whose precisely-timed arrival presented an opportunity for a demonstration of G-d's will at work in the world. Each aspect, guided by G-d, is a precious part of a greater wholeness, with each contributing something crucial and indispensable to the larger story. From this integral perspective, everything has a purpose, and every purpose is part of the perfectly orchestrated dance of creation, even if we fail to recognize it.

Divine by Design

Through this lens, the book of your life emerges from the unique aspects of your Divine design. Indeed, each and every one of us is constructed quite precisely. Not just certain parts of us but our entirety. Even what you may perceive as flaws and imperfections are in their own way perfectly imperfect features of your existence, because they were written into your life by the Hand of G-d. This is true no matter how small, simple, disconnected, or randomly appointed these characteristics may appear at first glance. By looking inward and reflecting on your inner makeup, natural gravitations, and dispositions, as well as your personality, character, passions, natural gifts, talents, and even vices and struggles, you will find that you have a host of internal indicators that become clues and tools to help you discover and fulfill your Divine purpose. This is equally true of the various circumstances, events, people, places, and challenges that occur throughout your life.

Through the kaleidoscopic lens of Chasidut, we begin to see the world as more than just a random place of indifference, or as Joseph Heller described it, "a trashbag of coincidences blown open by the wind." Rather, *Hashgachah Pratit* consciousness reveals the world and history to be a convergence of subtle orchestrations and gentle nudgings arranged to help us discover the higher purpose in every moment, event, and encounter in our lives. This elevated and elevating perspective reveals to us that, in fact, there is a Divine plot that informs our human storyline, and our purpose is realized at the intersection of Divine Providence and human initiative.

With this in mind, the circumstances of our lives begin to shine in a new way. In telling stories about how you met and married your spouse, for example, you may emphasize that you were drawn by their sense of humor, beauty, intelligence, or note that you met by chance at your favorite coffee shop one afternoon. And while all of that may be true, there is a deeper truth to be found in the qualities and circumstances that brought you together. This is the truth of Divine Providence—that your appreciation of blue eyes and a good sense of humor, and your gravitation toward the coffee shop where you would eventually meet, were written into the book of your life as plot devices in the story of your unfolding Divine purpose.

Whatever the details or circumstances, awareness of Divine Providence emphatically asserts that no part of us, nor anything that happens to us, is superficial or inconsequential. Of course, we are always free to choose how to react to our external circumstances and natural dispositions—what we make of and from them. But the raw materials, as it were, were given to us by G-d and arranged by Divine design.

A Task Done Well

The circumstances we are born into and encounter throughout our lives are preordained and are all perfectly coordinated and choreographed to create the conditions for us to achieve our ultimate purpose.

As the Rebbe taught:

> "Whoever has faith in individual Divine Providence knows that *Man's steps are established by G-d*—that this particular soul must purify and improve something specific in a particular place. For centuries, or even since the world's creation, that which needs purification or improvement waits for this soul to come and purify or improve it. The soul, too, has been waiting—ever since it came into being— for its time to descend, so that it can discharge the tasks of purification and improvement assigned to it.[58, 59]

Indeed, for each of us, somewhere out there is a marriage of soul and circumstance waiting for us to intercede.

This was the lesson sent in a letter by the Baal Shem Tov to his disciple, the great scholar R. Chaim Rapaport, who was instructed to travel to a specific place in the forest outside the city and study Torah there in depth, recite afternoon prayers, and then return home. Despite not knowing the purpose behind the numerous instructions, the disciple followed them, traveling to the forest to begin his studies. After studying for a while, R. Rapaport became very thirsty and sent his companions to search for water. While searching amid the forest undergrowth, they discovered a fountain that provided fresh water, which they brought back to relieve the rabbi's thirst. After drinking, he also used the water to wash his hands before praying, after which they all returned home.

Soon after, the rabbi visited the Baal Shem Tov and told him that ever since returning from that forest, his eyes and heart had been opened in Torah study and the service of G-d like never before. He thanked his teacher for sending him there.

The next Shabbat, during a meal attended by his close disciples, the Baal Shem Tov addressed R. Chaim, saying, "With G-d's help, you succeeded in your holy task, [and] with this journey, a very significant mission was accomplished! It is written in the holy *Zohar* that ever since G-d separated the lower waters from the upper waters on the second day of creation, the lower waters have been weeping and begging to appear before the Holy King, that they be used for holy purposes, such as hand washing before prayer, immersion in a *mikveh,* or having a drink of water that is preceded and followed by words of thanksgiving to its Maker.

"Near the place where I sent you, there was a fountain that had been weeping for five thousand, five hundred nineteen years—since the creation of the world: Why should it be less than all the other fountains in the world? Why should its waters be denied their elevation? Since the Holy One, Blessed Be He, created it, no one had ever made a blessing over its waters, and they had never been used for holy purposes. That day, when you drank its water and used it to wash your hands for prayer, you elevated that fountain. This was all the working of Divine Providence. Every creature and creation has a time for its elevation, and it is preordained when it will occur and by whom. And that is true for each and every soul; it, too, has its time for elevation."[60]

The insistence that everything in the world is part of G-d's Providence was a cornerstone of the Rebbe's teachings, and it inspired him to constantly repeat the teaching of the Baal Shem Tov that everything a Jew sees or hears must serve as a lesson in one's service of G-d.[61] As the Rebbe once wrote, "I have grown accustomed to searching for the *Hashgachah Pratit* in every opportunity."[62]

Recognizing *Hashgachah Pratit* at every step of our lives unlocks abundant opportunities to live better, more productive, purposeful, and optimistic lives. By following the threads with which we are woven into creation, we find a wholeness and sense of fulfillment that no other pursuit can provide.

No matter where you are in your life, from the lowest lows to the highest highs, G-d is there, guiding you and everything that surrounds you with Divine precision and loving intention. By choosing to view life through this clarifying lens, you are positioned to both read and write the *Book of Your Life*, borne by a stream of perpetual grace that is carrying you and everything else toward ultimate fulfillment and completion. Indeed, start right where you are. In all likelihood, it is exactly where you are supposed to be.

CHAPTER 6

Finding Your Focus

A TORMENTED MAN ONCE WROTE to the Rebbe regarding his recurring dreams about the world's many atrocities. In these dreams, the man wrote, he was overwhelmed by the never-ending injustice in the world. The solution presented in his dreams was to "ascend," that is, to take his own life. No amount of dream interpretation or expert counsel had helped him understand the meaning behind his dreams. In writing to the Rebbe, he sought guidance about how to discern their deeper meaning.

The Rebbe replied:

"…It is certain that the message of your dream is not about injustices in *the* world in the literal sense. For such issues are completely beyond your ability to rectify. Rather, the straightforward meaning of your dream is clear: You are being shown that you need to be 'angry' about the fact that *your* world—your personal life, over which you exercise full control—is being conducted 'unjustly...'"[63]

The implications here are profound, and they provide a paradigm shift for anyone struggling to discover a personal sense of purpose amid the myriad problems of the world.

Indeed, finding individual purpose and meaning is among life's greatest challenges. It is so challenging that we may avoid the question altogether by escaping into our momentary and immediate existence—whether that be work, relationships, or passions.

But the question of our life's purpose will always catch up to us.

And in this historical moment, those ready to face the question of their life's purpose can experience incredible difficulty. Thanks in large part to global information technologies, the question of our individual place and purpose in the world has become exceedingly overwhelming, and it is measured on a global scale.

Until very recently in history, the vast majority of us lived and died within fifty miles of the place where we were born. And even then, it was difficult to discern one's life's direction and meaning.

Today, mobile technologies put the world, its problems, and its possibilities in our hands. The number of registered mobile broadband subscriptions around the world increased from two hundred sixty-eight million active users in 2007 to an estimated 7.3 billion connections in 2023.[64] Meanwhile, a weekday edition of *The New York Times* contains more information than the average person was likely to come across during a lifetime in seventeenth-century England.[65] In 2012, more data was transmitted across the Internet each second than was stored in the whole Internet during the previous twenty years.[66] As our awareness of the world dilates faster than most can keep up, the question of our individual purpose and contribution can become paralyzing.[67, 68]

This state leaves the typical individual unmoored and disoriented, struggling to find their proverbial footing.

Increasingly, solutions to the resulting feelings of powerlessness are sought in mythologies defined by hyperbolic heroism. This trend can be seen in the exploding global popularity of comic books and their cinematic spinoffs. More and more, these mega-mythologies depict unlikely heroes arising from obscurity to save everything from one threat or another. Comic book storylines have expanded their scope exponentially, with "your friendly neighborhood Spider-Man" abandoning his local neighborhood to save the whole planet, other planets, galaxies, or even the entire universe.

Increasingly, emerging mythologies encourage us to emulate such outsized heroics. It is implied that if the stars align and you do the right things with enough audacity, you, too, can save the whole world from looming disaster. And while these stories may occasionally encourage real-life heroes to emerge, they can just as often leave us feeling overwhelmed, disempowered, and diminished.

In this world of overwhelming opportunity and possibility, the Rebbe repeatedly taught those struggling to find their personal mission and meaning to begin their journey by asking not, "How can I change *the* world?" but "How can I change *my* world?"[69]

Signature Sparks

This seemingly pragmatic perspective emerges from the deeper, metaphysical premise that G-d chooses a particular part of this world for each of us to nurture, impact, elevate, and illuminate. In the language of Kabbalah, before descending into this world, each soul is allocated a portion of the world, *chelko ba'olam,* and tasked with elevating certain "sparks" in specific locations at precise times that are intrinsically connected to our soul and its mission.[70]

Hidden within our personal mission and life story are heavenly orchestrations that gently direct us to the places, people, endeavors, and opportunities that are uniquely ours to uplift. Within Kabbalah, it is said that these unique opportunities—these sparks—have been waiting since the beginning of creation for our particular souls to redeem them. In fact, the mystics teach that these sparks have our names written on them, so to speak, and that no soul, prior to or following our stay on earth, can do the sacred work that is destined for us. It is here, inhabiting our part of this exquisitely crafted cosmic tapestry, that we discover our purpose in life. And this principle, however modest it may seem in its ambition, is absolutely essential in helping us design the focus of our impact.

Here, some may ask, "In an age of overwhelming injustice and global catastrophe, how could anyone choose to focus their efforts anywhere but everywhere?"

And herein lies a potential trap that can ensnare us as we search for our life's purpose.

The Rebbe spoke to this in the late 1960s, at the height of the Vietnam War, when he was approached by a Jewish chaplain on a college campus who asked how much time he should invest in anti-war and human rights demonstrations. Essentially, he wanted to know from the Rebbe how much of his time was too much if his participation in anti-war efforts came at the expense of his service to the local Jewish student body he was responsible to serve?

The Rebbe replied:

"...You have a responsibility to bring benefit to every human being. At the same time, you must consider the priorities presented to you by your current circumstances. If two people were drowning, and one was a stranger and you could save only one of them, wouldn't your brother come first?"[71]

Here we have a man deeply affected by a violent international conflict that had awoken global outrage and massive demonstrations that had their own sort of gravity, pulling anyone with a conscience toward them. For the socially and politically conscious, helping to end the war in Vietnam was depicted—and for many emphatically believed to be—a moral responsibility for anyone available to participate.

In response, the Rebbe brought the focus back to the chaplain's personal and immediate circumstances and responsibilities, punctuated by a starkly clarifying series of questions:

"How can I better my immediate surroundings? How can I best address the needs and dreams of those whom Divine Providence has brought into my personal orbit and sphere of life; my family, my friends, my community, and my people?"

This fundamental principle is rooted in an essential Talmudic passage that teaches:

"If you have the choice between supporting those who are poor in your family or the poor of your city, the poor in your family take precedence. [If the choice is between] the poor of your city and the poor of another city, the poor of your city take precedence."[72]

Such a localized approach to social change provides the basis of the Jewish notion of *Tikkun Olam*—repairing the world.[73]

This was the message the Rebbe shared with Janice Robertson, a leader in the Black community who was running for City Council. One Sunday morning, she joined the Sunday Dollars line and approached the Rebbe to ask for a blessing.

The Rebbe blessed her and said:

"By bringing more peace in one part of New York, you're automatically increasing the measure of peace in all of New York and after that in all of the United States. May G-d A-mighty bless that there be peace in all the nations around the world."[74]

Ripple Effect

This model of reverberating influence championed by the Rebbe—the kind that infinitely ripples out beyond its initial point of impact—begins with one person living out their unique purpose.

This point is powerfully reinforced in a story told by R. Chaim Gutnick about his efforts to organize a series of women's classes on the advice of the Rebbe. As it happened, just one woman arrived week after week to receive his teachings. A year later, during a follow-up visit, the Rebbe asked about the success of the classes. R. Gutnick related how he and his wife organized and promoted the event and worked hard to prepare for it. Yet, despite all their labor, only one woman showed up to the classes, leaving him feeling that all that effort had been a waste.

The Rebbe grew serious as he asked, "R. Chaim! Tell me, how many mothers did Moses have?"[75]

The Rebbe was teaching R. Gutnick, and each of us by extension, that we must never underestimate the power of even a single individual. We can never know what long-term impact our one blessing, one teaching, one smile, one good deed can have on the person we're interacting with, and its ripple effect on all the people with whom they come into contact.

This was the message offered to R. Sholom Ber Lipskar, the *shliach* to Bal Harbour, Florida, who is renowned for his oratory and eloquence.

"A certain benefactor was very inspired by our work and offered me an unlimited amount of money to spread 'my' message of accessible Judaism in a massive campaign across the country. The Rebbe rejected the idea outright.

"National media campaigns might be nice, but real impact is made organically, from the ground up, when a *shliach* makes a real connection with a person, who goes on to form more connections himself. That's how real change and success happens."[76]

The Rebbe explained this crucial point further in discussion with a young rabbi who was involved with outreach projects as well as a fledgling business and was feeling overwhelmed. He visited the Rebbe to discuss which of the areas he should focus on.

To his surprise, the Rebbe replied, "Not only should you not cut back on your activities, but you should increase your outreach efforts, your rabbinic work, and also your business."

"I'm humbled by your faith in me," exclaimed the rabbi, "but I don't feel it's realistic for me to manage all these tasks at once!"

The Rebbe looked at him warmly and said, "I'll tell you what your difficulty is. You are viewing human interactions like chemical interactions. When two elements interact, they result in the creation of a third compound. But people aren't chemicals. When people interact it's like a nuclear reaction.

"A nuclear reaction has a center, from which further reactions spread in all directions. As the outer rings of that sphere get larger, the number of reactions grows exponentially. Likewise, when you touch the heart of one person very deeply—even if only for a moment—he in turn will touch many other people, triggering a nuclear explosion of positive influence."[77, 78]

Here, we can see the so-called "butterfly effect," representing an aspect of chaos theory that suggests that in complex systems such as weather dynamics, even the smallest changes can have tremendous, far-reaching impacts. To explain this mathematical theorem, founder Edward Norton Lorenz used the poetic example of how a tornado's path can be shifted by tiny changes in the atmosphere, such as those generated by the beat of a butterfly's wings.

Act Locally, Impact Globally

The Torah offers its own example of this exponential effect in the story of Joseph, who rose from slavery to become the viceroy of Egypt, gaining international acclaim when he single-handedly saved the country and its neighbors from devastating famine and economic ruin.

During a talk he gave in 1973, the Rebbe offered the following penetrating insight.

If we are to pinpoint the event that set off Joseph's dramatic and meteoric rise from prisoner to second-in-command over that ancient superpower, it would undoubtedly be a conversation that took place between Joseph and his cellmates one morning in a dark Egyptian prison cell.

Upon encountering the despair written all over the faces of Pharaoh's ex-butler and baker, Joseph asked compassionately, *"Why are your faces downcast today?"*[79]

So attuned was he to their emotional state that he detected in their despondent demeanor a further deterioration from yesterday to today. *"Why are your faces downcast today?"*

He then proceeded to help them by interpreting their dreams, future, and fate. And it was as a result of his accurate predictions that he was later enlisted to help Pharaoh interpret his own dreams.

And the rest, as they say, is history.

Joseph proceeds to implement a system that saves Egypt from starvation, transforms its economy, and ends up providing safe passage for his family, who immigrated to Egypt to escape the famine in Canaan.

But on the morning that Joseph's fate would change, he wasn't busy thinking globally, about politics, power, fortune, or fame.

On that day, he didn't wake up asking himself, "How can I change *the* world?"

Instead, he asked himself, "How can I change *my* world, and my surroundings," which at the time consisted of a prison cell and two miserable cellmates.

Joseph understood that true success is defined by the quality of your response to the needs of the people in front of you and in your ability to faithfully hear G-d's call in those challenges you never sought and those situations you never planned for.

This principle is again articulated in the very first Biblical scene in which we are introduced to Moses, who is inarguably one of the most influential men in history. Moses did not begin his illustrious career in leadership looking for greatness or grandeur. His soul was stirred to action by an injustice he stumbled upon and chose to respond to.

As the Torah recounts:

In those days, Moses grew up and went out to his brothers and observed their suffering. He saw an Egyptian man striking a Hebrew man of his brothers. He turned this way and that way, and he saw that there was no man; so he struck the Egyptian and hid him in the sand.[80]

In other words, Moses did not wake up that morning, look in the mirror, and ask, "How can I change *the* world and go down in history as the man who brought Egypt to its knees and gave voice to a downtrodden people?"

Instead, he asked himself, "How can I change *my* world? How can I stop the injustices taking place in my neighborhood, to my people, to the man being beaten before my eyes?"

Ultimately, real world-changing leaders such as Joseph and Moses rarely set out to be powerful and influential figureheads. They simply respond to the call of the hour and their immediate environment, and in so doing, they discover their personal calling and mission. This casts the popular slogan, "Think Globally, Act Locally" in a wonderful new light, demonstrating the counterintuitive spiritual truth that those who think locally, can, in the end, act globally and change the world in the process.

CHAPTER 7

Personality, Passion, and Purpose

A YOUNG MAN NAMED MEIR Bastomsky once visited the Rebbe in search of guidance regarding his professional future. He had invested much time in training to become a mechanical engineer, but he remained unsure that this path was for him.

The Rebbe advised, "If financial matters are not your main concern, then choose a career in education."

Meir was initially taken aback by the Rebbe's answer; after all, it seemed like such a waste to abandon all the effort he had put into his previous training. But the Rebbe's words reminded him that in high school, Israeli psychometric examinations had shown that he had a natural aptitude and was more drawn to humanities than to science.

Summarizing the impact of the Rebbe's advice, Meir recalled in an interview:

"The Rebbe understood that I was more suited for education than engineering. I learned that for financial gain, a person may find himself working in a profession that does not fit his natural talents and makeup. He might have economic satisfaction but not emotional satisfaction. Only when a person works in a realm that truly suits him will he feel that he is fulfilling his true mission in this world. This insight changed my life. The Rebbe revealed to me that my life's mission—and indeed my emotional wholeness—lay in a profession that was more spiritual. How right he was!"[81]

In a world driven by the pursuit of material gain, status, and power, it's all too common to bypass our own personalities and passions in deciding what to do with our lives. But as the Rebbe counseled countless times, there are few more important or reliable indicators of your Divine purpose than the natural passions and personality that G-d gave you.

Without these critical indications to guide us, it is easy to be mesmerized and misled by opportunities that do not suit us. As we become lost in a sea of possibilities, we can drift far from the purpose that is meant for us.

This was precisely the point of advice provided by the Rebbe to a rabbi who was keen to become an emissary of Chabad. Having received invitations to several enticing *shlichut* opportunities, he wrote a letter to the Rebbe describing the various positions that had been offered to him, and he asked for guidance in making his final choice.

In response to the diverse array of proposals the young man presented, the Rebbe asked, "How is it possible for one person to be suited to all of the above positions, which vary completely?"[82]

The Rebbe then explained that when a person is trying to settle on a vocation, he ought to first consider what he is most suited to, what he is capable of, and what is most practical given his natural aptitudes and inclinations. From this place of inner alignment, one is more able to clearly discern when an opportunity is suited to their purpose.

The Rebbe impressed this truth upon Jewish law student Michael Tabor, who had been invited by his friend, R. Shmuel Lew, to visit 770, during which time he was given an opportunity to meet the Rebbe. During his one-on-one, he mentioned that his two great passions were chamber music and Chasidic melodies, and that he was a proud leader of the orchestra at the London School of Economics. He also mentioned that he would wear his yarmulke when playing, but he still felt a bit guilty that he was indulging his love of music instead of studying Torah.

"Isn't it a waste of time?" he asked the Rebbe.

The Rebbe answered, "If you feel that music is important to you, then focus on that. You have a gift—so put it to good use. But while you're in the orchestra, do more than just play....I want you to go out of your way to influence the non-Jews there to live life according to the Seven Noahide Laws."

Later, when interviewed about the encounter, Michael recalled, "I could have fallen right through the floor. Here was the Rebbe in New York worrying about the morality and spiritual lives of non-Jews playing in a school orchestra in London."[83]

Indeed, the Rebbe often challenged the entrenched assumption that one's passions are somehow opposed to a life of religious devotion.

For example, when Eli Lipsker was a student in the Lubavitcher Yeshiva in Brooklyn, he played music enthusiastically as a hobby. His school's administrators, however, frowned on his extracurriculars, fearing they would come at the expense of his studies. Their concern about his divided focus later came to a head when Eli was caught skipping school to attend classes at the Juilliard School of Music in Manhattan. At that point, they began the process of expelling Eli from the *yeshivah*. Customarily, however, no student was expelled unless the dean received the Rebbe's approval.

When the dean went to see the Rebbe to discuss Eli's case, he was surprised when the Rebbe asked him whether the *yeshivah* had provided Eli an allowance to help cover costs of music lessons outside of *yeshivah* hours!

Eli would go on to achieve musical renown, with his celebrated children's choir regularly performing at events in the local community. In fact, Eli, whom the Rebbe would come to refer to warmly as "my musician," would often perform at rallies and gatherings held at 770, and he led the main services there during the High Holidays.[84]

With customary insightfulness, the Rebbe recognized the Hand of G-d in these young men's love of music, teaching them that serving G-d and following their dreams were not mutually exclusive. Quite the contrary—their dreams and passions were G-d's way of pointing them toward the souls and circumstances that were intrinsic to their unique purpose waiting to be fulfilled.

Follow Your Heart

In addition to looking at our personal passions and proclivities, another way to discover our purpose in life is to identify and follow the pull of causes that resonate deeply in our souls. For, according to spiritual teaching, those resonances were planted in your soul by G-d to lead you to the broken parts of the world you are intended to mend.

Shavi Slodowitz had found her spiritual home in Brownsville, New York, at Bais Rikvah, a Chabad school. She met the Rebbe for the first time when she was twelve years old, and he immediately became a beacon on her spiritual journey.

One Friday, while walking in Brooklyn, Shavi encountered a stray kitten that had been abandoned and left crying in the street. Shavi had always been obsessed with animals and often brought home strays, to her parents' frustration. Despite the threat of her parents' disapproval, she picked up the kitten and continued on her way home. As she walked, Shavi encountered the Rebbe, who looked at her and the kitten, broke out in a huge smile, and warmly wished her: "*Gut Shabbos!*"

"I was in heaven," Shavi later recalled in an interview. "I ran home and told my mother that, no matter what happened, I was going to care for this kitten. I felt that my feelings for animals had been legitimized by the Rebbe's response."

Several years later, Shavi got involved in publishing her high school's yearbook and was invited by her principal to write an article in Hebrew.

"My initial response was, 'I can't write in English, let alone Hebrew!,'" she recounted. "So I refused. He wouldn't take no for an answer and offered me all kinds of incentives, but I was a very stubborn girl and held my ground."

Shortly thereafter, in a private audience with the Rebbe, he asked Shavi how school was going, and she mentioned the conflict over her refusal to write the article.

The Rebbe replied, "There must be some subject that you care deeply about and would want to make the effort to write about."

"What I have strong feelings for are animals," she replied.

"Then why don't you write about *tzaar baalei chayim*, the commandment not to be cruel to animals," he suggested.

Driven by the Rebbe's inspiring suggestion, Shavi wrote an article about all the instances in which the Torah stresses the importance of being kind to animals.

The Rebbe's validating guidance set Shavi on a lifelong path of caring for animals in her professional and personal lives. Commenting on the Rebbe's profound impact on the course of her life, she said:

"I have worked for the RSPCA and was a parrot breeder for many years. Now that I have retired from education, I spend my time caring for other people's animals and educating people how animals can help disabled children and the elderly as a very effective form of therapy.

"Looking back, I have to say that the Rebbe definitely raised my self-esteem and self-awareness, and he also shaped my unusual life and the way I perceive things. He had an amazing ability to motivate me—just as he has motivated many people—and encourage me to do things I never thought I was capable of or even wanted to do. Being able to tap into each individual's uniqueness, and to advise and guide them accordingly is what made the Rebbe so great. To have had the privilege to be one of those individuals is what I will always be grateful for."[85]

The Rebbe often reoriented people toward their purpose by shining a light on their unique abilities and where and how they might be matched to the needs around them.

A notable example of this illuminating influence was shared by Chief Rabbi Jonathan Sacks in the following reflection on his life's journey:

> "I did not want to be a rabbi at the beginning of my career. I had an aspiration to be an economist. I had an aspiration to be a lawyer. I had a dream of being an academic. I didn't think of becoming a rabbi until really quite late. I was very conscious that we were short of rabbis. That's what needed to be done. But I never saw that that's what I wanted to do until [the Rebbe] lit that little spark, that flame in me, and all of a sudden what I wanted to do became what needed to be done, and so I became a rabbi."[86]

Summing up the wisdom he received from the Rebbe, R. Sacks concluded:

"Where what you want to do meets what needs to be done, that is where G-d wants you to be."

Whatever your personality, passions, or pursuits, know that you were crafted perfectly to fulfill the role you are here to play. Whatever external opportunities beckon in your search for purpose, remember to look first at, and into, yourself, your unique strengths, truest desires, gifts, passions, and cherished pastimes. Take the time to feel their gravity, because they are drawing you gently toward your life's greatest purpose and possibilities.

CHAPTER 8

Your Talent Is Your Instrument

H AVING SURVIVED THE MURDER of his family by the Nazis, fighting for Russia in World War II, fifteen years of imprisonment in a Soviet work camp for helping his family flee from the Soviet Union, and finally immigration to the United States, gifted painter Chenoch Hendel Lieberman arrived in Paris, where he finally settled within the growing Lubavitch community.

At the time, the sixth Lubavitcher Rebbe, R. Yosef Yitzchak Schneersohn, was living in New York. Seeking counsel, Lieberman wrote to him across the Atlantic, asking for help reconciling the two things in his life that still held meaning—his art and his religion—which he had often felt were at odds.

R. Yosef Yitzchak immediately understood the needs of the troubled artist, and he responded with his own spiritual perspective on the arts.

Like most called to the creative life, he wrote, Lieberman needed the opportunity to remake the world as seen through his own unique lens. He explained that for the true Chasid, all aspects of life must be integrated into a harmonious whole, and that the means by which each Jew approaches and understands G-d is unique, including the way of the artist.

Thanks to this poignant response, Lieberman felt the tension between his artistic drive and Chasidic way of life dissolve, and he began painting again with previously unmatched dedication, employing the now harmonized aspects of art and spirit to initiate a new vision for his work. Paris, meanwhile, turned out to be the perfect place to nourish his reawakened inspiration.

Over the years, the traumatic memories of war and unimaginable personal loss returned to haunt the artist, and with those memories came renewed doubts about whether painting was an appropriate vocation for a Chasid. By then, R. Yosef Yitzchak had passed on, so he wrote to the Rebbe, who had since taken the mantle of Chabad leadership, for guidance.

The Rebbe responded by reminding him that the artist plays a uniquely holy role in creation, and that his purpose in life was to reveal the inner dimensions of the world through the lens of his particular artistic vision. In this way, the artist facilitates a special brand of redemption and *tikkun*, revealing beauty in things that most people take for granted, and thereby elevating the sparks concealed within the subject of each work.

The Rebbe wrote:

> "Our mission in life—based on the simple faith that *there is none else besides Him*—is that we should approach everything in life from this perspective. That we should each strive to reveal, as much as possible, the Divine essence in everything, and minimize, to the extent that we are able, its concealment by the externalities of creation…"[87]

Ignited by the Rebbe's reply, Lieberman moved to the growing Chasidic community in Crown Heights, Brooklyn. There, he took great comfort from the religious understanding that Chasidism provided. Now living in physical proximity to the Rebbe, he flourished even more. He was overjoyed to be occupying an honored position behind the Rebbe at prayers and *farbrengens*. The artist soon became an important figure in the Chabad-Lubavitch community, and he went on to enjoy great success and recognition for his talent.

Years later, while reflecting on his career, Lieberman

quoted the Rebbe's life-changing message that set him on his path:

"Each person on this earth is allotted a task. You have a talent...use it. True, in the old days, painting was not considered an acceptable way to achieve this aim [of bringing people to faith]. Today, it is. It is your way."[88]

In line with the premise that the first place to look for our personal mission in this world is within our own inner composition and makeup, one of the major and recurring themes of the Rebbe's guidance to individuals seeking their Divine purpose was to analyze and actualize the innate talents they were given by G-d.

The Times They Are a Changin'

In earlier times, it was not standard belief in religious Jewish communities that artistic talents are Divine instruments that should be developed and used for a higher purpose.

This is because the world of creative arts throughout Europe following the Enlightenment—from music, to art, to literature and film—was known for pushing, rather than preserving, social and moral boundaries, introducing new voices and ideas that challenged the prevailing establishment. For hundreds of years, the secular arts were known for confronting and mocking traditional beliefs and ways of life, all in the name of uninhibited exploration. It is understandable, then, that there was resistance and suspicion in conservative religious communities regarding the arts. This misgiving, in turn, led to a general discouragement of artists indulging and developing such talents within their communities.

The Rebbe, however, believed that times had changed, and, in discussions with numerous people who sought his guidance regarding their unique artistic aptitudes, often echoed the words of his father-in-law, the sixth Lubavitcher Rebbe, R. Yosef Yitzchak, who said:

> "Talent is a gift from G-d. Some people are endowed by G-d with a talent for singing; others with a talent for oratory and elocution, or a talent for instructing; and some people are graced by G-d with a talent for educating, and so on. Talents are [expressions of the] the soul's spiritual powers—its limbs.
>
> The soul's essence extends into these limbs, animating them according to their particular character and enabling them [thereby] to carry out their unique tasks."[89]

Indeed, according to the Midrash, one's talent is more than a gift to be used or discarded at will; it's an invitation, and even a directive, from on High to use their G-d-given instrument to bring light and healing to the world.

As the verse states in Proverbs: *Honor the L-rd mei-honecha—from your possessions.*[90]

The word *honecha* in this verse literally means "your

wealth" or "your possessions." The simple meaning of this text is thus understood to mean that we should honor G-d by using all of our material possessions for a G-dly purpose. For example, by using our money to feed the poor, we honor G-d.

The Midrash takes this line of thinking a step further by interpreting the verse to mean that we should not only use all of our material wealth to serve G-d, but our wealth of *talents,* as well.[91]

A beautiful example of this can be seen in an exchange between the Rebbe and beloved Cantor Joseph Malovaney.

Malovany is a world-renowned tenor vocalist and distinguished professor of liturgical music at Philip and Sarah Belz School of Jewish Music whose concerts have been attended by presidents and prime ministers alike.

In 1973, Malovany took the post of cantor at the Fifth Avenue Synagogue in New York. After some time there, Malovany was invited to a *farbrengen* at 770, where he first met the Rebbe. The Rebbe would often offer blessings for success in his career and urge him to use his talent to hold concerts around the world, including performances specifically dedicated to raising charity.

On one occasion, the Rebbe said, "You should honor G-d with your voice," explaining, "According to our Sages, the verse [from Proverbs], *Honor G-d with all of your possessions*, can be read to mean, *Honor G-d with your voice*, which applies to a cantor."[92]

The Rebbe quipped, "If I would try, I don't know if I'd succeed—the audience might run away. But when you sing, more people come, and they increase their donations as well."[93]

From the Rebbe's point of view, your talent is G-d's way of placing you on the doorstep of your life's purpose. Whatever your skill set, artistic or otherwise, and whatever capacity it provides to do good in the world, your talent is a G-d-given instrument that empowers you uniquely. This power is both a blessing and a responsibility. Using your talent isn't merely allowed or worth the risk. Talent is a gift from G-d, and it comes with a commensurate, sacred duty to put it to use for the greatest possible good. In this way, we become co-creators of a better world.

A Letter from the Grave

The following story illustrates just how deeply the Rebbe believed that steadfast and dedicated use of one's talents will inevitably yield spiritual fruit.

Following the conclusion of Rosh Hashanah one year, Natan Yellin Moor, a secular Israeli writer, arrived at 770 to receive *kos shel brachah* from the Rebbe.[94]

Born in Vilna to religiously observant parents, Natan had studied at the city's world-renowned Jewish academies. As a young man, however, Natan abandoned the beliefs and practices of Judaism in favor of secular Zionism, eventually becoming a staunch activist and fighting for an independent Jewish state. After the establishment of the modern State of Israel in 1948, Natan became disillusioned with the cause for which he had fought, and he began to regularly publish articles defaming everything Jewish, particularly the Jewish state and its policies.

Natan arrived before the Rebbe thanks to his acquaintance with the late Gershon Jacobson, editor of the New York-based Yiddish newspaper, *The Algemeiner Journal*. To the frustration of many of his readers, Jacobson had invited the self-proclaimed atheist to write for the *Algemeiner*, often publishing the venomously anti-Israel and anti-Jewish articles on his behalf. When Gershon suggested to Natan that he meet the Rebbe, the writer reluctantly accepted the invitation.

After introductions, the Rebbe turned to Natan, smiled broadly, and said: "I've read your articles."

Natan was taken aback that a Chasidic Rebbe had read his inflammatory and often heretical articles. He was even more surprised when the Rebbe appeared to endorse his work!

"When G-d blesses someone with a talent such as yours," the Rebbe said, "one must utilize it to the fullest. This is a Divine calling and an immense responsibility. It is your G-d-given power and duty to make full use of your capacity to reach out to others and influence them with your writing."

Confused, and thinking perhaps the Rebbe had mistaken his identity, Natan asked: "Does the Rebbe agree with what I write?"

The Rebbe replied with a smile: "One need not agree with everything one reads." The Rebbe then shifted the conversation back to his essential point. "What is most important is that one utilizes one's G-d-given talents. When one does so, one will ultimately arrive at the truth."

Before the writer could process the Rebbe's unexpected encouragement, the Rebbe asked a question that awakened something in his heart.

"Tell me," the Rebbe said in a gentle tone, "what is happening in regard to your observance of Torah and *mitzvot*?"

Not wanting to deceive the Rebbe, Natan replied, "A Jew contemplates..."

"But in *Yiddishkeit*," the Rebbe said, quoting a familiar Talmudic maxim, "it's most important *to do* [i.e., not just contemplate]. 'The primary thing is the deed.'"

Several months later, Natan was diagnosed with terminal cancer, with doctors giving him just months to live. Shortly before his death, he sent a sealed envelope to Gershon Jacobson with a note asking that it be published posthumously.

Gershon agreed, and following Natan's death, the article was printed in *The Algemeiner Journal.*

"My dear reader," Natan had written. "As you read this article, I am standing before the heavenly court and being judged for all the actions I took and the choices I made in the course of my life. No doubt, I will be judged for living a life totally antithetical to anything Jewish. In fact, I have severe doubts that I will even be allowed to speak in my defense. This is why I asked your editor to print this now, as I stand before the heavenly court, in the hope that what is being read and discussed at this moment on earth will attract the attention of the Supernal Judge. For I do have one merit I wish to present to the court in the face of all my failings and transgressions."[95]

Describing his exchange with the Rebbe, Natan concluded, "The Rebbe told me that I have a G-d-given talent, and that it is my sacred duty to utilize it to influence others. This I did to the best of my ability, however misguidedly. This is the only merit I can claim; may it lighten the destiny of my soul...."

The Rebbe believed that the merit and incorruptible potential that accompanies each person's unique talents never expires. Even in the twilight of a life that had been lived in direct conflict with traditional Judaism, the Rebbe saw a spark of heavenly fire and marvelous possibility. He believed that as long as you live, and even after, you can always become what G-d made you to be and put your talents to work for the benefit of the world and humanity.

Whether award-winning authors Herman Wouk, Chaim Grade, or Chaim Potok; sculptor Jacques Lifshitz; or renowned musicians such as American tenor Jan Pierce and Bob Dylan, the Rebbe repeatedly encouraged every individual to use his or her unique talents, artistic or otherwise, to promote goodness and G-dliness in the world.

Each talent, he repeated often, comes with a distinct responsibility. Of course, the magnitude and bearing of that responsibility changes depending on the talents and capacity bestowed on the individual by G-d. But no matter what the talent, aesthetic, or skill level, the Rebbe's call was clear—your *sui generis* talents are remarkable vehicles to fulfill your personal mission in the world, and their power must be used, as with all other blessings, for the sake of revealing the light of G-d in the world. In this way, your G-d-given gifts will find their highest expression, bear their greatest fruit, and fulfill the world-shaping holy purpose for which they were intended.

CHAPTER 9

Why Me?
The Hidden Blessing
in Struggle

O NE OF THE MOST transformative and enduring texts of Jewish spirituality is the *Tanya*, written by the founder of the Chabad Chasidic movement, R. Schneur Zalman, known as the Alter Rebbe. Having achieved great renown, he had become so inundated by thousands seeking his counsel that he decided to write a book that would articulate Judaism's approach to many of the most universal and pervasive human struggles. In his introduction, he describes the purpose of this holy work as replacing the need for face-to-face private audiences. In this way, the *Tanya* was essentially the first Jewish self-help book ever written.

In Chapter 27, the Alter Rebbe addresses the spiritual

seeker perpetually struggling to achieve righteousness amid the relentless temptations and machinations of their indwelling negative inclination.

At his wits' end, this proverbial spiritual struggler, the *beinoni* of the *Tanya*, despairingly laments: "I feel like I am endlessly treading water; lots of motion, but no progress."

The Alter Rebbe provides the following uplifting counsel: "One should not feel depressed or troubled at heart, even if you are to be engaged in this battle every day of your life."

He then offers perhaps the three most radical words in the *Tanya*:

"*Ulay l'kach nivra.*"[96]

That is, "Perhaps you were created *in order to struggle.*"

Put simply, here we learn that Jewish spirituality sees struggle as part of *our very purpose in life.*

This profound teaching turns our understanding of life's many challenges on its head. In it, we learn that life's struggles, both inner and outer, are not impositions to be avoided or solved. Rather, each challenge is a providentially placed opportunity to extract and transmute the light hidden in even the most trying of circumstances.

As a contemporary Chasidic thinker put it:

"Some think life is all about doing good and keeping away from evil. To them, struggle has no purpose of its own—to have struggled is to have failed. Success, they imagine, is a sweet candy with no trace of bitterness.

They are wrong, tragically wrong. Struggle is an opportunity to reach the ultimate—when darkness itself becomes light. In the midst of struggle, an inner light is awakened. Light profound enough to overwhelm the darkness, encasing it and winning it over."[97]

Epic Fail

The story of humanity's very first struggle, as recounted in the Torah, represents arguably the most far-reaching tragedy of all time. Adam and Eve's inability to obey G-d's command to refrain from eating the forbidden fruit, and their subsequent banishment from the Garden of Eden, are generally understood to be the root source of humanity's perpetual struggle with temptation.

During a talk given on Simchat Torah in 1963, the Rebbe explained the deeper meaning embedded in this quintessential story, which was previously obscured by prevailing interpretations.

According to the Rebbe, Adam's test was the archetypal trial of the human condition, and the Garden of Eden was the proving ground for humanity.

Would the first human beings obey the first Divine commandment ever given?

Given the significance of those primordial conditions,

Adam's every move would impact and set the course for human history from that moment forward.

The stakes couldn't have been higher.

According to the Rebbe's rendering, it was precisely because of the enormity of Adam's responsibility that the snake, symbolizing the human inclination to disobey the Divine, exerted such enormous energies and focused all of its strength on sabotaging Adam's mission.

Seen through this lens, the story of Adam's struggle with the serpent teaches that the more resistance we encounter when faced with a particular challenge to do something noble, the more essential overcoming that challenge is to the fulfillment of our purpose in life.

The Rebbe concluded the talk, saying:

"We find this to be the case in our own lives as well. A spiritual or moral matter that objectively should be a simple and easy matter for a particular individual to accomplish—and, indeed, is simply and easily accomplished by others—proves incredibly difficult for that person to achieve. Precisely because it is critical to that person's individual mission in life to accomplish this matter, the difficulties and challenges he or she faces are proportionally formidable."

Rather than discourage us, the greatness of our challenges in life should serve as an indicator of how important it is to persist in our efforts, and it should reassure us that since we were presented with such a challenge, we were certainly also granted the resources and fortitude to surmount it.[98]

This powerful teaching highlights an essential aspect of the principle of specific Divine Providence. Namely, and perhaps counterintuitively, that *the more difficult the struggle, the more integral that struggle is to your life's mission.*

The Bigger They Are, the Harder They Call

The Rebbe saw all kinds of opposition and challenges to the path of righteousness as surefire indicators that one is on the right path, going so far as to say that the more opposition one encounters when doing something positive, the more certain one should be that such a challenging endeavor is connected to their purpose in life.

For example, in 1968, after initiating a campaign encouraging all Jewish men to wear *tefillin*,[99] he received fierce criticism and pushback from a particular Rebbe of a different Chasidic court. He later commented that he found the backlash comforting, because historically, whenever a meritorious movement arose within Judaism, opposition would come not only from the negative inclination but from holy circles, as well.

The Rebbe shared the same perspective with R. Menachem Hacohen after he was elected to the Knesset in the 1970s and experienced severe opposition from certain political parties because he didn't toe the party line. When the attacks reached their peak, Menachem came before the Rebbe and shared that he was thinking of retiring due to the increasing intensity of the personal attacks.

"Maybe I'll just leave this entire business. What do I need it for?" he asked.

"What you are doing is good; you mustn't stop. And you shouldn't be afraid of anyone," the Rebbe replied, adding: "The Chasidic movement became stronger because it had opponents. When a person no longer has any opponents, they need to examine themselves; perhaps they are not doing what they are supposed to."[100]

The same insight helped invigorate R. and Rebbetzin Binjamini, who had been sent repeatedly to revive and establish Jewish schools throughout Brazil, each time facing considerable opposition from local communities.

"Why is everything so difficult?" the *rebbetzin* once asked the Rebbe.

The Rebbe replied: "Since you are fighting assimilation, the forces of negativity are trying to fight back. It is like a candle; just before a flame goes out, it suddenly starts to sputter and jump. It's not a reason to be dismayed, but to do even more."[101]

An Enviable Position

No matter the nature of one's struggle—whether it be internal or external, perpetual or fleeting, physical or spiritual—G-d provides us with the commensurate abilities, tools, and strength to help us overcome them.

A beautiful example of this empowering perspective can be found in the story of a traditional Jew who found himself in a relationship discouraged by the Torah. Arriving before the Rebbe, he explained that he desperately wanted to live in alignment with the Torah and G-d's will, but he had powerful inclinations that persistently led him astray.

After describing his situation, the man fell silent and prepared himself for admonishment, expecting to be told in no uncertain terms how gravely he had failed to live up to G-d's commandments.

The Rebbe remained silent for a moment and then finally said softly, "I envy you."

Surprised and confused, the young man clearly did not know what to make of the Rebbe's reply.

The Rebbe explained:

"There are many ladders in life; each person is given his or her own. The ladders present themselves as life's challenges and difficult choices. The tests you face are the ladders that elevate you to great heights—the greater the challenge, the higher the ladder. G-d has given you this difficult test because He believes you can overcome it, and He has endowed you with the ability to do so. Only the strongest are presented a ladder as challenging as yours. Don't you see, then, why I envy you?"[102]

Why Me?

Each of us is given our own ladders to climb. Their many rungs comprise the personal hurdles of morality and circumstance that we must overcome to reach our highest potential and achieve our true purpose. Seen in this light, life's challenges become rungs to ascend rather than roadblocks to avoid, providentially placed in our path to help us reach our greatest spiritual heights.

By overcoming the challenges that wait along the path of our purpose, we unleash inner strength and manifest capabilities that a life of ease and privilege could never impart or invoke.

"Every flower must grow through dirt," goes the saying.

This perspective emerges from the Rebbe's unalterable awareness that the Divine permeates every aspect of existence. Even the direst circumstances and personal challenges are infused with Divine sparks waiting to be unleashed. As far as the Rebbe was concerned, there is no struggle that is merely a burden. Indeed, the Rebbe believed that the greatest challenges conceal the greatest light and that the deepest depths also house the greatest spiritual rewards.

A breathtaking example of this spiritual truth is found in the Rebbe's exchange with a young man who was suffering from excruciating personal spiritual challenges.

He penned a letter to the Rebbe, asking one simple question: "Why me?"

The Rebbe responded:

"We do not know. The mysteries of people's journeys are beyond our human finite comprehension."[103]

The Rebbe then offered a revitalizing insight, saying: "One observation that can be suggested… If an individual experiences a particularly difficult, or trying, situation, it may be assumed that Hashem has given him extraordinary powers to overcome the extraordinary difficulty. The individual concerned is probably unaware of his real inner strength; the trial may therefore be designed for the sole purpose of bringing out in the individual his hidden strength, which, after overcoming his problem, can be added henceforth to the arsenal of his revealed capacities, in order to utilize both for infinitely greater achievements for the benefit of himself, and others."

Put simply, sometimes a person possesses an incredible inner light that can change the world. There is no way for this person to discover that secret power within himself and call it his own without being compelled to overcome a major challenge.

It is often the case that we ourselves are unaware of the inherent power and truest potential of our own souls. It isn't until we are forced by adversity to dig deep and find our greatest strengths that we are empowered to change the world. We are thus impelled to travel to an uncharted place in ourselves, which would have otherwise remained undiscovered. In that process, we unleash the true power and light of the soul, which, when integrated, can illuminate our lives and our world in incredibly powerful ways.

Where others might have looked down on the young man with disdain or pity, the Rebbe saw someone graced with tremendous spiritual strength, signaled by the very struggles that made others doubt his inherent sacredness. Where others saw a tragedy of morality, the Rebbe saw an opportunity to reach for unmatched spiritual heights. The young man wasn't crippled by a crisis of virtue—he had been sent as an emissary into the deepest darkness because his potential to shine the light of G-d was of a greater magnitude.

Indeed, it would have been easy for G-d to clear the way for us, allowing us to coast effortlessly along the paths of our lives. But in His infinite wisdom and benevolence, G-d orchestrated for each of us to encounter roadblocks and obstacles that invoke our greatest potentials.

In this way, the uphill battles of our lives become spiral paths leading us ever higher and closer to G-d and to fulfilling our most sacred purpose.

CHAPTER 10

The Virtue of Vice

T HE PROVIDENTIAL DESIGN OF our personal struggles is not only found in external challenges. Indeed, some of our greatest challenges originate from within. Chief among these internal challenges are our entrenched and enduring vices and character flaws—anger, lust, greed, arrogance, and indifference, to name a few. Counterintuitively, our Sages tell us that our inborn vices are also invitations that serve as critical signals pointing us toward our mission in life.

As opposed to a purely pragmatic approach, which would suggest evading the areas of personality you struggle with most, the mystical teachings of Judaism convey that part of our sacred purpose in life is to face, channel, and redeem our natural vices, character flaws, and the difficult or "broken" parts of our personalities.

Based on the belief that "G-d does not create anything

superfluous,"[104] time and again, the Rebbe insisted that every part of us can be harnessed in the service of G-d and humanity. In fact, even the seemingly undesirable aspects of our personalities—including our shadows, not just our sunshine—have potential for elevation. As such, rather than seeing our character flaws as curses to be excised or avoided, we are taught to see them as gifts from G-d waiting to be "unpacked" and put to good use.

Paradoxically, it is our shadows that represent some of the most powerful instruments in our personal toolkit for bringing our individual light to the world and fulfilling our purpose in life.

In the words of the Rebbe in *Hayom Yom*: "Every soul has its own [designated] Divine service in the realm of intellect and emotion, each according to its nature and disposition. It is written, *Make me wise from my enemies*—that is, from the negative leanings that a person senses in his own undeveloped character traits, he can gain wisdom and know how to tackle his tasks of self-refinement, and how to harness his personal strengths to G-d's service."[105, 106, 107]

The following stories demonstrate the Rebbe's persistent application of this principle.

A Chasid once complained to the Rebbe that his righteous behavior was often motivated by concerns about his public image.

"I am often consumed by thoughts of what others will say or think about me," he said.

The Rebbe replied:

> "That's not a bad way to think—if used as a motivator. Next time you are debating whether to stay and study longer, think to yourself, 'What will people say about me?' and this will cause you to study for longer."[108]

In an ideal world, our positive behavior would be motivated by our values rather than by the way we are perceived by others. However, if we use our ignoble intentions as fuel, we can, to use the above example, harness our seemingly shallow hunger for status and attention to propel us beyond where we might have reached based on our own "pure" motivations. One might call such a process *spiritual composting*—processing our psychic refuse and putting it to work for productive ends.

In another instance, a man asked the Rebbe: "Rebbe, what should I do to get rid of my inflated ego?"

"Why get rid of it?" the Rebbe replied. "Why not live up to your own great expectation of yourself? Be the amazing person whom you believe you are."

Traditionally, Chasidic thought emphasizes and values *bittul*, the negation of one's ego or entitled self. In fact, *yeshut*, the strong sense of selfhood, which is predicated on a skewed sense of self-importance, is most often considered by the Chasidic masters to be the nemesis of holiness.

However, according to the Rebbe, ego can also be channeled for holiness; in fact, it must be used properly. From this perspective, one's ego is not inherently negative. To the contrary, if integrated within a broader spiritual structure, it can play a catalyzing role in actualizing our purpose in life by providing the confidence and internal horsepower required to become your greatest self.

Yet another example can be found in the story of a Chasid living in London whose son Yaakov was melancholy by nature. Yaakov was withdrawn and did not seem to get very excited about anything.

"What can I do to change my son's nature?" the distraught father asked the Rebbe.

The Rebbe replied, "Your son's nature does not need to be changed. He can use this part of his personality toward positive ends—for example, to help advance his studies."

"Introversion is good for focused study and contemplation," the Rebbe explained, adding that a penchant for critical judgment is beneficial for self-refinement and, more broadly speaking, locating what is lacking and articulating what is necessary for progress.[109]

Sacred Mistakes

In the same way that all aspects of the personality can be channeled and elevated, the Rebbe insisted that all aspects of our life experience—even our misdeeds—are an essential part of our life story and can be harnessed and used for the greater good.

This was the empowering message shared by the Rebbe with a group of Jewish inmates who came to see him. The visit had been organized by R. Sholom Ber Lipskar, who, inspired by the Rebbe's teachings, founded an organization called Aleph, which helps provide spiritual and moral support for Jewish prisoners and their families.

R. Lipskar shared[110] that during their encounter with the Rebbe, "the Rebbe talked about the concept of jail and about the fact that men and women who were incarcerated have a mission from G-d that is extraordinary; otherwise G-d would not put them in such a situation where they are in an 'exile within an exile'[111]...[The Rebbe then] talked about the [unique] opportunities and mission that these men are on."[112]

Put simply, while it's true that the *cause* of these individual's incarceration was related to crimes they committed, the *reason* they found themselves in prison was that their souls had been handpicked by heaven and sent into a place of exile and existential darkness for the purpose of bringing Divine light into a place of dire hopelessness and despair!

Here, in this radically redemptive approach, the Rebbe asserts that even our mistakes and poor choices can be seen as Divine indicators and invitations meant to help us fulfill our unique Divine purpose.

Unexpected Yield

Indeed, the Rebbe saw the same potential even in the most unexpected of places—sin and transgression—recognizing the explosive power for return and renewal embedded within our spiritual and moral failings.

Always rooting his teachings in classic Judaic texts, the Rebbe often quoted the Talmudic teaching[113] that through proper *teshuvah*, even sins can be transformed into merits and *mitzvot*. Much like the velocity created by pulling back a slingshot, the spiritual distance and subsequent yearning caused by sin becomes the very force that propels us powerfully toward greater engagement with our soul and spiritual purpose.

A beautiful illustration of this redemptive dynamic is found in the case of a woman who became religious later in life. As a student, the woman had spent many years in the Far East engaging with various spiritual practices, including different forms of idolatry. When she was inspired to return to Judaism, she felt immense remorse, lamenting the degradation of her soul that had occurred while she searched for spiritual truth and meaning.

Writing to the Rebbe, she told her story and received a heartfelt response, referencing a teaching of the Sages that says, "If one claims: 'I have toiled and did not find,' do not believe them. If they said: 'I have found without having toiled,' do not believe them. If they say: 'I have toiled (*yagati*) and I have found (*matzati*), believe them.'"[114]

The Rebbe concluded:

"Since *yagati* has definitely been fulfilled, certainly the promise of *matzati* has also been fulfilled."[115]

With this life-changing perspective, the Rebbe reframed the woman's time and energy spent in India as an integral part of the spiritual "toil" that eventually led her to "find" the truth of Judaism.

Before her encounter with the Rebbe, this woman may have viewed this errant period of her life as a wasted and irredeemable chapter that had corroded her soul and compromised her Divine purpose. But from the Rebbe's perspective, this woman's initially misguided and fervent search for truth is what ultimately led to her earnest embrace of Judaism. Without her profound drive to seek spiritual truth, however initially misdirected, she may very well have lived a life of spiritual mediocrity and complacency, and she might have remained forever disconnected from G-d, her people, and her heritage. In this way, the idolatrous detour she traveled ultimately led her to the path of deep, authentic engagement with Judaism. It was, as the Rebbe emphasized, *yagati*—a struggle that was essential to the discovery and fulfillment of her life's purpose.

Here we see how every aspect of one's life experiences,

including the most excruciating and unsettling *yagati*-struggles, can become integral parts of our journey—necessary developmental stages on the way to fulfilling our life's purpose.

Hard-Won Lessons

In addition to the powerful momentum generated by spiritual deviation and alienation, the hard-won experiential lessons and insight we gain from a sinful past can be used to help others in their journey avoid the moral pits we fell into.

In the following story, the Rebbe shared this redeeming insight with R. Betzalel Kinn, a *baal teshuvah* who felt insecure about his former non-observance and considered himself unworthy of being a role model and teacher.

"I don't feel righteous enough to teach Jewish children," Betzalel said sheepishly before the Rebbe began laughing merrily, his eyes twinkling.

"If you wait until you are perfect, it will take a long time. So get on with it. If you don't fulfill your mission in this world, when Mashiach comes, he will ask you why you didn't do what you were sent down to earth to do. Make no excuses. Get on with it," the Rebbe replied, closing with the following advice, "Because you fell in a quagmire and lived, you will lead others through the quagmire with a lantern in one hand, pointing out the stepping stones with the other hand. You will get them across to a good place. That is your job."[116, 117]

From the Rebbe's perspective, this man's mistakes were not detrimental to his purpose. Rather, they imparted essential lessons that would enable him to help others safely navigate their own journeys. In this way, he was not only suitable but powerfully and uniquely positioned to excel in his role as teacher.

According to the Rebbe's redemptive way of viewing the world, our vices, character flaws, misdeeds, and transgressions are not just unfortunate banes and burdens to avoid or regret, but they are also bespoke Divine signposts placed on our path by G-d to help direct us to the most precise locations where our unique purpose awaits.

CHAPTER 11

Traditionally Yours

M R. ELLIOT LASKY, A spiritual seeker, once came to see the Rebbe with a burning question.

"In our prayers, we proclaim, *Hear O Israel, Hashem is our G-d, Hashem is One*. Rebbe, *Hashem is One* seems like a universal statement. Why does the Torah single out the people of Israel? How can it be said that the Creator of all is 'our' G-d? Isn't there only one G-d for all peoples, whether you're a Jew, an African, or an Indian?"

The Rebbe replied: "The essence of an African is to be who he truly is as an African; the essence of an Indian is to be who he truly is as an Indian. And the essence of a Jew is to be bound to G-d through His Torah and *mitzvot*."[118]

Here, the Rebbe reveals an essential clue in our quest to unearth our sacred purpose. Your life circumstances, such as family, community, tradition, and the environment into which you were born, are an intrinsic part of your self-hood as fashioned by G-d. You were born into a cradle of circumstance intended to help nurture you into the person you were made to be, starting with the spiritual tradition into which you were born.

In contrast to this providential approach to one's roots, religious traditions for millennia have invested in growing their numbers and seeking to convert people from other traditions to their own. At the heart of these efforts is the satisfaction and validation of drawing others into your world, as well as the pride of having delivered salvation to the members of an opposing tradition.

The Jewish approach is decidedly different. While Judaism is welcoming to converts, it does not proselytize.

This is because Judaism does not believe you must be Jewish to find G-d, spiritual enlightenment, salvation, or to live righteously. From the Jewish perspective, there are seven laws handed down since Noah that represent a universal code of morality, and by following these laws, every human being can live a life in accordance with G-d.[119] Judaism believes that every human being is created in the Divine image, that each has a mission to fulfill, and that one need not be Jewish to fulfill their G-d-given purpose.

This was the message provided to renowned psychological researcher and Yale Professor Reuven Feurstein when he came before the Rebbe with a unique moral and cultural dilemma.

At the time, Feurstein had been working with the Navajo tribe to develop programs that would help them preserve their tribal cultural knowledge across generations. In the process of learning about the tribe's symbolism and icons of worship, the question arose for Feurstein— as an observant Jew, should he be involved in training the Navajo to transmit their unique mythology? After weeks of wrestling with the question, Prof. Feurstein decided to seek the Rebbe's counsel and received the following response:

"[So long as one is not facilitating idolatry], it is our duty as Jewish people to reinforce and encourage other cultures to fulfill the *Sheva Mitzvot Bnei Noach* (the Seven Noahide Laws). This duty is of great importance. They must be what they are...it is our duty to teach them these seven laws."

Leaving space for everyone to be who G-d made them to be is among the reasons that Jewish wisdom prohibits proselytizing and rejects those who would petition to become converts three times—to ensure that the tremendous commitment of conversion is understood and honored, and that G-d's plans for the would-be convert are not circumvented in pursuit of a tradition that is not part of their Divine design.[120]

For example: Once, a non-Jewish spiritual seeker who

was considering converting to Judaism shared her interest with the Rebbe and sought his advice about whether she should proceed.

The Rebbe replied that she was already good as she was and need not convert to find meaning and purpose in life, as she had already been given a mission by G-d. The Rebbe concluded by encouraging her to continue forward in her current tradition, living a meaningful life according to G-d's unique plan for her, and reminding her of the Seven Noahide Laws meant for all peoples on earth.[121]

Another time, when approached by a young, non-Jewish woman who was insistent on conversion, despite her parents' strong opposition, he responded:

> "Why would you engage in a major, emotionally-straining split and conflict with your parents and with all your childhood friends, to take upon yourself the yoke of Torah and *mitzvot* [which would impact] every single step of your life—something that you are not obligated to do in your current status? [Instead], keep the Seven Noahide Laws properly, be kind to other people, and make complete amends with your parents."[122]

In situations like these, the Rebbe often encouraged people to reconsider changing their spiritual identity and tradition, reminding them that their primary responsibility is to G-d, and that honoring that responsibility is often best served by exploring the tradition into which they were born.

Like a Fish in Water

The Rebbe was also frequently approached by Jews who had come to doubt the primacy of their own spiritual inheritance and wondered if they might find more beauty and depth in other traditions.

His response was simple: Jewishness is an honor and a gift, and it represents the most natural source of vitality and nourishment for the Jewish soul. The Rebbe saw the Jewish soul as being healthiest and most fulfilled when in alignment with Torah.

> "...The inner peace and harmony of a Jew is closely associated with living Jewishly in the fullest measure, for, as our Sages put it, Jewishness for a Jew is what water is for a fish. And just as a fish cannot feel happy and content when it gets out of its natural element, so it is with a Jew who, for one reason or another, becomes neglectful of the proper Jewish way of life."[123, 124]

In a letter he wrote to a young man who had lapsed in his practice of Judaism, the Rebbe clarifies this point further:

> "I must take exception to what you call at the conclusion of your letter, 'my lost Judaism.'

The expression 'lost' does not really fit here,
for no person can lose something that is his or
her true essence and inner nature."[125]

Again, the Rebbe reminds us that our commitment to ourselves and our own personal growth begins with honoring the tradition given to us by G-d. No matter what value is to be found in the beauty of other cultures and traditions, our purpose is wed to the tradition into which we were born, and that should be the first place we go looking for it, no matter how challenging.

This was the case with a Jewish girl who had joined the Rebbe for *yechidut* at the behest of her parents. Upon arrival, she made a point of declaring her belief that no one has the right to impose a worldview on another.

The Rebbe listened and then asked gently, "Why did you come here?"

"Because I was brought here," she replied.

"But didn't you say that one shouldn't follow others' directives?" the Rebbe probed.

With this question, the girl softened her tone. She then asked the Rebbe whether she should travel to India to familiarize herself with way of life of other peoples, or whether she should stay in the United States and continue her studies.

"If you will heed my advice," the Rebbe counseled her,

"stay here. In India, you will learn other people's lifestyles; here, you will learn your own."

Touched by the Rebbe's words, she decided to stay in New York, and she later built a beautiful Chasidic family.[126]

Native Soil, Native Soul

Notably, the Rebbe encouraged many different Jews who came to him for guidance to deepen their connection to their own specific variation of Jewish tradition, custom, culture, and heritage. It would be easy to assume that as a Chasidic Rebbe who was deeply committed to the Chabad approach to Judaism, the Rebbe would use every opportunity to encourage those who were keen to adopt Chabad customs. But, perhaps counterintuitively, the Rebbe encouraged individuals to maintain their rich, unique Jewish customs rather than trade them in for the particular ways of Chabad.

One example among many is found in the story of Moshe Rappaport, a descendant of great Chasidic rabbis of Poland, who approached the Rebbe with a conundrum regarding prayer traditions. Just eighteen years old at the time, Moshe had become enamored with the Chabad customs of prayer, despite being born into the Radomsker tradition. His fascination with Chabad, and his desire to begin praying according to its customs, had met with fierce opposition from his father, who was dedicated to the traditions of his native Chasidic dynasty.

The Rebbe replied, "Since your family's customs are also based on the teachings of the Arizal [the great sixteenth-century Kabbalist R. Yitzchak Luria], it is advisable that you continue to keep them and that you pray according to *nusach Sephard*."[127]

The young man did as he was instructed by the Rebbe and continued to pray in the manner of his father and homeland.[128]

The Rebbe gave similar advice to members of every conceivable tradition and custom, reminding them to honor the profound sanctity of their unique way, among the many ways of being Jewish. In fact, he warned that attempts to subsume diversity were ill advised, even in the name of peace and community.

The Rebbe's advocacy for honoring one's tradition spanned the globe and became part of a multi-dimensional, lifelong effort to help people of all Jewish traditions preserve and thrive in the native soil into which G-d had planted them in order to most productively germinate their purpose in life.

For example, R. Avraham Alashvili recounts that when his father, R. Rafael Alashvili, immigrated from his native Georgia to Israel, he made a detour to New York to seek the Rebbe's guidance on adjusting to his new life in the Holy Land.

During that audience, the Rebbe asked the elder R.

Alashvili to describe Shabbat in the village of Kulashi, from whence he came. Beginning with preparations on Friday afternoon and evening, he described in detail the unique and precious practices in his community, noting that in Georgia, the Shabbat spirit fills the entire day to the extent that there is no time for anything else.

When the Rebbe heard this, he said, "If only our Shabbos was like this."

The Rebbe expressed his satisfaction and admiration that a group of Soviet Jews, isolated from the rest of the Jewish world, were so passionate and diligent in keeping Judaism alive, despite the difficulties involved. The elder R. Alashvili then asked the Rebbe whether he should use the Chabad prayer books and adopt Chabad customs, or whether he should keep his Georgian traditions alive and continue in the ways of the place he called home.

The Rebbe replied, "If you, the rabbis, were to change customs, people might think that these traditions aren't worthwhile and drop everything. It would have a negative impact. You may see it as a positive move, but they could lose everything. You must continue your tradition and pray from your prayer book so that your community will also maintain all of its traditions. Don't change anything."[129]

No matter where you were born, no matter what you came to this earth to do, your journey begins at home and emerges from the tradition into which you were born, which has already shaped you in countless, imperceivable ways. If you, like so many today, feel a deep desire to expand your spiritual horizons, consider journeying deeper into the tradition that G-d chose as part of your Divine design. There are so many glorious, exotic, and beautiful paths to G-d, but the path your ancestors walked is precious. Despite the novelty and pull of today's plethora of options, there is no substitute for deep roots, holy heritage, and a sense of belonging when seeking your place and striving to fulfill your unique purpose in the world.

CHAPTER 12

The People in Your Life

RABBI SHALOM BER LIFSHITZ arrived in New York on a Thursday after a long flight from Israel with plans to continue directly to Canada. At the time, R. Lifshitz led an organization supporting Jewish educational institutions in Israel; he was traveling to attend a fundraising event with the hope that spending a Shabbat with the local community would engender some much needed support.

But the Rebbe had other plans for his emissary. Before he was able to leave for Canada, R. Lifshitz was tracked down by the Rebbe's secretary and given an unexpected mission. An old classmate of R. Lifshitz's had fallen into a depression, and the Rebbe requested that he stay in New York over Shabbat and visit the man to help lift him out of his pit of despair. Although he hadn't been in touch with his former classmate for many decades, he immediately agreed to the Rebbe's request, arranged a place to stay, and pushed his ticket reservation forward a few days.

True to his word, R. Lifshitz visited the man several times over Shabbat and tried to lift his spirits.

On Sunday, the rabbi was summoned to a private audience with the Rebbe. The Rebbe emphasized the importance of what he had done and showered him with many blessings for his willingness to compromise his plans and sacrifice his convenience to help an old acquaintance in need. The encounter left a lasting impression on R. Lifshitz, who would tell the story often as a reminder of the supreme importance and responsibility to prioritize the well-being of those who have been placed in your life by Divine Providence.[130]

Here we find yet another precious signal directing us to an essential aspect of our soul's journey. The people in your life are not there merely by coincidence or circumstance; rather, they were woven into your life by Divine Providence for the sake of mutual blessing and personal growth.

In the Rebbe's words, delivered during a *farbrengen* on Shabbat Parshat Matos 5741 (1981):

> "For every Jew is apportioned a section of the world that he must refine and make anew, and from it, make a dwelling place for Him, may He be blessed... And therefore, when he meets another Jew [through particular Divine

Providence], this is evidence that the other's work of refinement is connected with him, and he must work with him.[131]

Spiritual Co-Travelers

The Kabbalists teach that before our souls descend, it is determined which souls we will encounter, engage, and travel with, and each of them hold sparks that will be our responsibility to help activate, illuminate, and elevate, and vice versa.

This includes all of the people in your life, including the seemingly random people you come into contact with, from schoolmates, friends, acquaintances, and clients to complete strangers. Regardless of the circumstances surrounding your encounters with others, the Rebbe insisted that the people in your life represent precious aspects of your purpose on this planet.

In his own life, the Rebbe embodied this principle to an extraordinary degree, taking personal interest and responsibility for anyone who entered his orbit of influence. One example among countless others occurred during the winter of 1973, when an erratic Jewish man arrived at 770 and began debating religion with the *yeshivah* students. One night, as the Rebbe hosted visitors for *yechidut*, the man stormed into the Rebbe's room, only to be stopped by one of the secretaries. The Rebbe told him to let the man pass and took time to speak with him. At some point during the months that followed, the man told the Rebbe that he planned to convert out of Judaism. The Rebbe sat with him for a while and invested immense energy in trying to change his mind.

At a subsequent Shabbat *farbrengen*,[132] the Rebbe shared a story of the Mezritcher Maggid, who stopped a disciple from converting by quoting a verse from the Torah, *A soul that reflects*. As the Rebbe told the story, he began weeping.[133]

The man left a handwritten note for the Rebbe expressing his thanks and sharing his intention to leave 770 and follow through on his plans, G-d forbid:

"Thank you for your love and concern which you have so freely shown to me during my stay here...Thank you for the many things I have learned from your life...I plan to leave tomorrow. My only goal, I hope, is to find the Perfect Will of G-d."

The Rebbe circled the words "I plan to leave tomorrow" and wrote in reply:

> "This is...certainly not G-d's will. Remain here until after Tishrei [some six months later], so that we will be able to celebrate all the *Shalosh Regalim* [Pesach, Shavuot, and Sukkot] together (and also my birthday)— including Simchas Torah. Utilize your time to study Torah in depth and with energy, to the extent that you will be able to energize

others as well. G-d will grant you success in this regard, because *this* is G-d's will."[134]

The man ended up suspending his plans after receiving the note, which included the Rebbe's personal invitation to his birthday celebration, an extremely rare occurrence. All in all, the man spent nearly a year at 770, where he remained a cherished guest.[135]

If this degree of loving-kindness and dedicated responsibility is warranted in the case of the seemingly "random" individuals brought into your life, how much more so when it comes to those who are more explicitly and inextricably built into the architecture of your life, such as parents, siblings, spouses, and children.

Sacred Roots

Naturally, among the most important people chosen to be part of our journey are our parents. As quoted previously from the sixth Lubavitcher Rebbe, R. Yosef Yitzchak Schneersohn, in Chapter 10:

"The life story of a person is a book that one must study. That book must be a guide in a person's life..."[136]

Among the ten aspects that contribute to the book of a person's life, according to R. Yosef Yitzchak, are "to whom this person was born..."

In this way, if the ten aspects composing a person's Divine design are the book of their life, then a person's parents and their influence are the very first page. From this point of view, your parents are not just the caretakers entrusted with your well-being and development into a healthy, independent adult. The souls of your parents (and by extension your siblings[137]) are foundational components of your life's trajectory.

Their role as caretakers, guides, protectors, and nurturers creates the conditions that reveal the inborn connection they have to your soul rather than the other way around. In other words, it's not what our parents (and siblings) contribute to our lives that creates their bond with us. Their nurturance and influence, rather, is an expression of the preordained and intrinsic bond they share with you.

This spiritual dynamic explains in part why the commandment to honor one's parents[138] is included in the first five of the Ten Commandments, all of which relate specifically to our relationship with G-d, rather than in the second five, which relate to our fellow human beings. Its inclusion among the commandments pertaining to our relationship with G-d reflects the fact that it is not social in nature. It is mystical, metaphysical, and intrinsic to your soul's design and its purpose in descending to this world.

Climbing in Love

Another fundamental relationship that many establish along their providential pathway is with a spouse or life partner. On the surface, this relationship may seem less obviously orchestrated by Providence due to the underlying belief that we "choose" our life partners—sometimes to our detriment. Especially in those cases where the partnership becomes challenging, we may reframe the relationship as a poor choice that only revealed itself after we learned the truth of the one we chose.

From a mystical point of view,[139] however, this is rarely the case. We may "choose" our partners in life, but the reasons for the choice—the specific virtues and qualities we were looking for, and the fact that the person we chose possesses them—were designed and hardwired into us by G-d in order to bring "two halves of one soul together."

This empowering perspective becomes a philosophical bedrock that supports our efforts to learn and grow through challenges that inevitably arise in any relationship, and to continue working on a relationship even when it appears to have outlived its value to the individuals involved.

The extraordinary extent to which our life partner is connected to our life purpose and mission can be seen in the Rebbe's letter to a man who was struggling with marital discord.

> "I wrote to you in my previous letter about the fact that you will certainly find challenges and difficulties especially in relation to domestic (marital) harmony, and this is *precisely where one's most urgent effort is required.* For from the intensity of the difficulties in question,

it is evident that *this is a prime locus of your essential life-task of refinement*, as is understood from the writings of the Arizal, and as made clear in Chasidut. For aside from a few exceptions, the souls of our generation have already been in the world and are returning now as a *gilgul* (reincarnation). Their main purpose is to rectify what they did not do among the 613 *mitzvot* in their previous lifetimes on this earth.

"...When it comes to those *mitzvot* that the person performed previously, the evil inclination does not put up its strongest opposition. It merely opposes sufficiently so that free choice remains. This is because this person has already affected refinement in these matters.

"However, in those matters where their service was lacking in previous lifetimes—meaning, in the specific portion of the world and their psyche that they failed to refine, the evil inclination's opposition is at its fullest strength...

"With respect to practical action, which is the essential point: I will once again [seek to] inspire and implore you to make the greatest effort possible to establish a peaceful home, even though this requires concessions (as these are not concessions in Torah or *mitzvot*)..."[140, 141]

To be sure, our most intimate relationships are rarely smooth and easy. In fact, these are the very relationships with which we often struggle the most and which cause the greatest emotional stress and turmoil, testing us to the extreme.

And that is precisely the point.

True goodness, including depth of character, virtue, and nobility, often emerges specifically in response to challenges presented by those closest to us, requiring us to dig deeper and tap into our true strength and greatest potentials.

Lifting the Veil

There is no relationship in the Torah where this idea is better illustrated than in the relationship between Jacob and his two wives, Leah and Rachel.

The Torah relates that Laban had two daughters, Leah and Rachel. Jacob loved Rachel, her character, and her manner, and he was so enamored that he offered to work for seven years to earn her hand. When the seven years were up, Laban substituted Leah for Rachel on the night of the wedding, a treachery that Jacob discovered only the following morning. Jacob accepted his fate and remained with Leah, but he also married Rachel, his bride of choice, and indeed loved her more than Leah.

Why did the marriage that formed the foundation of the Jewish nation—the marriage that produced the twelve tribes of Israel and every Jew since—have to come about in such a convoluted way?

According to Chasidic interpretations of the story, the Biblical characters of Leah and Rachel represent two dimensions that exist within each of us and offer a lesson for everyone.

Rachel, the beautiful woman, symbolizes the attractive, charming, and desirable characteristics in the people we love—and within ourselves.

Leah, whose name means "weariness" or "exhaustion," represents the challenging and broken aspects in our loved ones and ourselves, becoming a living symbol of our psychological, moral, and spiritual battles.

The second Lubavitcher Rebbe, R. DovBer, known as the Mitteler Rebbe, explains that Leah is far deeper than Rachel.

Rachel represents the conscious and revealed self—the self that is projected, manifested, and expressed outwardly. Leah, meanwhile, represents the unconscious self, the shadowy components of identity that roil beneath the surface of our conscious experiences.

Indeed, we each have a "Rachel" and "Leah," within ourselves, within our spouses, within our children, within our parents, siblings, and friends, within our entire lives— and within our relationship with G-d.

Rachel symbolizes those dimensions of your loved ones

and life that you easily comprehend, appreciate, and naturally connect with.

Leah represents the components of your life and loved ones that challenge you—the aspects that confront you with the need to unearth and address the ways you love, live, and relate to the world, and the dimensions of identity that lurk beneath the surface and take you by surprise when they arise.

It is especially in our closest relationships that we must learn to embrace and even love the unexpected aspects of the people in our lives, as well as the surprises that disrupt our carefully curated and comfortable existence. We must, because these unexpected and difficult aspects contain the most precious sparks to gather and redeem. Indeed, those aspects of your self, spouse, children, or siblings that frustrate you most may hold the key to precious discoveries about yourself and your very purpose on earth.

Of course, there is a predictable inclination to favor Rachel and to be wary of Leah as we move through life.

But if we persevere, we are likely to discover that the challenging aspects of our lives and loved ones are gateways to becoming the person we're truly capable of becoming.[142, 143, 144, 145]

In the end, it is the providential relationships that challenge us most that serve us best, and that we ultimately remember and look back on with pride, pleasure, and purpose, because they were ultimately what forced us to dig deepest, to extract our most precious insights, to refine our greatest potentials, and to fulfill our greatest calling.[146]

CHAPTER 13

Family First

ONE OF THE MOST common and fraught arenas of conflict between *my* world and *the* world, as referenced in Chapter Six, is the home. While searching for our place in the world, it is all too easy to seek meaning, fulfillment, and a sense of purpose far from those who are closest to us.

This was the case with a troubled mother who confided to the Rebbe that she felt lost and without purpose. The Rebbe replied:

> "I received your letter...In it you write that you really do not understand your place in the world, etc. At the same time, you begin [the letter] with the good news that you and your husband have been blessed with good children.
>
> The above already contains the answer to your question...you can well understand that

having been blessed with the greatest gift, the gift of children, [and having been blessed] to bring them up as "children of Hashem [G-d]," you have been provided with the necessary capacities to carry out this great privilege and pleasure in the fullest measure, and with joy and gladness of heart."[147]

Today, a growing number of people are deprioritizing their family lives in the name of their career and other pursuits—social activism, personal accomplishment, and material success, among others. This, in part, accounts for statistics showing that nearly ninety percent of the world's population now live in countries with falling marriage rates.[148]

This is symptomatic of an emergent social phenomenon that author, columnist, and political scientist Derek Thompson calls "workism," which he defines as the "belief that work is not only necessary to economic production, but also the centerpiece of one's identity and life's purpose."[149] For so many people today, family simply comes second—or even third or fourth.

One's professional success used to be considered a necessary means to an end. Work was once seen as a way to support and sustain one's family life. But for a growing number of people in our society, a career has become an end unto itself.

This phenomenon is also prevalent among service-driven individuals, whose natural inclination is to serve causes outside the home. How many therapists, philanthropists, activists, politicians, and community leaders have dedicated their lives to the care of others, only to lose sight of, or fall out of touch with, the people closest to them?[150]

And while hard work, personal growth, social activism, and financial success are all undoubtedly worthwhile and necessary pursuits, the Rebbe repeatedly reminded those blessed with family and children that no ambition should be pursued at the expense of those closest to home.

It is worth noting that this cornerstone of the Rebbe's worldview follows the Mishnaic teaching about how to prioritize one's charitable giving:

> "If you have the choice between supporting those who are poor in your family or the poor of your city, the poor in your family take precedence."[151]

This notion is the basis of the well-known aphorism: "Charity begins at home."

Just as G-d granted each of us a set of unique sparks scattered throughout the world to engage and elevate, so were we assigned a short list of other *souls* to elevate. First and foremost among these precious souls are our families—spouse, children, parents, and siblings. These souls were hand-picked by G-d and entrusted to us—as we were entrusted to them—to be primary among those we are responsible to help support, shepherd, and shape. Accordingly, caring for these souls ought to be the paramount focus and locus of our purpose in life.

As the Rebbe once told a man experiencing domestic strife:

> "The true greatness of a person lies in fulfilling their mission in life and acting in a way that brings joy and peace to the members of one's family."[152]

One Mission Above All

This paradigm was especially crucial to emphasize during the earliest days of the Rebbe's leadership, which began just five years after the declared end of World War II. During this time, the majority of the Chabad-Lubavitch community lived a relatively insular existence, protected and ensconced in the Crown Heights neighborhood of Brooklyn. Following the trauma of the war, Crown Heights had become a cultural and spiritual safe haven for many in the Chabad community. Boldly, the Rebbe turned the intense, community focus of his Chasidim outward to impact the world beyond their *shtetl*. He directed his students to leave the comforts of their homes and familiarity of their community behind and travel to the farthest corners of the earth to care for Jews who were seeking guidance or were estranged from their spiritual heritage.

As described by the late Chief Rabbi Jonathan Sacks, "The Rebbe undertook the most daring spiritual initiative ever undertaken in the history of humanity, [he made it his mission] to search out every Jew with love as they had once been hunted down in hate."[153]

This was to be the work of the Chabad *shluchim*, a radical expansion of the original impetus of Chasidism as outlined by the Baal Shem Tov: To bring teachings and acts of loving-kindness to the farthest reaches of the earth.

The Rebbe knew that those sent on such missions would be called on to give of themselves tirelessly day and night. They would need to be available to the entire Jewish community for all of its needs, and, in many cases, they would be the only Jewish point of contact in their city, state, or even country. Knowing that their lives would likely be overtaken by their missions, the Chasidim who accepted were reminded time and again that another mission must be honored above all others—that of nurturing their families and raising their children to live by the highest standard of Chasidic values and integrity.

The Rebbe offered this truth to R. Nosson and Miriam Gurary before they left for their posting in Buffalo, NY, in 1971. He wished them success in their mission and in establishing a home. He then emphasized in no uncertain terms:

"The ultimate objective *of everything* [of your entire

relocation from Brooklyn to Buffalo on *shlichut*] is to experience *Chasidishe nachat* (spiritual fulfillment) from your children."[154]

Here the Rebbe distinguished what the Gurary's *main shlichut* was while living in Buffalo. It was not, as one might assume, strictly the hallowed outreach they would perform in the community. Rather, it was the sacred inreach they would do with their own children, in their own home.

Casualties of Work

Oftentimes, one of the first casualties of living a life devoted to communal service is the relationship with one's spouse. When life gets hectic, it is all too common to overlook the needs of our most intimate partner and privilege pressing communal commitments in the name of "saving the world." We might tell ourselves that our spouse is self-sufficient and thus reserve only the remnants of our energies for them. Here, again, we find the potential pitfall of allowing *the* world to eclipse *my* world.

In advising others, and by his own living example, the Rebbe repeatedly highlighted the need to prioritize one's spouse above all else with unwavering, sacred emphasis.

He illustrated this cardinal value once to R. Gershon Mendel Garelik, who had been sent to Milan in 1959 as one of the pioneering *shluchim*. During *yechidut* with the Rebbe, R. Garelik said he was struggling under the tremendous weight of his responsibilities in Italy. After describing his struggles, the Rebbe gently asked, "And how is your relationship with your wife?"

The Rebbe then made an unusual request. He asked R. Garelik to write a note describing the dynamics of his marriage and how it was holding up under the stresses of their work.

At the end of his note, in which he had elaborated on his wife's many virtues, R. Garelik wrote: "Perhaps I should not have been so profuse in describing my wife's qualities."

The Rebbe crossed out the word "not" and underlined the word "should," leaving the sentence to read:

"I <u>should</u> ~~not~~ have been so profuse in describing my wife's qualities."

Without a single word, the Rebbe underscored for the overburdened Chabad luminary responsible for Jewish life throughout all of Italy that his *foremost mission* is, and will always be, to care for and cherish his wife.

The Rebbe further reinforced this sacrosanct value in conversation with R. Garelik as he was leaving for Milan after a visit to New York. Asked by the Rebbe's chief secretary, R. Hodakov, if he was going to return home with a present for his wife, R. Garelik said he had bought her some cakes from a legendary local bakery, as such kosher delicacies were not available in his new hometown. R. Hodakov suggested that he should buy her a present that better reflected her preciousness—perhaps something made of gold. After some deliberation, R. Garelik decided to buy her a watch.

Remarkably, the Rebbe took a personal interest in ensuring that this present was special. A jeweler who had recently opened a store nearby was invited to 770 to bring some options to consider. The Rebbe then proceeded to assist R. Garelik with his choice. At one point, the Rebbe duly emphasized to R. Garelik the importance of treating his wife as though she were the most important person in the world, despite all of the demands of his communal role.

"I don't know what to say," Rebbetzin Garelik said in response to the powerful influence the Rebbe had on her husband. "I just know that I have a very magnificent husband who treats me superbly...[this he learned from] the Rebbe being so *meyaker* [cherishing of] his wife, which made its importance especially clear to him..."

Stories of the Rebbe's own example are many, and they are particularly moving in light of the tremendous weight of his global responsibilities: from answering letters by the thousands, to directing international outreach efforts, to receiving countless people seeking guidance in private audience, all in addition to leading his vast community on a daily basis.[155]

And yet, the Rebbe viewed the precious time spent with his dear wife and life partner, Rebbetzin Chayah Mushka, as absolutely sacred and on par with one of the greatest Biblical commandments.

As he once told Dr. Ira Weiss, a cardiologist who treated both the Rebbe and the Rebbetzin and enjoyed a close relationship with both of them:

> "The time I set to have tea with my wife every day is as important to me as the Biblical commandment to put on *tefillin* every day."[156]

Father of One

When considering the true magnitude of our holy command to honor family above all, the Rebbe drew inspiration from Judaism's very first *shliach*, if you will, Abraham. In his attempt to spread the word and light of G-d in the world, Abraham pitched his tent in the wilderness, welcoming all passersby without exception, extending them love and connection, in an effort to help draw them closer to the teachings of monotheism. Soon after the passing of his wife, Sarah, Abraham married a woman named Keturah, who is identified by Rabbinic tradition as his former wife, Hagar, Sarah's arch-nemesis and a source of deep trauma during her lifetime.[157] So contentious was their relationship and the threat posed by Hagar's son Ishmael to the life of Sarah's son, Isaac,[158] that Sarah had them banished from their home, leading to their estrangement from Abraham.

This begs the question: Given their troubled history, how could Abraham desecrate Sarah's memory by returning to Hagar so soon after her passing, especially considering that Hagar had returned to her idolatrous past upon leaving Abraham's home?[159]

But that is precisely the point. Despite having influenced thousands to adopt the truth of monotheism, Abraham had somehow not succeeded in bringing his own former wife Hagar and son Ishmael into the fold. This would seem to be a classic case of one taking care of *the* world while neglecting *one's own* world. This is why, after Sarah's passing, Abraham followed his long-held desire to reconcile with his estranged family and do everything in his power to help them find their way.[160]

Abraham may have been destined to be *Av Hamon Goyim*, "Father of Many Nations," and the most influential human being to have walked this earth, with more than half of the planet's population considering him their spiritual father to this day.[161] But he was also the father of his *own* world, including his estranged partner and child. As long as they remained astray and estranged, Abraham had failed to meet his holiest obligation.

In the end, it was not Abraham's worldly accomplishments, extraordinary courage, or moral integrity that made him special in the eyes of heaven. Nor was it his legendary kindness or even his spirit of activism and sacrifice that made him worthy of fathering the Jewish nation. Instead, it was his continued focus on the ultimate priority of family. As the verse states clearly:

> "I have selected him for he shall instruct *his children and household* after him to keep the ways of G-d, to do charity and justice."[162]

We can all learn from Abraham's example. No matter what monumental task pulls us in another direction, we must always turn back home and remember that no priority is greater than loving dedication to the family with which G-d has blessed us. Indeed, no aspiration is greater than the nurturance of the souls entrusted to us as living foundations of our sacred purpose.

CHAPTER 14

Location, Location, Location

I N HIS YOUTH, R. Aharon Serebryanski was one of just a few students at a *yeshivah* run by his father in a small town about twenty miles outside Melbourne, Australia.

Under his father's guidance, the *yeshivah* had grown steadily, albeit slowly. And while the younger Serebryanski enjoyed his role as a mentor there, he remained hopeful that he might someday travel to New York to study near the Rebbe.

Hoping to receive approval to travel to 770 and begin his studies, the ambitious student began corresponding with the Rebbe, but he was told time and again that he should remain precisely where he was, much to his disappointment.

In one exchange, the Rebbe summarized his reasons for redirecting Serebryanski's requests, explaining that since Divine Providence had brought him to Australia, he must remain and do more work teaching Chasidut there before he was able to move on to the "more enjoyable work" of learning in 770.[163]

Even after achieving great success and asking once again to travel to New York, the Rebbe withheld his approval, noting that his success, along with the fact that no one else was available to replace him, suggested that R. Serebryanski had "found his mission in the world."

"Why would you leave and travel elsewhere?" the Rebbe asked, concluding that he should not let "foreign thoughts"[164] disturb the important work he was doing.

Eventually, the young rabbi was invited to 770 and was inspired and exhilarated by his experience, including a chance to meet with the Rebbe for *yechidut*, where he was praised for his dedicated efforts in Australia.

After returning to his relatively unfulfilling life back home, Serebryanski began to feel restless again, and on the day before Rosh Hashanah, he wrote to the Rebbe to explain that ever since experiencing the High Holidays in 770, the services in Australia left him yearning to return to Brooklyn.

Two days after Rosh Hashanah, the Rebbe wrote back. Citing several relevant Chasidic discourses, he explained that Serebryanski was right about the difference between where he was and where he wanted to be, but this is a matter of perspective. Certainly, being at 770 would be a pleasure for *him*. But staying in Australia brings pleasure to G-d. How could he complain?

Indeed, one of the most important clues provided to help you discern your mission in life is waiting for you right where you are. Your immediate, physical location, whether that means the place where you were born or the place where you may now find yourself, is a fundamental indicator of where you are called to invest the lion's share of your efforts and energy.[165]

By reflecting on and committing to the location where Divine Providence has placed you, you are likely to come face to face with the reason you arrived there, and the role it plays in fulfilling your purpose.

An Outstanding Debt

This spiritual symbiosis is a natural product of the numerous, multidimensional resonances that develop between you and the place that shaped who you have become. You are an integral part of the place where you find yourself, even though it may be easy to take for granted. The allure of the exotic and unfamiliar often emerges from a failure to see the value we bring to the place where G-d arranged for us to arrive and thrive.

This was the guidance offered by the Rebbe in a

correspondence with a group of students at a Jewish camp in Be'er Yaakov, Israel, who asked for the Rebbe's view on their efforts to encourage American Jewish students to immigrate to Israel.

The Rebbe replied by explaining that each student owed a spiritual debt to the community that had nurtured them into becoming upstanding young Jewish adults. It was their duty, he wrote, to pass on the good they received so that others could follow in their wake.

> "...A young person with yet untapped vigor and who still needs to enter life and to be an active part of society and his surroundings must give priority to devoting himself to the community around him from which he received his potential...How much more so is this true when the society [where he was raised] is in a precarious position and when those working to establish its foundations are few in number—then it is understood that the necessity for this is [even more] profound...Only after one has repaid his debt to the place in which he was raised is he able to think about what he might do for his Jewish brethren in another place.[166, 167]

This was the truth impressed upon Yerachmiel Glazer, who was born to a non-observant family in Johannesburg, South Africa, and raised near Zambia, in the Jewish community of Ndola. The once-thriving community had dwindled significantly since its peak in the 1950s and was lacking opportunities to learn about Judaism.

In 1967, Glazer traveled to Israel to volunteer on a kibbutz. It was there that he began deepening his Jewish roots and enrolled in the *yeshivah* for *baalei teshuvah*, returnees to the traditions of Judaism, in Kfar Chabad. Two years later, he visited New York, where he had the opportunity to meet the Rebbe for the first time. Prior to his departure, Glazer sent the Rebbe a letter that included a description of the scarcity of Judaism in his hometown.

> "I went into a private audience with the Rebbe," he recalled in an interview. "The Rebbe read what I had written about my family in Zambia and my studies in Kfar Chabad. Suddenly, the Rebbe raised his holy eyes and said to me: 'I would like you to return to Zambia and involve yourself in spreading Judaism there.'"

Glazer was visibly taken aback at this unexpected request, prompting the Rebbe to provide further instruction. The young man was to continue learning in Israel, but he was to begin writing letters home to his community with guidance about each upcoming festival to hang up on the synagogue bulletins.

Six months later, Glazer's father asked him to return home to help with the family business. The Rebbe directed Glazer, "You should fulfill the request of your parents and visit them for a few months, and surely this will be used for the spread of Judaism."

During his stay in Zambia, Glazer was instructed to travel around Ndola to teach the local Jewish population about Jewish practice.

Meanwhile, the Rebbe continued to send Glazer letters of support and instruction, showing the young man a level of respect usually reserved for those who were already established community leaders.[168]

Why would the Rebbe, whose life was marked by a strong commitment to Jewish education, deter a young man from relocating to a place that would enrich his own Jewish studies?

This was because the Rebbe believed in the providential link you share with the place where you were born, the profound responsibility you bear to the souls who reside there, and that ultimately your mission in life is wed to both.[169]

At Your Station

Indeed, in many encounters, the Rebbe reminded leaders who were eager to relocate to places seemingly more conducive to their personal development and quality of life that their current location is exactly where their particular mission awaits. What on the surface appeared to be an imposition was actually a privileged opportunity to release the hidden Divine sparks specifically marked for their individual soul in that particular place. If they were to depart for greener pastures, who would tend the proverbial flock and raise those resident sparks?

This was the message at the heart of a letter sent by the Rebbe to Professor Marcus Arkin, director-general of the South African Zionist Federation:

> "We have seen this happen time and again, when the leaders of a community have been persuaded to make *Aliyah*, with the inevitable result that the community dwindled rapidly, physically, and spiritually. In a small community, the departure of a single influential member, whether a rabbi or layman, may make all the difference."[170]

The Rebbe shared a more penetrating iteration of this truth with a prominent Jewish activist in the United Kingdom who wished to relocate to Israel, hoping to redirect his energies and activism toward the Holy Land.

The Rebbe strongly discouraged him, explaining:

> "...Another important reason is that each and every one of us has been mobilized by Divine Providence to wage the battle for Judaism in a specific place. And it's not for a military man to forsake his post, and all the military personnel around him and the cities on the scene that he is to defend, because he has found (in

his opinion) another place where the battle is easier."[171]

Again and again, the Rebbe reaffirmed the profound responsibility we bear for the place where G-d planted us, reminding leaders and laymen alike that what we want or think we need should not be conflated with what is needed from us.

Grow Where You Are Planted

At the age of 13, Adeena Bernhard was excited to learn that her father, R. Nachman Bernhard, had chosen to relocate the family from their home in Johannesburg, South Africa, to Israel. The family had been asked to leave the country due to R. Bernhard's vocal and stalwart opposition to apartheid.

Her excitement turned to frustration when Adeena learned that the Rebbe had intervened on behalf of their family and arranged for her father to remain. Crestfallen, she decided to write the Rebbe the following impassioned letter:

"Dear Rebbe:

"During the past nine years, my father has proved himself to be a great scholar and Torah leader. Like many other *tzaddikim*, he has a great wish to go and live in Eretz Yisrael... I, too, can think of nothing better than going on *Aliyah* to Israel. I do not want this because of the fun and excitement of moving, but because it is not like settling in just another land...it is settling in the Holy Land, a Promised Land and a Land in which you do not have to be ashamed to be a Jew.

"In Eretz Yisrael my father could still have a lot to do with saving Jewish souls, even if he were not a practicing rabbi. As a girl of thirteen who wants to see her father and family happy, I implore you please to take into consideration my feelings about living in Israel when the matter comes up...

"Sincerely, Adeena Bernhard"

The Rebbe replied:

"Miss Adeena Bernhard

"Blessings and greetings:

"First of all, I am gratified to note your concern, indeed profound concern, for your parents. This does not surprise me of course, knowing your father and your upbringing, but it is nevertheless gratifying to see it expressed in a letter.

"As for the subject matter of your letter, it is surely unnecessary to point out to you that when one thinks about the well-being of any person, including above all his inner harmony and peace, one must obviously think not in terms of the immediate days and weeks, but also how it will be in the long run. This should be the consideration in regard to all affairs, but especially so when it is a question of where to settle down.

"This is a very serious question, even when one is at the crossroads, and much more so when one has already been settled in a place and contemplates changing it. Now, with regard to your father and knowing him, I have no doubt that he could feel in his element only in a place where he can fully utilize the knowledge which he has acquired and the qualities which G-d has bestowed upon him. That is, to utilize them in the fullest measure for the benefit of the many. By comparison with this, personal amenities—and I mean this also in a spiritual sense—are not the decisive factor, and perhaps no factor at all...

"On the basis of what has been said above, supported by what you and all the other members of the family have seen of your father's success, not only in your city, but South Africa as a whole, you will surely realize without any shadow of a doubt that your father will feel in his element and be truly happy if he continues his present situation in your country."[172, 173]

In this exchange, and countless others, the Rebbe taught that there is an often-overlooked benefit to doing the work placed before us in a particular location and moment in time, even if it comes at the expense of our comfort, satisfaction, or presumed personal development. By standing firmly in the place where your Divine purpose resides, you will ultimately receive spiritual rewards that far exceed those you think may be waiting for you somewhere else with more immediate appeal. By growing where you are planted, the fruit born by your efforts will be a thousandfold, or even more.

CHAPTER 15

Yours and Yours Alone

BEFORE ASAF ABRAMOVITCH REACHED the age of thirteen, he received bar mitzvah instruction from a young R. Rachamim Jerufi. As his studies and immersion in the culture of Chabad deepened, he became curious why the Rebbe remained in Brooklyn, New York, rather than relocating to Israel. He posed the somewhat impertinent question to his rabbi, who encouraged him to write to the Rebbe and ask him directly, which he did.

Sometime later, Asaf received a visit from R. Jerufi, who arrived with a response from the Rebbe, which included blessings on the occasion of his bar mitzvah and a footnote that read:

> "Regarding what you have asked about where one lives, the deciding factor is not where it will be personally best for the individual,

or most pleasant to live, but where one can accomplish more good and *where one is most needed.*[174] Take, for example, a doctor. A doctor should live in a place where they are needed, where people require their help, not simply in a place where their life will be pleasant. And in truth, every person needs to heal their surroundings, to bring more light and holiness."[175]

There seems to be no end to causes and initiatives beckoning each of us to address the needs of those both near and far. In an age when a world of opportunity awaits, how do you decide which opportunities are most beneficially yours to pursue?

The Rebbe offers an essential principle that can help us clarify which opportunities are meant for our particular souls. Namely, a task that *only you can fulfill* trumps all others when deciding which needs to prioritize.

Especially in cases where specific individuals were uniquely suited to serve a particular need in the Jewish community, the Rebbe directed them to prioritize those needs, even if it meant sacrificing other competing commitments.

For example, R. Sholom Ber Lifshitz once wrote to the Rebbe during the vigorous growth of Yad L'achim, an organization he helped found in 1950 to serve the needs of an influx of Jews who flooded Israel soon after its statehood was established. Noting in his letter that his efforts had initially borne impressive fruits, he added that public response and support had fizzled, leaving him to bear the weight of responsibility. His Torah study, meanwhile, had suffered as he did his best to continue building the organization.

Writing for guidance, he asked the Rebbe, "Am I required to abandon my soul's needs in order to attend to the souls of others?"

The Rebbe replied:

> "...I was astonished at this question, coming after the Holy One, Blessed Be He, has made you successful and has given you the chance to save the souls of sons and daughters of Israel and help them remain faithful to G-d and His Torah. And here comes your evil inclination, inciting you, saying, 'Who knows if this is the right thing, and maybe it's better for you to get involved in other activities, and then it would be possible for you to thrive in Torah [study], etc., etc...'
>
> "There is a well-known legal ruling in the Gemara that a mitzvah that cannot be done by others takes precedence over Torah study (*Moed Katan* 9b)."[176]

It would be easy to listen to the whispers of the negative inclination as it seeks to instill subtle doubts about where we are needed most. But even the most sacred practices must be set aside if there is an urgent task assigned to us uniquely by Divine Providence. No matter what is tugging us in another direction, we must remain steadfastly focused on the work that is uniquely ours.

The Rebbe and the Nazi Hunter

As a young man, Tuviah Friedman was helpless as the Nazis invaded his home in Poland and sent him and his family to live in the Radom ghetto. His family was murdered in the gas chambers of Treblinka, while he was sent to a labor camp from which he escaped with one ambition beyond survival—to bring the architects of the Holocaust to justice.

What began as a singular effort to capture the SS officers who oversaw the Radom ghetto would become his life's work. During the course of his storied career, Friedman worked with various agencies and efforts to capture hundreds of war criminals, including Adolf Eichmann, the chief architect of the Final Solution.

Thanks to the support of his wife, who served as the family's primary breadwinner and funded the bulk of Friedman's hunt, he was able to continue doing the work that he believed to be so important for a long time.

After more than twenty years, his wife began insisting that he had done enough and that she could no longer fund his efforts; she asked him to call off the hunt. Still reluctant, Tuviah decided to visit the Rebbe in New York, hoping that he might help Tuviah find another way to fund his work.

"I will describe the situation to the Rebbe and hear what he has to say. If he can't suggest another way for me to fund my work, I'll stop and go into business," he promised his wife.

When he met with the Rebbe for *yechidut*, Friedman learned that the Rebbe knew of his work but was curious to learn more. He offered stories about the many Nazis that he had brought to justice before segueing into the issue that brought him to the Rebbe, saying, "Here is my problem: I have no income. My wife has been supporting me for the past twenty years, and we can no longer afford it. Although I want to continue, I have no way to fund my work."

The Rebbe replied, "Can you really stop? How many people are still at it? You and Simon Wiesenthal? Look at what you have accomplished so far. If you abandon this work, the Nazis will rejoice that they've won. Can you name someone else who is willing to take over for you? In the past twenty years, has anyone else volunteered? No. No one is interested—there is no one else! So what choice do you have?

"You must go from city to city in Germany, bringing them all to justice. This is very important for the history of the Jewish people—all the Nazi criminals must be punished for what they did. And if you don't do it, who will?

"As far as supporting your family, here's what I suggest: Take your book, *We Shall Never Forget: The Final Solution* [about the trial of Adolf Eichmann], and translate it into English. Wherever you go to speak in Jewish communities across America, take twenty copies with you. The book will sell, and you will make a living... Look at the millions of creatures in this world; they all eat and survive. G-d looks after all His creations; He will look after you, too."

Friedman followed the Rebbe's advice, returned home, and took a course to improve his English. He then went on a speaking tour of Jewish communities in America, giving many paid speeches and presentations. He also issued and sold an English edition of his book, *The Hunter,* which together with earnings from his tours generated enough income to continue his work and even to buy a new house. Thanks to the Rebbe's timely advice, he was able to continue his work for another forty years, and he later founded the Institute for the Documentation of Nazi War Crimes.

In an interview, he would observe, "If it weren't for the Rebbe, I would have stopped after twenty years, and some one thousand Nazis would have gone unpunished for their crimes. The fact that they didn't was thanks to the Rebbe's guidance."[177]

Where You Are Needed Most

This point of radical responsibility was a cardinal consideration for the Rebbe himself when deciding among the endless causes that came his way.

"People wonder why the Rebbe takes on causes that appear to have nothing to do with the Chabad movement—matters of world Jewry, Russian Jewry, events in Israel—especially when they seem like impossible causes," a journalist once asked the Rebbe boldly.

The Rebbe replied by citing the verse: *In those days, Moses grew up and went out to his brothers and observed their suffering. He saw an Egyptian man striking a Hebrew man of his brothers. He turned this way and that way, and he saw that there was no man; so he struck the Egyptian and hid him in the sand.*[178]

The Rebbe wondered aloud, "Why did Moses look all around, and only when he saw no man did he strike the Egyptian? In this time of crisis, was Moses so concerned about his own well-being?"

"*He saw that there was no man* can be interpreted to mean that he saw *no man who cared*—no one was concerned about the travesty being perpetrated against their fellow man. This is why Moses stepped in—to do what was necessary to protect innocent people from cruelty and oppression.

"When we witness an injustice and look around and no

one seems to care," the Rebbe concluded, "we must act."[179, 180]

The Rebbe often rooted this principle in a halachic teaching that says: "If you come across a mitzvah that only you can do, the performance of that mitzvah takes precedence over any other."[181]

This was the guidance the Rebbe provided R. Dr. Abraham J. Twersky, a prominent rabbinic psychologist known for his pioneering work to address addiction and other areas of mental health in the Jewish community.

Years before achieving great renown, he was a young rabbi on the verge of becoming a practicing psychiatrist, and he went to speak to the Rebbe regarding his career. The Rebbe suggested that he move to New York so that he could serve members of the local Jewish community in need of his help, which drew immediate protest from Twersky.

"But if I am the only religious psychiatrist in New York, the load will be so immense that I may never have time to study Torah again!" he replied.

Acknowledging his rabbinic background, the Rebbe gently pushed back, citing the above-mentioned halachic principle, "A good deed that can only be performed by you takes priority over Torah study."

"Are you the only one who can do what needs to be

done? If so, then that is G-d's way of saying, 'This is yours to pursue!'"[182]

Not So Easy Does It

From the beginning of his leadership in 1950, the Rebbe began a spiritual revolution in the Chasidic and wider Jewish world by sending young Chabad couples to the far-flung corners of the world to seek out their fellow Jews. But even in the late 1960s, almost twenty years into his initiative, it was still challenging to generate momentum for the effort.

And for those who were already in the field, there was still the occasional doubt about the value of their personal toil and the hardships they endured, being so distant from their family, community, and spiritual center.

In the following moving talk, the Rebbe addresses a seeming curiosity at the heart of the Chabad mission to create outposts everywhere in the world, including remote locales with very sparse Jewish populations.

From one perspective, this was not the best use of resources. It would appear far more efficient and strategic, one could argue, to send *shluchim* to the most heavily populated Jewish cities, where their impact would likely be much more pronounced. Why send *shluchim* to all corners of the globe, including in many instances to places with meager, forlorn Jewish populations?

At a *farbrengen* in 1968, the Rebbe offered the following response:

> "Jewish leaders have endeavored—and most significantly of late, the Rebbes of Chabad, especially my father-in-law, the Rebbe—to disseminate Torah study and Jewish observance to all corners of the earth, even to the most remote places. Now, if one could benefit more Jews closer to home, why is it that so much effort [is expended] to reach one solitary Jew, one single family, or a few families? First of all, we are advised, especially in this era, 'Grab whatever food and drink comes your way!'—meaning, *every opportunity*, for Torah and *mitzvot* is the sustenance, the 'food and drink,' of a Jew. 'If a mitzvah comes your way, do not delay!' If news reaches you that there is an isolated Jew far away, 'G-d does nothing in vain'—*the very fact that you learned of it indicates that you're expected to act upon it.*

> "Now, one may make calculations: 'With the same effort required to succeed in a distant country, I can achieve many times more in closer proximity.' First of all, you may be wrong...and it confuses and distracts you from your responsibility to rescue a fellow Jew. Additionally, Jewish law states that a mitzvah that cannot be accomplished by anyone else

must be your top priority. For someone living in a populated Jewish area, there are plenty of observant Jews to reach out to him. But if you, who knows of a remote solitary Jew, do not take action, who will come to his rescue?"

Here the Rebbe refutes the utilitarian perspective that claims it is better to save many than few, declaring that if one learns of the plight of a single individual anywhere in the world, and that individual's fate can be bettered through your efforts alone, this is G-d's way of saying, "This is part of your mission and responsibility, especially when no one else can help." This becomes "a mitzvah that only you can perform."

"Let this be the double consolation for the *shluchim* who are paving this unbeaten path. At times they are frustrated—whether it is kept to themselves, expressed privately to their Creator, or spoken to someone else: 'Is it fair that I be fated to be alone, or as a couple, to save some obscure town or country, to make them aware of G-d and his Torah? In this place I can share only the most basic concepts, because anything subtler is above them.' ...You must realize that this is G-d's own mission. G-d selected you to fulfill this mission specifically in this distant place, and only through this can you achieve personal wholeness; the spiritual heights you can attain there, you could never reach if you were to remain in a place where Torah study and Jewish observance come easily."

Your personal mission, whatever and wherever it may be, is not affected or determined by how much your soul will seemingly gain or be nourished, or even by how much, according to your calculations, you might contribute to the greater good.

In fact, the Rebbe adds:

"Here [in a more vibrant Jewish city], perhaps, one could study an extra page of Talmud or observe an additional stringency...But fortunate indeed is the lot of all those who enthusiastically journey for and fulfill this mission with joy and happiness...Their success will certainly be above and beyond nature, for G-d Himself is there with them, and my father-in-law, the Rebbe, is with them there. And if only other Jews could merit what the shluchim attain in the farthest of lands..."[183]

This final, passionate point was offered as part of the Rebbe's effort to change the mindset of his Chasidim and, by extension, the Orthodox Jewish community in general, who all-too-humanly measured their spirituality in terms of personal spiritual growth, and the heightened spiritual consciousness and engagement that comes with living in a thriving Jewish community.

In a world where one's religious aspirations were inextricably linked to studying and mastering as much of the Torah as possible and performing *mitzvot* with ever growing piety and punctiliousness, leaving behind the spiritual incubator of one's beloved community seemed likely to compromise rather than complement their holiest pursuits.

This was especially true of the Chabad nexus in Brooklyn, where the Rebbe resided and presided. To be sent on a mission far away seemed, for many, daunting at best, and at worst as a fracturing of their idyllic spiritual life. The Rebbe, however, taught otherwise without wavering. If we are here for a purpose, he declared over and over again, we must ask not what I need or want from this life, but why was I sent here, what is G-d's plan for me, where am I most needed, and how can I best serve in the place and the way that was designed for me specifically?

CHAPTER 16

Your Circle of Influence

———————

D URING A PRIVATE AUDIENCE with a journalist for a large Jewish newspaper in Texas,
the Rebbe once asked, "Does your paper's reach
extend to remote regions as well?"

The journalist replied, "Indeed, it does. In fact, we
deliver papers to two Jewish families in outlying areas of
Texas."

The Rebbe asked, "Do you realize your responsibility to
these two families? In addition to providing the news, your
paper is the only link and lifeline these two families have
to Jewish life and community!"[184]

Much like talent and opportunity, your sphere of influence is a gift from G-d that must be fully utilized. By
specific Divine Providence, those souls whom G-d has
placed in the concentric circles of your life are an integral
part of your Divine mission and responsibility.[185]

Indeed, just as there are sparks of G-dliness embedded in the universe, and each one of us was given our own personal portion of the world to cultivate and elevate, so, too, each of us was entrusted with certain precious souls to nurture and uplift.

Along with other indicators of our Divine purpose, such as location and the circumstances into which we are born, we can further assess the scope of our mission by identifying the ways and means with which we have been empowered to shape the lives of others in our orbit.

Seize the Moment

A powerful Biblical example of this, referenced by the Rebbe on many occasions, is the story of Queen Esther, who unexpectedly rose to power and became the queen of Persia through a series of seemingly random events orchestrated by Divine Providence.

Initially, when Mordechai encourages Esther to reveal her Jewish identity and use her position to influence the king to rescind his genocidal decree against the Jewish people, she demurs, as she would be putting her own life in danger.

Mordechai then said the following immortal words to Esther:

> *Do not imagine to yourself that you will escape in the king's house any more than all the Jews. For if you remain silent at this time, relief and*

rescue will arise for the Jews from elsewhere, and
you and your father's household will perish. And
who knows if you have attained royalty for a time
such as this.

In a talk given on Purim 5744 (1984), the Rebbe elaborated on the ways in which Mordechai's galvanizing message can inform us all as we seek to use our influence to its utmost.

"When a Jew finds himself in exile and then suddenly finds himself sitting at the gate of the king, he must know that this is happening due to particular Divine Providence, so that he will fulfill his true purpose—to affect those in the royal household and the king himself, and through this...every good matter in that entire country.

"...One must remember that this is a great personal privilege, for with respect to the essential action that must be affected in the king's household, relief and rescue will come to the Jews from somewhere else, but in that case, you and your father's house will be lost—meaning that you would lose the merit associated with this matter.

"Similarly, for a Jew whose is able to affect a certain portion of the country, or a city, or a neighborhood, all the way to a Jew who is able to affect only his family group or even just his own inner world and microcosm—even in such a situation, it is within his ability to take such actions as would tip the balance of the scales of his own life and of the entire world for the good, bringing '[world] salvation and rescue,' to quote Maimonides' legal ruling."[186, 187]

The Provenance of Prominence

From statesmen to students, the Rebbe taught that whatever your ambitions or magnitude of influence, you have a Divinely imparted responsibility to put it to use for the greater good. The Rebbe saw every individual, not just those inhabiting grand roles, as leaders of their own kingdom, no matter the size or scale.

For example, Dena Horn [nee Mendelowitz] did not expect to receive much attention from the Rebbe when she accompanied her mother for *yechidut* when she was eighteen years old. She was humbled and deeply touched, however, when the Rebbe took the time to ask about her studies and activities at New York University, where she served as vice president of the Jewish Culture Foundation. Some weeks after returning to school, she was surprised when a letter arrived from the Rebbe addressed specifically to her rather than to her mother. The letter, which would change the course of her life, read:

"Your visit some time ago gave me the pleasant opportunity of touching upon an important topic, which deserved more time than I had at my disposal....

"Any thinking person must frequently ask himself, 'What is my life's purpose?'

"...The Torah...gives us a true definition of our life's purpose, and it shows us the ways and means of attaining this goal.

"...The extent of one's duty [as outlined in the Torah] is in direct proportion to one's station in life. It is all the greater in the case of an individual who occupies a position of some prominence, which gives him, or her, an opportunity to exercise influence over others, especially over youths. Such persons must fully appreciate the privilege and responsibility which Divine Providence vested in them to spread the light of the Torah and to fight darkness wherever and in whatever form it may rear its head."

Emphasizing the power that even a single person carries to affect great change, the Rebbe added:

"...Discouragement or a spirit of defeatism [should not] be permitted to creep into one's mind, such as, 'What can I do? I am alone in the field,' etc. Our father Abraham has taught us what one individual can achieve. For *one was Abraham, yet he inherited all the earth* (Ezekiel 33:24). Our age, which some people prefer to call the Atomic Age, has further demonstrated that in the minutest quantity of matter tremendous stores of energy may be found. All that is necessary is to discover them and then harness these stores of energy for constructive purposes, and not, G-d forbid, otherwise."[188], [189]

Great Expectations

In keeping with the aphorism attributed to Voltaire, "With great power comes great responsibility," the Rebbe consistently taught that the more *influence* vested in the person by Divine Providence, the greater their responsibility to use it for the betterment of humankind.

The Rebbe elaborated on this principle during a talk given on his birthday, 11 Nissan 5744 (1984), saying:

"A person who has reached an elite [position of influence] in society—say, in government, whether [at the national, state, city or neighborhood levels]...

"Such a person cannot be content being merely involved with things that are good, just, and upright, just like every [other upstanding member of society], because he has [a greater ability to influence others] in all these matters than those around him.

"He is not able to argue: Why should there be a commotion if I do not use some of my potential and opportunities?

"For those potentials and opportunities are not things of his own making; rather, they were given to him by the Holy One, Blessed Be He, and it is certain that they were given for a purpose and goal—to spread justice and uprightness throughout the whole world.

"There is no doubt at all that your...talents are not there because *My own strength and the might of my hand made this success for me*[190]; rather, it is because *the L-rd, your G-d, is the one Who gives you the power to succeed.*[191] It is the Creator and Director of man Who gave you this advantage. *From G-d are man's footsteps established*[192]—what has brought you to this place, both 'place' in its simple sense and 'place' of importance and elevation and power to influence, is only in order [for you] to carry out the mission of the Holy One, Blessed Be He.

"...Therefore, this matter of using one's potential fully is dependent on your choice. For *I have placed before you life and the good,*[193] and the opposite, G-d forbid. But the Holy One, Blessed Be He, commands you and implores you, *Choose life!*[194] Here, this means utilizing fully and completely the powers that have been given to you by the Holy One, Blessed Be He."[195]

Heavenly Beckonings

Even when not directly related to one's primary role or vocation, the Rebbe taught that if by Divine Providence you discover a way to use your influence for the good and benefit of others, it is likely a sign that you should follow those heavenly beckonings.

For example, Israeli Prime Minister Menachem Begin met with the Rebbe several times.

At the end of one of these audiences, the Rebbe turned to Begin and asked if he would do him a personal favor. Begin replied that he would.

The Rebbe then told him that he had received a letter from a French girl's parents who wrote in great pain about their daughter, who was planning to marry outside of the faith. The parents had tried every thinkable way to intervene, but with no success.

Feeling hopeless, they turned to the Rebbe for help and advice.

"I am sure," the Rebbe told Begin, "that if a prominent individual such as yourself, especially as you speak French, will speak to her about her choice in marriage, she will respect your words, and it will influence her in the right direction."

Begin accepted the mission, and the Rebbe gave him the name, address, and phone number of the girl, and insisted on paying all the travel expenses.

Begin traveled to France and spoke to the young girl. His words entered her heart, and she decided to move to Israel, where she eventually built a beautiful Jewish family.[196]

A Surprising Request

In his own life, the Rebbe embodied this principle again and again. Whenever he became aware of a cause or a need, no matter how small, and saw a way he could use his influence to advance the greater good, he took it up, even when the greater good had nothing to do with advancing the goals of his own movement.

A beautiful example of this can be seen in the Rebbe's encounter with a state senator from New York who sought the Rebbe's counsel concerning certain issues involving the Jewish community. After offering advice with regard to these matters, the Rebbe asked if he could request a favor.

"'Here it comes,' I thought to myself," the senator later recounted. "'Just like all the others, he's looking for the payoff.'

"But what did the Rebbe ask of me?

"He said, 'There is a growing community in Chinatown.

These people are quiet, reserved, hard-working, and law-abiding; the type of citizens most countries would treasure. But because Americans are so outgoing and the Chinese are, by nature, so reserved, they are often over-looked by government programs. As a state senator from New York, I suggest that you concern yourself with their needs.'

"I was overwhelmed. The Rebbe has a community of thousands in New York, and institutions all over the state that could benefit from government support. I was in a position to help secure funding for them, but the Rebbe didn't ask about that. He was concerned with Chinatown. I don't think he has ever been there, and I'm certain that most people there don't know who he is, but he cares about them. Now that's a true leader!"[197]

In this case, and in countless others, the Rebbe was guided by the deep-seated belief that any opportunity to use influence for the benefit of others is G-d's way of saying, "This is part of your purpose. These are your sparks. Don't conserve or hold back! Use the gift of influence I have given you."

Friends in High Places

We see the same in the following story of the Rebbe's encounter with a budding community leader from Tel Aviv.

In 1972, R. Avraham Chaputa was appointed as the leader of Yeshivat HaRambam U'Beit Yosef, a Sephardic *yeshivah* in Tel Aviv, when he was just twenty years old. Under his leadership, what had been a modest *yeshivah* grew so much that the rabbi began to look for opportunities to expand. Toward this end, he traveled to the United States to raise money to cover building costs, and he was subsequently invited by some of his donors to join them in meeting with the Rebbe while in New York.

Arriving with his well-heeled and important companions, the young rabbi remained silent during the entire meeting, not uttering a word.

He was surprised when the Rebbe addressed his companions, saying, "The rabbi who is with you should stay," at which point he stood and addressed the quiet rabbi directly. "Are you R. Avraham Chaputa?"

Thus began a long, impromptu *yechidut* in which the Rebbe asked about the rabbi's students, the *yeshivah*, and the plans for its expansion. After their meeting, R. Chaputa returned to Tel Aviv, and shortly thereafter, he was surprised to receive notice that city officials had offered a plot of land on which to build his new building. The grateful rabbi attributed the surprising donation of land to his work on the Tel Aviv Religious Council.

It was only thanks to a chance encounter some thirty-four years later that R. Chaputa learned of the true source of his boon. Having been invited by Chabad to participate in an evening of study, he was taken aside at one point and shown a letter from the Rebbe written shortly after their impromptu *yechidut* many years prior. It was addressed to Yehoshua Rabinovitz, then mayor of Tel Aviv. Noting some of the red tape that had troubled the expansion of the *yeshivah*, the Rebbe had written to ask the mayor to help clear the way for their expansion!

"I was astounded," R. Chaputa recalled later in an interview. "The Rebbe was requesting that the mayor give us a plot for our yeshivah! In that meeting, he had heard me say that I needed a plot of land so that we could expand and admit more students. But I had not asked him to help me, nor did I expect him to. Yet he took it upon himself to do what he could to secure this plot for us. His eyes were open and watching over so many places—he was not just a Rebbe to his Chasidim; he cared about the entire Jewish world."[198]

Divine Promotions

In the following, we find examples of the Rebbe's insistence that promotions, advancement, and other avenues of increased influence bring additional responsibility to serve the One Who helped you rise.

When William Horowitz was elected to the Board of Trustees at Yale University, the Rebbe sent a letter reminding him that, along with bringing honor and accolades, his new position was a Divine invitation to put his expanded influence to use:

"I was gratified to learn of the distinct honor which has been bestowed upon you in your election as a trustee of Yale University. I know from the report that the event made history inasmuch as it broke with 'tradition,' you being the first Jew elected to this body.

"...Needless to say, every event in one's life is meaningful in other ways than personal, especially an extraordinary event. I trust therefore you will see in this appointment not only a well-deserved personal tribute, but also an added obligation to utilize your new opportunities for the good of many.

"I understand that there are many Jewish students at Yale, that they have special problems, such as relates to Sabbath and Yom Tov observance, and the like. It is to be hoped that they will find in you a sympathetic and understanding friend, and that you will take a personal interest in their academic problems.

"No doubt a distinction of this kind goes with a feeling of humility and gratitude to G-d, to which you will surely wish to give full expression.[199, 200, 201]

Similar encouragement was provided by the Rebbe throughout the career of noted scientist and professor Dr. Velvel Green. When Dr. Green was promoted to a professorship at the University of Minnesota, the Rebbe wrote to him and his wife a letter of congratulations with the following important reminder:

> "This is undoubtedly a true promotion, both professionally as well as in the opening up of new horizons in your work for the spiritual benefit of the many, and when the two are coupled, it is indeed a true and complete promotion.
>
> "May G-d grant that this be the forerunner of further advancement in the same direction which is indeed a natural aspiration, as our Sages declared, 'He who possesses one hundred desires to possess two hundred, and he who possesses two hundred desires four hundred.' This indicates that the ambition grows with success, and having advanced, one is not satisfied with the previous increment. The same, at least, should be true in the spiritual sense."[202], [203]

Naturally, upon receiving a promotion, one might be content to merely meet the demands of one's newer, greater workload. The Rebbe taught otherwise, insisting that as we grow and achieve, so does our strength. When we are blessed with additional influence, we also receive the commensurate responsibility and increased abilities to use that added influence to spread goodness and kindness.[204]

A Question of Impact

Even our choices about which opportunities to follow should be guided by their potential for providing the greatest degree of influence. For example, a congregational rabbi who was at a crossroads in his career once visited the Rebbe for guidance. He had been offered a teaching job and was passionate about Jewish education, but he had reservations about leaving the rabbinate. "Should I stay on as a rabbi or should I become a teacher?" he asked. The Rebbe replied, "The question you need to ask yourself is this: 'Where will I be able to have the greatest impact on the largest group of people?'"

"In the classroom, you will have twenty or thirty students per year, whereas through your work with the community, your sphere of influence extends to many more. If G-d has given you the ability to lead a community, this is the correct choice for you."[205]

Here the Rebbe couches an individual's duty to exert influence in quantitative terms—if you can reach thousands, it is a clear indicator that this is the place for you to focus your efforts. But, as the following story illustrates, influence also has a qualitative dimension, which we must seek to maximize for the benefit of others.

When pioneering psychiatric researcher and author Dr. Ruth Benjamin was working on her master's thesis in psychology, she wrestled with the question of whether to continue her graduate studies and pursue a PhD. The Rebbe offered his encouragement, saying that her doctorate was important for the sake of "prestige."

"After reading so many Chasidic teachings that stress humility, wouldn't 'prestige' be the wrong motivation?" Dr. Benjamin asked.

The Rebbe replied, "What I mean is that if an individual came to ask for your advice, he or she would be more likely to listen because you had a doctorate. That's why I say it is important to have a PhD. for prestige."[206]

A Model Citizen

In the end, the ultimate way to maximize and manifest our influence is by modeling lives of faith, commitment, and purpose ourselves, which in turn activates the same in others.

For example, while vacationing on his private yacht, American Jewish businessman and philanthropist David Chase would put on *tefillin* gifted to him by the Rebbe.

At sea, Chase would regularly ask his captain, Dick Winters, what direction the boat was facing so that he could face eastward toward Jerusalem while praying, as is customary.

After a few days, Winters was perplexed by Chase's repeated questions and asked if his employer had been learning the principles of marine navigation.

"Oh, no," Chase replied, explaining that he needed to know the information for religious purposes.

The following Sunday, when the yacht docked at Block Island in the Atlantic Ocean, Winters made an unusual request to leave his post for an hour, together with his wife.

"Of course," Chase replied, inquiring why Winters wished to leave his duties.

"When I discovered that you recite daily prayers," Winters explained, "you made me feel guilty that I don't follow my own faith. So I would like to leave for one hour to attend church with my wife."[207]

Chase later shared the incident with the Rebbe. At a subsequent public talk, the Rebbe told the story to the thousands of Chasidim present, using it as a living lesson of how a Jew who is committed and comfortable in his observance can positively influence those around him—Jews and non-Jews alike.[208] Together, all of these examples provide a clear illustration of a powerful truth the Rebbe repeated often: "A person's purpose in life is only truly attained when they make full use of the influence they have to impact those around them for the good."

Meaningful acts of auspicious influence can take on a viral nature, impacting myriad lives in a perpetually unfolding chain of positivity and growth. As we activate and direct our influence consciously and constructively, its ripples continue to spread, setting in motion a chain reaction of goodness and blessings.

CHAPTER 17

Maximum Impact

O N THE OCCASION OF her birthday, a woman wrote to the Rebbe, mentioning her efforts during the past year to share the beauty of Judaism with her community.

After warmly noting her achievements, the Rebbe wrote, "...bear in mind, however, that a person who was granted the ability to impact one hundred people and reaches only ninety-nine has not yet fully realized their G-d-given potential."[209]

Previously, we learned that each of us is born with talents that help inform our life's mission, and that our gifts find their most potent expression when we use them to heal and uplift our world. As we courageously live out our personal sacred mandates, an essential question to consistently ask is: *Am I truly giving my all, or do I have more to give?*

This line of introspective questioning formed the basis of a nightly ritual practiced by the Rebbe.

As he once shared with R. Yochanan Gordon:

"Every night, before saying *Krias Shema She'al Hamitah* (Shema Before Bed), when I make a spiritual accounting of the day, I ask myself: *Did I give away everything I have to this day?*"

The Rebbe repeatedly insisted that each of us, along with our particular constellation of individual talents and strengths, is placed in the world with a personally tailored *capacity and wherewithal* for impacting the world. Energy levels, general health, ability to deal with stress or lack of sleep—each of these things impact your capacity to strive and serve. Some can do more, some less. In either case, your capacity is as unique to you as your purpose, and, hence, an integral part of fulfilling your purpose involves using your G-d-given capacity to its fullest, whatever that may be. In the Rebbe's own words:

> "...If someone has the ability to influence a thousand people and only influenced 999, then it's likely that he will be rewarded for his work, but he did not fulfill the purpose for which he was created!"[210]

All in the Details

During a Purim farbrengen in 1973, the Rebbe used the example of Persian King Ahasuerus to illustrate just how far we must go to live up to our inborn potential. Drawing attention to the fine details of a lavish feast provided by the king to his subjects, the Rebbe explained:

> "...it is not at all clear why the Megillah must relate, and we must read all the details of, how King Ahasuerus arranged his royal feast...
>
> "To know that the king was merry is one thing. But of what significance are the *tapestries of white and blue fine cotton*,[211] or the *golden couches*,[212] or all the details of what was given to the guests who participated in the king's feast?
>
> "...The point we learn from this narrative is that when a person does something, he must do it to the *fullest of his abilities*—not to calculate that since such and such an effort is sufficient for someone else, then it is enough for me to do only a little more. Rather, since your potential is greater, it is not enough to make an ordinary celebration; rather, it should be a celebration *in the court of the garden of the king's palace*.[213]
>
> "The lesson we learn from this...[is that] a person...must contemplate: You have a mission from G-d! It is not enough to do just as much as someone else who has less abilities than you...

"No! You must use *your* full potential! You must measure your own abilities—and then exceed them!"[214]

All too often we are tempted to calculate our capacity based on the contributions and expectations of others. But your level of effort and engagement, like so many other aspects of your purpose, are meant to be discerned by looking inward rather than outward.

As the Rebbe once stated emphatically, "Living a full life means using all the unique abilities that G-d grants an individual—man or woman—and to harness them in the fullest measure, in a manner that is most beneficial to yourself and others."[215, 216, 217]

In the Presence of Greatness

This was the empowering message the Rebbe shared with an individual who was struggling to find motivation and energy while pursuing his life's purpose:

"One of the effective ways of overcoming this difficulty is by thinking deeply about the fact that G-d is present everywhere and always, as the Alter Rebbe [R. Schneur Zalman] explains in the beginning of Chapter 41 of the *Tanya*:

"'And behold, G-d stands over him'...and He looks upon him and 'searches his mind and heart' (to see) if he is serving Him as is fitting...

"The point is to remember that inasmuch as G-d gives one the great gift of time and mental ability, etc., one must not waste these great gifts given by G-d.

"By way of illustration: Suppose a great and majestic king personally and graciously gave you a gift, and he stands by you, watching what you will do with it; what would it look like if you would drop it with complete disregard, and go out for a walk or engage in some other pastime, etc.?"[218]

The G-dly purpose that you carry can only be developed and delivered to the world by you. No matter what may be standing in the way of maximizing the impact of your holy mission, know that G-d looks to you for a return on the investment he made in crafting the miracle of you.

Dynamic Growth Potential

The same is true of new opportunities that invite us to stretch our existing capacity.[219] While it may be tempting to remain in our comfort zone, new opportunities that come our way are Divine invitations to further expand the scope of our service. These growing pains, uncomfortable as they are, are simply a matter of course and should be viewed as opportunities to reach deeper and shine brighter.

This was the challenge facing R. Yitzchok Dovid Groner, whose easygoing life as a rabbinic employee in

New York had been upended by an assignment that placed him in charge of establishing a Chabad outpost in Melbourne, Australia.

In a letter to the Rebbe, R. Groner's wife, Devorah, expressed her frustration with the burden of her husband's new assignment, noting the comparative ease of his previous job in New York, where he had enjoyed ample support and appreciation from his colleagues. Noting the couple's longing for their previous, uncomplicated life, the Rebbe responded in depth:

> "...concerning the lack of appreciation, etc., ...which gave rise to your thoughts on the relative disadvantages of your husband's present position by comparison with his previous one...the difference between his present work and his previous work is not a difference of place or surroundings, but a difference of the essential quality and character of the work itself. For previously he was in the capacity of an employed 'clerk,' and as such, there were certainly a number of advantages.

> "A clerk has definite hours, and upon completion of his day's work, he can dismiss it from his mind, knowing that the responsibility lies squarely on the shoulders of his superior. He needs only to do the task given to him, in the best way, and he can then feel no worries,

responsibilities, or other commitments. Furthermore, such a job arouses a minimum of envy, less nervous strain, etc.

"On the other hand, when one has the task of an executive, upon whom the full responsibility rests, all the more so being at a great distance, and having to make decisions, and especially when he takes up such a job willingly and enthusiastically and is successful, it is bound to call forth envy.

"Obviously, one whose capacity limits him to a secondary position, such as that of a clerk, there is little he can do about it, as this is all that he can accomplish. [However,] one who has the capacity to be an executive and in charge of a responsible undertaking—if such a person should confine himself within the framework of a clerk's job, it would be a gross injustice even for himself, not to mention to the cause.

"It is written, 'More knowledge, more pain,' and the more knowledgeable and advanced person is inevitably involved in more complicated things. One can say, 'I don't want to be on the higher level, so that I can be spared the pain.' But this would be like a person saying, 'I don't want to be a human being; I want to be like an animal and be spared all the pain associated with human life.'

"...Furthermore, in a country where Judaism is still in its infancy...what a challenge and opportunity such work offers to the qualified person!"[220]

Assuring her that he meant no rebuke, and that their previous position would always remain available should they choose to return to New York, the Rebbe concluded:

"The important thing is that if the task is to be done successfully, the work must be carried on willingly, without compulsion.

"On the other hand, I would be remiss in my duty if I were not to point out the essential differences between one job as against the other, in the light of the quotation mentioned above, 'More knowledge, more pain.'"

New Capabilities

From the Rebbe's perspective, our capacity is dynamic, growing as we go from strength to strength. As our capacity grows, so does our responsibility and power to shine the light of G-d in the world. It may be tempting to define the scope of our present endeavors based on the demands and achievements of the past. But this approach is similar to basing our ambitions on those of someone with fewer capabilities or resources than we possess. It is important to avoid the folly of using who we were yesterday to decide how much we might be able to accomplish today.

Meanwhile, every challenge to which we rise opens new channels of Divine energy and blessings.

The Rebbe crystallized this point to the wife of R. Avraham Alter Heber, who wrote to the Rebbe about the overwhelming demand that accompanied their communal work to establish a new community in the city of Kiryat Malachi.

At the time, she was deeply entrenched in promoting the various *mitzvah* campaigns the Rebbe had launched, and she confided that she sometimes felt like the demands that were made of her were beyond her abilities.

The Rebbe responded by sharing an adage of his father-in-law, the Previous Rebbe, who taught that "when someone decides to go beyond what they are normally capable of, that very decision opens up new channels of energy, granting them more abilities than they previously possessed."[221]

From this perspective, even tasks that seem beyond us in the moment can be surmounted, as G-d promises to provide everything we may need to complete the tasks He assigns as part of our Divine purpose.

Never Enough

At this point, it makes sense to ask: *When am I permitted to sail into the sunset?* Modern convention would say that, at the very least, we are expected to retire in our so-called golden years. This reward, for many, is a given—a final payout for a life of tireless toil. But time and again, the Rebbe fervently rejected the idea that there is ever a time to say, "Mission accomplished."

As far as the Rebbe was concerned, there is always more good to be done in the world, and we are always beholden to the mission G-d gave us, no matter what comfortable alternative beckons to us.

For example, a Jew from Montreal once approached the Rebbe with a question about his life as a businessman. After dedicating much of his life to his work, the man sold his business with plans to retire. But a recent opportunity to buy the business back had thrown his trajectory into question, and he wrestled with the notion of returning to the demands of his previous work.

"How much is enough?" he asked.

"Enough of what?" the Rebbe asked.

"We sold our business," the visitor explained. "We have an offer now to buy it back. I am trying to understand: When should one feel that he has enough for himself and his family?"

"If you have experience in business, you must use it," replied the Rebbe.

The visitor was still unsure.

"And [what are you supposed to do] when you have

enough, and you feel that there's enough for you, and you have reached your goal?" he asked again.

"That is not possible for a Jew!" exclaimed the Rebbe. "Because he [the Jew] has an endless message and mission from G-d A-mighty!"

Here, the Rebbe's question, "Enough of what?" was not meant to clarify but to challenge the very notion of "enough," and whether such a rubric even exists in the context of one's purpose in life.

This is not to discount the Rabbinic teaching: "Who is wealthy? He who is happy with his lot."

Indeed, in accord with this maxim, it seems that the businessman's question, "How much is enough?" was his way of asking whether, having achieved material success, perhaps it was time to move on to more spiritual pursuits.

However, from the Rebbe's perspective, where everything available to us, including influence and wealth, can be used as a conduit for bettering our world, there is no separation between spiritual and material capacities, and there is therefore no such thing as enough. If someone has opportunity and skills in business or otherwise, they are called upon to use those tools to influence the world for the better. As long as we have the opportunity, we have a G-dly mission to shine.[222]

Accelerating with Age

For the Rebbe, who remained extraordinarily active

into his nineties, the idea of retiring was never a consideration. He saw every single day as an opportunity to further reveal G-d's presence and Providence in the world.

The Rebbe lived this philosophy to an extraordinary degree. On his seventieth birthday, for example, he received tens of thousands of letters from well-wishers around the world. Among them were many letters that suggested it was perhaps time he considered "slowing down" and "taking it easy" after many blessed decades as a global leader and activist, to which he responded at a public birthday gathering: "I have been asked: 'Now that you have attained the age of seventy, what are your plans? It would seem that this is an appropriate time to rest a bit....'[223] My response to that is that *we must begin to accomplish even more.*"

The Rebbe then announced the launch of a campaign to open seventy-one new educational institutions in the course of the coming year alone, virtually doubling the Chabad worldwide outreach network.

A decade later, at a *farbrengen* marking his eightieth birthday, the Rebbe did the same, calling for a massive expansion of Chabad activities.

Never Let Go

In story after story, the Rebbe repeatedly and vehemently challenged the very notion that it was even possible for one to outgrow their usefulness.

The very fact that G-d has granted a person a single

additional day to reunite the scattered sparks of creation means they have not concluded their mission in life. The mere opportunity to achieve some betterment demands we must rise to the occasion.

The Rebbe shared this motivating message with Esther Mentz at the end of her long and successful term as president of N'Shei Chabad in Crown Heights. She came to the Rebbe in a state of exhaustion, saying, "I can't do this anymore. This is the year. I'm letting go."

"Why are you letting this go? You're doing such a great function," the Rebbe asked.

"I'm tired. It takes all your strength out of you. There's no one who cooperates with me. I'm doing this single-handedly. I have to do it myself. I'm tired. I don't want to do it anymore."

"You're tired and you don't want to do it anymore?" the Rebbe asked.

"That's right," she affirmed.

"What should the Rebbe say?" the Rebbe asked. "The Rebbe is tired. No one helps the Rebbe. But the Rebbe continues doing it."

Esther replied, "I'm not the Rebbe."

"But you're not doing the job of a Rebbe. You're doing the job that you can do," the Rebbe replied. "Can you continue another year?"[224]

The Rebbe's dedication to squeezing every ounce of

potential from each moment can serve as a living example for every one of us. Whether you are a leader or a layperson, your sacred capacity is one of a kind—just like your Divine purpose. You don't have to match anyone else's contributions. You only need to live up to your own Divine potential and give your all to every day and opportunity granted by G-d to bring the world one step closer to its ultimate redemption.

CHAPTER 18

Expect the Unexpected

I N 1979, MIRIAM SWERDLOV attended a Chabad-sponsored convention for women and girls in Detroit. After the inspiring event, while waiting to board the plane for home, Miriam and about twenty other women learned that the flight was canceled due to a snowstorm.

The group rushed to a payphone and called Chabad headquarters in New York to report on the delay. The leader of the group, Miriam Popack, spoke with the Rebbe's secretary and told him that they were stuck in Detroit.

"He put us on hold, and a minute later he came back on the line. 'The Rebbe doesn't understand the word "stuck,"' he said." Mrs. Popack proceeded to explain what the word stuck meant, to which the secretary replied, "The Rebbe knows what stuck means. The Rebbe says that a Jew is never stuck."

Caught off guard by the Rebbe's response, the women immediately got the message and rose to the occasion. They spread throughout the airport and began handing out Shabbat candles to the Jewish women they met. As a result: "There are women and families today all over the United States lighting Shabbat candles because we got 'stuck' in Detroit."[225]

Purposeful Pitstops

Every path is filled with setbacks and detours. But even the unexpected pitstop has a place in your search for purpose. Often such deviations in life are perceived as distractions and detractions from the ultimate purpose to which we are committed. Feeling ourselves lost in a tangent, we may resist, react, or reset in an attempt to reclaim our carefully curated trajectory.

But according to Judaism, even setbacks and detours are governed by Divine Providence, which never introduces anything superfluous or unnecessary into our lives. Seen through this lens, we arrive at a crucial realization—while it does occur, most lives don't consist of one mission alone, but of various Divinely appointed tasks, some of which are sought out, and others that emerge from circumstances outside of our control. These are events and experiences that we may never seek out or want, but they are, nevertheless, sent to us by G-d. Hidden within these Divinely orchestrated encounters are sparks that are part of our soul's journey, despite their apparent randomness.

To paraphrase the Rebbe's words:

> There are two types of "sparks of holiness" that a person redeems in the course of his life. The first are those that he consciously pursues, having recognized the potential for sanctity and goodness in an object or event in his life. The second are those that pursue him: Opportunities that he would never have realized on his own—indeed, he may even do everything in his power to avoid them—since they represent potentials so lofty that they cannot be identified by his humanly finite perception. So his redemption of these "sparks" can come about only unwittingly, when his involvement with them is forced upon him by circumstances beyond his control."[226, 227, 228]

In short, there are sparks *we* pursue, and there are sparks that *pursue us*.

Divine Detour

The following story demonstrates how awareness of Divine Providence can transform moments when our chosen trajectory is obstructed, allowing us to find hidden purpose and potential for positive impact no matter where our path takes us.

Each day, the Rebbe's wife, Rebbetzin Chaya Mushka Schneerson, would go out with a driver for fresh air at a park in Long Island. One day, as they neared the park, they found their regular route closed off due to road work and were forced to take an alternate route. As they drove along trying to find their way, they passed a woman on the side of the road crying and protesting. When they stopped at the traffic light, the Rebbetzin turned to the driver and said: "I heard a woman crying. Can you go back and see what that was about?"

They turned around and drove back to the beginning of the street, where they saw a woman standing on the curb weeping, while workers were carrying furniture from a house and loading them onto the truck of the county marshal. The Rebbetzin asked the driver to find out what was happening. The marshal explained that the woman had not paid her rent for many months and was now being evicted from her home.

The Rebbetzin inquired how much the woman owed, and if the marshal would accept a personal check. The sum that the family owed was approximately $6,700. The marshal said that he had no problem accepting a personal check, as long as he confirmed with the bank that the check was covered. He also said that if he received the payment, his men would carry everything back into the house. Then, to the driver's surprise, "She took out her checkbook, wrote out a check for the full amount, and asked me to give it to the marshal." The Rebbetzin then urged the driver to quickly drive away before the woman realized what had transpired.

Amazed by what he had seen, the Rebbetzin's driver could not contain himself and asked the Rebbetzin what had prompted her to give such a large sum to a total stranger.

"Once, when I was a young girl, my father took me for a walk in the park. He sat me down on a bench and began telling me about Divine Providence. 'Every time'—said Father—'something causes us to deviate from our normal routine, there is a Divinely ordained reason for this; every time we see something unusual, there is a purpose in why we've been shown this sight.'

"Today," continued the Rebbetzin, "when I saw the detour sign instructing us to deviate from our regular route, I remembered my father's words and immediately thought to myself: We drive by this street every day; suddenly, the street is closed off, and we're sent to a different street. What is the purpose of this? How is this connected to me? Then I heard the sound of a woman crying and screaming. I realized that we had been sent along this route for a purpose."[229]

A Man on a Mission

There is no place or situation devoid of G-d.

Indeed, every step is a destination of its own. Every phase of our journey, even our detours, is meant to bring us exactly to where we need to be, if we would but remain present. This is the essence of Divine Providence—sanctifying each moment by granting it ultimate significance.

This perspective is especially helpful when we find ourselves lost or knocked off course. For it is then that we are most tempted to disregard our immediate surroundings, as our mind can be elsewhere.

In the mid-1970s, during the early years of R. Yisroel and Vivi Deren's *shlichut* in Stamford, Connecticut, one of their children became ill and was in the hospital for an extended period. With other children to care for, including a baby, one parent had to always be at the hospital while the other remained at home. It was a trying time for everyone, and getting anything done beyond taking care of the family was very difficult.

At a certain point, R. Deren called the Rebbe's secretary to issue a report of his activities, as was his custom. He humbly reported that because of his son's condition, he had spent almost all of his time at the hospital, to the neglect of his usual *shlichut* activities.

The line went quiet. A short while later, the secretary returned and said: "The Rebbe asked me to convey that certainly the *Eibershter* (G-d) didn't make such a thing happen so that you should suffer or be anguished because of it. Surely you have a *shlichut* to do there; go find it and do it."[230]

R. Deren took the Rebbe's lesson to heart and immediately began reaching out to Jews throughout the hospital—wrapping *tefillin*, giving inspiration, and providing comfort for those in need. In that one conversation, his view of his situation was transformed. Instead of seeing his unplanned stay in the hospital as a diversion from his *shlichut*, he internalized the Rebbe's message that "every moment and every situation is a part of your *shlichut*; your Divine purpose."[231]

Midlife Metamorphosis

This was a lesson impressed upon Micha Peled, who at the age of forty-four was diagnosed with a severe and malignant cancer and was advised to travel from his home in Israel to seek medical care at Mount Sinai Medical Center in Miami Beach, Florida, which specialized in treating his particular variety of melanoma.

Following his doctor's advice, he met R. Avrohom Korf, the director of Chabad of Florida, who offered to hire him to work at the local *yeshivah*. In addition to providing an income, the job ensured he would have health insurance in the United States.

Amid treatments, Micha began visiting the *yeshivah*. He was warmly received by the dean, R. Leibel Schapiro, who introduced him to the students, invited him to learn with them, and welcomed him into the fold. Having settled in Miami, Micha eventually made a trip to New York with his wife so that he could visit the Rebbe as he had on past occasions to receive dollars for charity, and in this case to receive a blessing prior to his next course of treatment.

When his turn came to speak with the Rebbe, he mentioned his association with the Miami *yeshivah*, drawing from the Rebbe an awe-striking comment, "Do you think you came to Miami only for medical reasons? Know that the real reason you came is to strengthen the *yeshivah*, to have a good influence on the young students, and to inspire them with your love for life, your passion, your positive spirit, and your optimism."

The Rebbe then gave a blessing that Micha would emerge from his life-threatening condition in good health.

A few years later, after making great strides in his studies, Micha traveled to Israel to be tested for and receive rabbinical ordination. He subsequently held several rabbinic positions in Miami and later Israel, where he settled in the hills of Mateh Binyamin to serve as the rabbi of Beit Horon. Reflecting on the winding path of his life, he would observe, "It was the Rebbe who set me on the path toward the rabbinate when he encouraged me to go back to *yeshivah* at the age of forty-four."[232]

Here we see a beautiful example of the extraordinary possibilities hidden within every seeming setback in life.

Thanks to the Rebbe's insistence that every apparent upset is also a potential gateway to finding the sparks that animate our unique purpose, this man's illness became the impetus for his transformation into a rabbi and spiritual beacon for others.

Permanent Station

Our final story speaks to those times in life when we find ourselves in between assignments or in transition, neither here nor there.

R. Avrohom Glick, a young rabbinic student from Melbourne, married a teacher from Worcester, Massachusetts, and on the Rebbe's instructions joined his wife there, assuming the role of organizing youth activities in the community. After a few years, a position opened up back in Australia, and he was invited to relocate to Melbourne by the Chabad emissary there. He asked for and received the Rebbe's approval and blessings.

However, once he began preparing for the move to Australia, he began to feel as if he were just treading water in Worcester. He had already wound up his activities there, but as he had not yet moved to Australia, he felt neither fully here nor there. He had yet to depart, but his mind was elsewhere.

During a *yechidut*, he confided his state of mind to the Rebbe, who replied:

"In the Torah we find that during the forty

years the Jews were wandering in the wilderness, they would sometimes set up the Tabernacle just for one day and then take it apart, which was obviously a very difficult job. However, for that day, it was considered permanent—they were in that place as though they were going to be there permanently. This was pertinent to many laws.

"Therefore, when a Jew finds himself in a place—even for only one day—he must treat it as though he were there permanently, and not as if he is there with a packed suitcase, ready to go."[233]

We are never just "passing through." We are always exactly where G-d needs us to be. We must always be mindful and ready to fulfill our Divine purpose in every place and time.

Obstacles or Opportunities?

How do you handle situations that disrupt your schedule? How do you deal with obstacles in your path? When plans do not go your way, what then? It is so easy to become disoriented when our lives take an unexpected turn. We know where we are going, and anything that veers from that course is met with resistance and even rejection. We are supposed to be in control, and we know best.

But what if we saw life in a different light? What if

there is more going on in our lives and in the world than we are aware of? By cultivating an appreciation for the role of Divine Providence in our lives, we can discover the hidden meaning and holy opportunity within any situation in which we find ourselves. Remember, every step has a purpose, every setback is an essential part of your story, and every detour contains sparks waiting to be redeemed and uplifted.

CHAPTER 19

No Such Thing as a Vacation

RABBI MOSHE HECHT, SHLIACH to New Haven, Connecticut, once asked the Rebbe for a blessing beforetraveling on vacation to Israel. The Rebbe replied, "I understand that there is an old-age home in Hungary with some elderly Jews, and kosher meals there are not an option. Can you travel to Israel via Hungary and use your oratory skills to persuade the owner to offer a kosher option to the Jewish residents?"

R. Hecht would later quip, "It's a bad idea to tell the Rebbe you're going on vacation..."[234]

Behind R. Hecht's tongue-in-cheek observation lies a profound insight into the Rebbe's perspective on the Divine purpose and potential present within every step of life's many journeys and destinations. In the previous chapter we learned that life's many setbacks and detours are Divine orchestrations, arranged to help us discover hidden meaning and deeper purpose amid the circumstances of our lives.

And what is true for unexpected detours is equally true for all journeys—even those we may define as "time off." From the Rebbe's perspective, there is no such thing as a vacation from our purpose in life. Each and every one of our travels, whether for business or pleasure, carries a Divine invitation to elevate our journeys and destinations. Indeed, in one encounter after another, we find the Rebbe encouraging people to recognize the opportunity waiting at every station, and to follow the Divine gravity that gently pulls us to select locations for the sake of revealing G-d's presence and Providence.

The Law of Attraction

As elucidated by the fifth Lubavitcher Rebbe, R. Shalom DovBer, known as the Rebbe Rashab, a person may sometimes feel drawn toward a specific place. They may not know why they want to go there, but they feel drawn there, nonetheless. What is the source of this motivation? The Rebbe Rashab explains that the desire to go to that place is the result of a providential pull toward a mission they are destined to fulfill there.[235]

As the Rebbe once explained to a traveling businessman: "The Baal Shem Tov taught that when a Jew travels to a given place, it is not of their own doing. Rather, G-d, Who *establishes the steps of man* has sent them there. If it were just about making a living, G-d could have allowed them to do so without the need to travel elsewhere. But because He desires for you to illuminate that place, and to bring the recognition of G-d's name there, He sends you to accomplish it and guides your steps so that He can 'delight in your way' as you go on the path He desires."[236]

The above teaching asks us to acknowledge and embrace this providential dynamic. Doing so empowers us to carry out our uncharted missions more effectively, and it opens us up to unforeseen moments of serendipity that enable us to accomplish more than we could possibly have imagined.

Much Needed Uptime

On the precipice of a well-earned sabbatical, R. Benjamin Blech, who was serving as the rabbi of Young Israel of Oceanside, was once redirected by the Rebbe toward the sacred, unanticipated opportunities that awaited him during his "time off."

"At that time, I was taking a sabbatical from my pulpit and from my teaching responsibilities because there was a book that I wanted to write," Blech recalled in an interview.

"Before I could embark on that project, however, I got a call from the Rebbe's secretary, R. Yehuda Leib Groner."[237]

"I hear that you're going on a sabbatical," said R. Groner. "The Rebbe wants to see you."

Having had no personal relationship with the Rebbe, R. Blech could not understand why this global Jewish leader would call on him for a meeting.

Upon meeting, the Rebbe explained that he wanted R. Blech and his wife to visit a number of locations across the Far East where Jews were in need of spiritual connection and nourishment.[238] What had been scheduled to be a time of rest and rejuvenation from the strenuous demands of his communal role quickly transformed into a three-month mission to Jewish communities in Australia, New Zealand, Singapore, Bangkok, Hong Kong, and Tokyo. R. Blech accepted the Rebbe's mission, and he was astounded by the many acts of Divine Providence he encountered along the way, and the many Jews he inspired to turn or return to a life of Jewish engagement.

"After I came back from my trip...I met with the Rebbe again, and he congratulated me on what I had achieved," R. Blech recalled. "He said, 'I am very happy with what you have done, and I want to tell you something—whether you know it or not, you are a Chasid in camouflage.'"[239]

The unexpected opportunity and success found by R. Blech on his "sabbatical" reminds us of the supreme importance of infusing every step we take with Divine purpose and intention. Typically, we separate our lives into moments and endeavors that are sacred, meaningful, productive, and part of the purpose of our lives, and other moments and endeavors that are there to support those moments or provide respite from the sometimes heavy demands of everyday life. Operating from this perspective, we tend to compartmentalize our lives into different categories—leisurely vs. active, incidental vs. intentional, mundane vs. meaningful, secular vs. sacred, and so on.

But from the Rebbe's point of view, there is no such thing as "downtime." Rather, we should strive to see every moment of our lives as "uptime," dedicated to the elevation of creation.

At the Gates

Having survived the horrors of Nazi concentration camps and immigrating to Montreal, Canada, R. Nissen Mangel enrolled in the local Lubavitch *yeshivah*, where he studied diligently while applying for citizenship. When his citizenship was finally granted, freeing him to travel abroad, he quickly made plans to travel to Chabad headquarters in Brooklyn, where he hoped to meet the Rebbe. After his first *farbrengen* at 770, R. Mangel was invited to a private audience with the Rebbe, who inquired about his studies and aspirations before the discussion shifted to his return trip.

Mangel mentioned that because he could not afford to travel by any other means, he would be returning home by bus along a circuitous, meandering route.

Hearing of his protracted itinerary, the Rebbe proceeded to name several cities in Upstate New York that were along the young man's bus route and then suggested, "Wherever the bus stops, go to the local community. Speak there and relay some Chasidic teachings."

The nineteen-year-old *yeshivah* student wondered how he could accomplish a mission with such daunting logistics.

"Don't worry," the Rebbe assured him, as if reading his mind. "The Lubavitch Youth Organization will arrange it for you. Somebody will pick you up at the bus stations; you just need to speak."

Indeed, the Rebbe saw to it that a number of talks were arranged at several synagogues in Upstate New York, which were all enthusiastically received.[240]

Where the young man saw a long, inconvenient detour based on lack of funds, the Rebbe saw a providential opportunity arranged for the sake of ministering to outlying communities near stops along his wayward route. Far from an inconvenience, his journey and mode of travel were all Divinely orchestrated to place him exactly where he needed to be.

As the Rebbe taught[241]:

"If [G-d] guides your footsteps somewhere, at

a specific time, to a specific place, in a specific manner, it is so you can accomplish something there."

This perspective reveals the subtle depth of Jacob's famous statement, uttered when he awoke one morning amid his sudden flight from the Holy Land, driven by the murderous machinations of his brother, Esau. Having dreamed of a supernal ladder with angels ascending and descending to and from heaven, he proclaimed: *"Indeed, the L-rd is in this place, and I did not know [it]...How awesome is this place! This is none other than the house of G-d, and this is the gate of heaven."*[242]

Jacob's surprised reaction reflects his realization of a profound spiritual truth: There is no place and no journey—even one hastily undertaken in reaction to sudden, terrible circumstances—that does not have a deeper spiritual purpose. Behind the veil of everyday reality, there is a providential drama unfolding, waiting for us to recognize and reveal how every moment, encounter, route, and destination can become a "gate to heaven."

Every Step You Take

A beautiful example of this perspective was shared by the Rebbe in 1954 with R. Yochanan Twersky, who had traveled from his home in Israel to New York to attend the wedding of his son. Taking advantage of his time in

Brooklyn, R. Twersky hoped to renew his connection with the Rebbe, whom he had known during his youth.

During *yechidut*, the Rebbe asked R. Twersky whether he remembered a particular student in the underground Jewish school they had organized together in Nikolayev, Ukraine.[243] When the rabbi replied that he did, the Rebbe explained that the student had immigrated from the Soviet Union to the United States, where, over time, he had lapsed in his religious observance. The Rebbe said that Lubavitcher Chasidim had done their best to help him reengage with Judaism, but sadly, to no avail.

"Perhaps you will have an influence on him," the Rebbe suggested, and he asked R. Twersky if he could spend some time visiting with the young man. Saddened to hear of his former student's divergence, he promised to do what he could.

Seizing the opportunity, the Rebbe immediately picked up the phone and dialed the man's number.

"I have R. Yochanan Twersky sitting here. Do you remember him?" the Rebbe asked. The man indeed remembered his former teacher and agreed to meet with R. Twersky.

The former student traveled to Williamsburg to meet with the rabbi, and they shared a heartfelt reunion after thirty years apart, reminiscing about people from their past.

When the man asked the rabbi why he had come to New York, he replied that he had come for his son's wedding. The former student, assuming this was the reason for their meeting, took out a checkbook, wrote a generous check, and presented it to R. Twersky.

To his surprise, R. Twersky refused to accept the contribution.

"I won't take a check until I finish our conversation," he said firmly. "I want to discuss your Jewish observance."

The man replied that he was a respected member of his community and even went to his local temple on occasion.

"What about Shabbat observance?" asked the rabbi.

The man replied that although Shabbat was very important, he couldn't close his store while all his competitors were open on this busiest day of the week. When asked if he kept kosher, he said that it was hard to shop for kosher products where he lived, so he did not. When asked if he put on *tefillin*, he admitted that he frequently didn't have the time.

The rabbi's eyes filled with tears, and he cried bitterly.

"Was it for a 'Judaism' like this that we invested so much effort into you in the underground schools in Nikolayev? Each of your teachers put his life in danger so that you might grow up to be a committed Jew."

The man was touched by the rabbi's words and himself began to cry. "You are absolutely right! I promise that from now on I will endeavor to do *teshuvah* and keep the *mitzvot* as I learned them."

The rabbi was heartened by his student's promise and blessed him with success before they parted.

Several weeks later, while still in New York, the phone rang at his host's house, and R. Twersky picked up to discover the Rebbe on the line. The Rebbe reported to his delight that their former student had indeed returned to his roots.

"R. Yochanan," the Rebbe concluded poignantly, "do you think your trip from Israel to the United States was merely to marry off your son? You came here to help a Jew return to his heritage and roots."[244, 245]

Know Your Place

The Rebbe's penetrating observation about the Divine orchestrations drawing us to each destination is rooted in a Chasidic principle, beautifully elucidated by R. Levi Yitzchak of Berditchev:

> "Each person must clearly recognize that man's travels from place to place are not random, G-d forbid. Rather, they are directed by G-d with precision; *this* person has a specific portion to rectify in *this* place...
>
> "As the Baal Shem Tov explained the verse, *The L-rd establishes the steps of man*—G-d gives man the desire to travel to a specific place,

His intention being…that the person should engage in a particular Divine service, thereby rectifying what he must rectify.

"Therefore, when a person comes to a particular place, he must take this to heart and ask himself: 'Why am I here? For what purpose did G-d bring me here? Surely it is not in vain.'"[246]

Many of us go through life subscribing to an exclusively "human narrative"—i.e., interpreting reality based solely on our understanding of how the world works. We rigidly define our various travels and destinations in the narrow context of our quotidian reality. Vacations are for resting and recuperating. Business trips are for conducting business. Travel is for getting from point A to point B. We arrive at our destinations to fulfill whatever purpose we envisioned when we set out. But as the Rebbe reminds us, there is always a higher, Divine narrative behind every step we take. From this vantage point, the art of spiritual living begins by asking ourselves at every opportunity: What is the *higher purpose* behind this journey, detour, or destination?[247]

No matter where life's journey takes you, know that Divine opportunities await you there. There is no place, no time, no path that isn't brimming with immense, sacred possibility. Rather than looking at life as a diverse array of distinct, disconnected, segmented chapters, encounters, and journeys, the Rebbe taught that every route and destination should be viewed through a purpose-driven lens. Through this lens, every detour and destination in life becomes a piece of an integrated whole, infusing every step with Divine intention. There is no journey or destination that isn't holy. It is up to you, however, to recognize and reveal the light waiting to be revealed wherever you are sent.

CHAPTER 20

Your Life
Was Made for You

I N A SMALL VILLAGE not far from Berditchev there
lived a simple innkeeper named Mendel who made a
modest living serving the many travelers who stopped
for a meal or a rest on the side of a country road. Over
time, Mendel became restless and began to consider his
life's trajectory. He decided it was time to hand over
management of the inn to his son, with the hope that he
would then have time for prayer and study, which he had
neglected while running his business.

He summoned his son Shia, who was young and ener-
getic, and handed over the keys, saying: "I've managed the
inn for decades. The time has come for you to take over."

Shia left the village and moved to Berditchev, where
he dramatically overhauled his father's business, drawing

local nobility to frequent the inn, where they also began to host their meetings, parties, and events. From a business perspective, the transformation was an overwhelming success. But the simple passersby, who longed for the warm reception Mendel had always extended, stopped coming. They missed the modest meals and peaceful ambiance. But the inn's transformation had left it feeling alien and overrun to its former clientele.

When R. Levi Yitzchak of Berditchev heard of the changes, he reached out to Mendel and asked, "Why did you abandon your inn and hand it over to your son?"

"I am not getting any younger, "Mendel explained. "Who knows how many more years I will be granted? With what will I meet my Maker? Shall I remain without any Torah or prayer to accompany me?

"Now that my son is taking care of the inn, I feel better. I rise in the morning, wrap myself in my *tallit* and *tefillin*, and pray slowly with concentration. Then I study. I feel I am accumulating at least a small amount of merit that I can take to the heavenly court when my time comes."

R. Levi Yitzchak took time to consider Mendel's dilemma and then said, "Our Sages say, 'A wise man is someone who knows his place.'[248] A person ought to know the place that Divine Providence has destined for them. When one knows one's place, he or she ought to stay there and not try to take the place destined for someone else.

"G-d places each person at their post. He placed one person in the study hall and another in a small and remote village. You, Mendel, were selected by G-d to be posted at an inn at a crossroads, so that you could serve up some warm kosher soup to weary travelers on a cold winter night and a cold cup of water on hot summer days.

"No, Mendel, you will not stand before the heavenly court like a poor man. With no shame will you greet the angels. With you will be all the kosher meals you served to the travelers and all the warm beds you prepared. All the friendly smiles and kind words you shared will advocate for you. Return to the inn and fulfill the position that G-d assigned specifically to you."

Mendel followed the Rebbe's instructions and returned to the village. Shortly afterward, the inn returned to serving travelers, and the revelers found other places for their parties.

Mendel returned to his old work, reinvigorated and filled with the satisfaction of knowing he was serving G-d in alignment with his own unique purpose.[249]

Each of us has something to learn from the innkeeper's example, especially today. In a world where causes proliferate and beckon us at every turn, identifying and remaining focused on our particular mission is no simple task. The world is full of well-intentioned souls who devote their lives to good causes, sacred causes, honorable causes, only to end up leading lives that are not aligned with their own Divinely intended purpose.

Herein lies the subtle genius of the negative inclination, which seeks at all costs to sabotage the fulfillment of our life's mission. Instead of enticing us to do evil or waste our lives in hedonistic pursuits, it seductively directs us toward a mission that is not connected to our soul. As the Rebbe taught:

> When the negative inclination sees no other way to test a Jew, it resorts to a particularly cunning method, a special approach. It does not tell the Jew to refrain from doing good, nor does it tell him to transgress G-d's will, heaven forbid; rather, it pushes him into something that is not for him. This has two results: The Jew fails to do what he needs to do, and what he does do is not done properly or in the best possible way—even though he performs a commandment in the process—because it's not his mission.

You Do You

As the following story illustrates, the Rebbe would remind us often that if our mission is truly to serve the will of G-d, then it doesn't matter which job or role we perceive to be the most laudable, important, or meritorious in the eyes of the world. From the Divine perspective, the success of our lives is measured precisely by how well we inhabit and fulfill the particular mission that was designed and designated for our unique soul.[250]

Long before he became dean of the Chabad *yeshivah* in Los Angeles, when R. Ezra Schochet was nearing his fifteenth birthday, he wrote to the Rebbe to unburden himself.

Having heard stories of how the founder of Chabad, R. Schneur Zalman, known as the Alter Rebbe, wrote the *Code of Jewish Law* before he was twenty years old, and how R. Aryeh Leib Hakohen Heller wrote a brilliant commentary on the Talmud titled *Shev Shemateta* before he turned eighteen, and how R. Meshulam Igra had delivered a speech to the public that amazed all the great rabbis of his generation at just thirteen, Ezra felt that he simply could not compare to the accomplishments of these illustrious scholars.

He concluded his letter by saying that compared to them, he was getting nowhere, so why should he continue to learn?

The Rebbe replied: "As for your question regarding what is recounted in writing and orally about those who were geniuses in their younger years, what is the use of asking why all minds are not the same? It is explained in the *Tanya* that a person's grasp of Torah is dependent on 'his ability to understand and the source of his soul on high.'"

The Rebbe went on to cite the *Tanya*, adding, "The Mishnah states that 'you should feel humble before all people,' because each has an advantage over another [in some respect].

"It is the purpose of every person not to try to be greater than someone else but to serve G-d and fulfill the intention of the Creator, for which *he* was created."[251]

A well-known Chasidic story captures the essence of this perspective. As the last hours of R. Zushe of Anipoli's life drew near, his students found him crying bitterly as he pondered his life's achievements.

Puzzled, they asked, "Surely our teacher has led a righteous and worthy life. What does our teacher fear?"

R. Zushe replied, "When I am summoned to heaven, I am not afraid they will ask me, 'Why were you not like our great leader Moses?' For if they would ask that, I would respond: 'Was I blessed with the humility and vision of Moses?' What I am afraid they will ask me is, 'Zushe, why were you not more like Zushe?' What will I answer then?"[252]

Ultimately, the goal of all human existence, our raison d'être, is to serve G-d. There are numerous pathways to do so. Some are well suited for one particular path, while others are better suited for another path, but the end goal for all human beings is the same, no matter the path.[253]

Our unique abilities and life circumstances are G-d's way of teaching us which pathway toward that universal goal is right for us.

Lost Souls

In the *Hayom Yom* entry for 25 Nisan, the Rebbe writes: "Each individual's *avodah* (service of G-d) must be commensurate with his character and innate qualities. There may be one who can drill pearls or polish gems but works at baking bread. Though baking bread is a most necessary craft and occupation, this person is considered to have committed a sin (The Hebrew word for sin, *cheit*, can also mean deficiency).[254]

Here we arrive at one of the great secrets to living a meaningful and fulfilling life—learning how to discern between that which is right and that which is right *for you*.[255]

As the sixth Lubavitcher Rebbe, R. Yosef Yitzchak, once taught: "When a soul descends from above in order to be enclothed in a body, it has its *shlichut*, its mission, but [once it is] here below that person must see to it that he should not be one of the souls that 'go astray' [i.e., neglect their mission]."[256]

The Rebbe elaborated on the folly and danger of diverging from one's intended path during a talk he gave on 12 Tamuz 5724 (1964), marking the birthday of his father-in-law, the sixth Lubavitcher Rebbe, R. Yosef Yitzchak Schneersohn.

"My father-in-law, the Rebbe, related a story in the name of the Alter Rebbe: A wealthy man and his wagon driver were once on a journey to buy merchandise. As Shabbat approached, they stopped off in a village to spend the holy day. As is customary, they both went to the *mikveh* to immerse themselves in honor of Shabbat.

"On his way back, the wealthy man, having left the *mikveh* in his Shabbat best, noticed a wagon stuck in the mud. The Torah says, *You shall surely help him*, so he walked over to help drag the wagon out of the mud. Because he wasn't used to pulling wagons from the mud—not to mention that he was in his Shabbat clothes—he obviously wasn't much help. He got himself dirty and was injured in the process. He arrived at the synagogue filthy and battered. The wagon driver also left the *mikveh* in his Shabbat clothes. As it is praiseworthy to 'add to Shabbat,' he arrived early at the synagogue and recited Psalms there. Then he looked around for people in need of a Shabbat meal and invited them to join him at the inn where he was staying at his expense. When prayers concluded, synagogue officials wanted to assign the poor people to join Shabbat meals in the affluent homes of the city.

The poor people replied that they were taken care of—the wagon driver had already invited them.

When they passed away, the wagon driver and his boss stood before the heavenly court, which ruled that their souls should return to this world. This time the wagon driver would help his fellow pull the wagon from the mud, while the wealthy man would invite needy guests, which was his true calling."[257]

As laudable as both of these men's intentions and attempts to help those in need in this story were, it is obvious that had they remained focused on their own unique gifts and missions, they could have helped much more. Surely, the wagon driver had more experience and expertise in removing wagons from the mud, and certainly the wealthy man had more resources at his disposal to provide meals for hungry people in the synagogue. When weighing our options to impact and contribute to the world for the good, it is imperative that we consider our capacities to determine if we are truly the best person for a particular job.

Stay on Course

What is true for the individual is also true for institutions and organizations, where mission drift is an ever-present risk.

This was the essence of the Rebbe's penetrating response to an individual living in a troubled part of the world that was rife with political turmoil who wrote a letter demanding the intercession of Chabad emissaries.

He wondered cantankerously why the Rebbe's *shluchim* weren't doing more about the broader social problems that concerned him. The Rebbe replied:

> "…Your questions would be no more logical if you asked a physician why he is not actively involved in a matter related to engineering.

> "You should know that Chabad-Lubavitch representatives have a specific mission assigned to them, which is to spread Judaism in the communities designated to them. …Furthermore, there is very little—if anything—they can achieve in the area that interests you most.

> "Therefore, to divert their minds and to turn their energies and their time to something not related to their mission will be wasteful and diversionary to the work that they already do superbly."[258]

Love Your Life

Time and again, the Rebbe invited those who crossed his path to not only embrace their Divine design but to do so *with joy and satisfaction.* As he often declared:

"There are many ways to serve G-d. However, the ultimate way to serve Him is through joy."[259]

True joy and satisfaction, the Rebbe insisted, are born of accepting and choosing to love all aspects of our lives—including all elements of our personality, life experiences, challenges, and all.

Indeed, one of life's greatest joys comes from embracing every part of the life G-d designed just for you.

It's not enough to simply thank G-d for the gift of life, but for the gift of *your* life, in its entirety.

Put simply: Part of our purpose is to *rejoice* in our purpose.

As our Sages teach, *"Eizehu ashir? Hasame'ach b'chelko—* Who is wealthy? He who is *happy* with his portion in life."[260]

On a basic level, this teaching refers to material possessions. But on a deeper level, it redefines what it means to be truly wealthy in life as reveling and rejoicing in the unique portion of the world G-d gave us to elevate and illuminate—*chelko ba'olam.*

As we learn from the greatest Jewish teacher, Moses, about whom it says in the Shabbat prayers, *"Yismach Moshe b'matnat chelko—*Moses *rejoiced* in the gift of his portion [in life]."[261]

You don't need to live up to any standard but your own. It is there—in the all-encompassing embrace of your particular Divine purpose—that you will find your greatest focus and fulfillment, and you will subsequently deliver the greatest measure of G-d's love and goodness to the world.

CHAPTER 21

What Now?

T HROUGHOUT THIS SECTION OF the book, we have offered numerous teachings and perspectives of the Rebbe to help guide you through the labyrinth of possibilities toward your own Divine design and the unique purpose that comes with it.

Ultimately, these teachings are merely principles in the abstract. How they are applied and lived, however, is often as complex and multifaceted as the individuals in which they coalesce, and they are further complicated by the dynamic, tumultuous world in which we each live.

For example, what happens when a person has more than one mission, or when one apparent mission comes into conflict with another? What happens if you have a clear indicator that you are the only one suited for a task but lack the natural talent or resources to see it through? Do you spend your precious talents and resources on causes that suit you naturally and easily, or do you invest your time and energy evolving to become the person you need to be to meet a challenge beyond your current capacities?

In previous generations, there were great spiritual masters who would communicate directly from a higher source and direct people to their mission in life. But even then, it was rare to find explicit and clear guidance. In the modern era, when true examples of such guides are fewer and further between, where are we to turn?

The Rebbe addressed these pressing questions by turning to a foundational teaching from the Mishnah that says: "Designate for yourself a mentor, acquire for yourself a friend."[262]

In this directive, we are called to seek out two types of objective interlocutors—a mentor and a friend—who can help us find clarity amid the many conundrums and biases that would mislead us, drawing us away from our Divinely designated role in creation.

Chief among the many biases we must avoid with the help of a mentor is our own.

The Rebbe made this point during a private audience with the bureau chief for a national Jewish newspaper, who extolled his periodical, saying: "Our publication is independent and completely objective!"

The Rebbe replied pointedly: "Independent, perhaps—but

objective? There is no such thing. It is humanly impossible to be completely objective.

"Every person has a bias of some kind."[263]

The Rebbe's observation emerges from a deeply held understanding that each of us, whether we are aware of it or not, is too often driven by myriad, overlapping layers of self-interest, conflicting desires, and distortions of perception.

This is why the Rebbe insisted that an outside observer is required to help us sift through the dross of our egos and provide a clear and objective perspective.

On a number of occasions, the Rebbe pointed out that this "fact of subjectivity" applies to every human being. He noted that even those with the most refined, admirable character and vast wisdom—for example, Torah giants such as Chatam Sofer and the Vilna Gaon—would turn to other scholars to avoid personal bias in matters of law and character development.[264]

Noting the inherent dangers and blind spots of our biases, the Rebbe taught that everyone—from laymen to sages—must seek an outside perspective.

"How important, then, it is to have a qualified and objective third party, who will not be 'bribed by self-interest.' ...[The] Torah says that bribery blinds and distorts one's perception until he actually believes he has done what is good—to the point that he actually sees evil to be good and good to be evil; he sees sweet to be bitter and bitter to be sweet. Therefore, one must have an objective mentor."[265]

Toward this end, in his later years of leadership, the Rebbe introduced a system that encouraged everyone to choose a spiritual mentor for themselves called a *mashpia*, who would serve as an independent, objective guide for life. More than just a source of objectivity, the Rebbe taught that when we designate a mentor for ourselves according to the Torah-based instruction of the Mishnah, our chosen guide becomes an extension of the Torah's living influence and a personalized channel for Divine guidance.

During a talk he gave on *Shabbat Lech Lecha* 5746 (1985), the Rebbe elaborated on the need for a *mashpia*.

> "...[One] might argue: [In the effort to make this world more G-dly,] there are so many things that require dedication that it becomes completely confusing, and I don't know where to begin! And since this is the case, one doesn't need to do anything!

> "We say to this person regarding that line of thought: ...[Here] is some simple advice—go to someone wiser than you, present him your question, and he will instruct you what to do.

> "In this neighborhood there is a rabbi who is the local authority. Approach him and ask him! It follows from what you already do, and it is merely a case of 'all the more so.' For

when a dairy spoon falls into a meat pot, you go and ask the rabbi a question, even though you could simply use another spoon and another pot. If so, then when you have a question about your service of G-d this day or this moment, something so urgent it is impossible to delay, since if you do not do what you must today, a day goes to waste, because, 'Every day (and similarly every second of the day itself) requires its work,' then how much the more do you have to ask a rabbi a question about this matter!"[266, 267]

Character Is Key

All that being said, finding the right mentor is not always an easy task. In fact, the Rebbe notes that the Mishnah uses the term *asei*, make, which implies that this endeavor sometimes requires effort and perhaps even struggle. That is to say, even if you think you cannot find a guide more qualified than yourself, make every effort to find one, nonetheless. Don't wait for the perfect mentor to arrive, because you are not seeking a flawless guide but a clarifying perspective untainted by personal bias.

Toward that end, the Rebbe recommended avoiding people who are prone to envy, rivalry, and other corruptions of perspective that can potentially convolute their advice and inspiration.

Furthermore, the Rebbe offered several positive qualities one should seek in a mentor or guide:

> "...[They should be] modest, compassionate, kind, and giving...Such things cannot be hidden. One must be able to see openly how his mentor lives his life. If he is clearly modest, compassionate, and kind in his public conduct, these are the indicators that he is, in fact, a mentor...with all the requisite, sublime qualities."[268]

Here, beyond mere charisma or erudition, the Rebbe emphasizes the critical importance of good character in the role of the mentor. Humility, compassion, kindness, and generosity—these virtues are signs that a chosen guide is well-suited to the task of acting as a conduit for G-d's Divine instruction, which is the role that every *mashpia* inhabits by definition.

Additionally, as the following story illustrates, a *mashpia*, according to the Rebbe, is one who is capable of putting their own ego and interests aside when advising others.

During a private audience with the Rebbe, R. Herbert Weiner, author of *Nine and a Half Mystics*, once asked candidly, "How do you assume responsibility for the advice you give people on all matters, business and medical included?"

The Rebbe replied, "When a person comes to me with a problem, this is how I try to help him. A man knows his own problem best, so one must try to unite with him and become *batel*, as disassociated as possible from one's own ego. Then, in concert with the other person, one tries to understand the principle of Divine Providence in his particular case."[269]

Friendly Advice

Returning to the words of the Mishnah, we are also bidden to "acquire for ourselves a friend" who can be an existential mirror and provide spiritual insight and support based on their intimate knowledge of our personality and lives.

Like others who are placed in your path by Divine Providence to help you identify and actualize your Divine design, a true friend is an invaluable and precious resource to consult as you negotiate the complexities of your individual purpose.

The Rebbe emphasizes this point in a letter to Pinchas Joseph Saffran, who once reached out to the Rebbe to ask for help discerning his life's purpose. The Rebbe replied:

"I received your letter, in which you ask what is your mission in life.

"...Since one should not rely on his own judgment, it would be well for you to discuss the matter with your own teachers at the *yeshivah*, and they will give you further guidance.

"...*it would also be well for you to discuss the*

*matter with your friends, to whom you could
explain the problems in detail, and they could give
you some helpful advice.*"[270]

As guides, friends may even have an advantage over a traditional mentor.

Where a mentor is generally senior in age and acquired wisdom, as well as typically more removed from the intimate context of your daily life, a friend is deeply familiar with your quirks, circumstances, personality, and history. A friend knows you exactly as you are and can advise you in a manner that is informed by your actual self in addition to your aspirational self.

Even if your friend isn't a scholar or a sage, their providential bond, selfless care, and heartfelt connection to you makes them a precious guide. And like a *mashpia*, the Rebbe taught that the definition of a true friend is one who puts your interests and well-being above their own when offering support and advice, as emphasized in the following story:

A man once bluntly asked: "Rebbe, what exactly do you do? And why are you admired by so many?"

"I try to be a good friend," the Rebbe replied.

Incredulous, the man blurted out, "A friend? That's all you do?!"

Unfazed, the Rebbe responded with a question of his own: "How many friends do you have?"

"I have many."

"Let me define a friend for you, and then tell me how many friends you have.

"A friend is someone in whose presence you can think aloud without worrying about being taken advantage of. A friend is someone who suffers with you when you are in pain and rejoices in your joy. A friend is someone who looks out for you and always has your best interests in mind. In fact, a true friend is like an extension of yourself."

The Rebbe then asked with a smile, "Now, how many friends like that do you have?"[271]

Providential Emissaries

The extent to which the Rebbe emphasized the importance of true friends as providential emissaries sent to deliver the love and instruction of the Divine can be seen in the following story.

After getting married in 1965, R. Mayer Plotkin and his wife were deeply inspired to leave their home in Montreal to become emissaries of the Rebbe. Opportunities emerged for them to take positions in Detroit, California, or Florida, but before accepting, the eager rabbi wrote to the Rebbe seeking his blessing and counsel. The Rebbe replied simply that he should "consult with friends," and he did not offer his blessing for the couple to take up a post in any of the proposed locations. For their part, taking into account Mayer's personality and skills, his friends had repeatedly advised him to go into business.

Maintaining the conviction that becoming an emissary was part of his life's purpose, Mayer wrote several more letters to the Rebbe, insisting that, contrary to the advice of his friends, he wanted to go on *shlichut*. Time and again, he received the same reply—consult your friends. After writing what would be his final letter on this topic, explaining that he suspected that, despite his constant deferment, the Rebbe really did want him to become an emissary. The Rebbe responded:

"Where did you get that idea from? Haven't I already written, <u>once,</u> <u>twice</u>, <u>three times</u> that you should consult with friends? Stop sending letters here, because I am not going to answer. Make a decision straight away based on the advice of your friends, and may G-d grant you success."[272]

Here we see how seriously the Rebbe took the notion that one's mentor and friends are instruments of Divine guidance, even if the advice guided a student toward a life in business rather than one devoted exclusively to spiritual outreach, which was the Rebbe's primary passion.

The Sage Within

In addition to the importance of enlisting a mentor and/or friend, when we find ourselves at a crossroads in life, the Rebbe would also encourage people to spend time alone with themselves,[273] in reflection and introspection, in the deep-seated belief that we have untapped reservoirs of inner wisdom, which should be included in any consequential conversation relating to our life's mission.

In fact, the Rebbe cautioned strongly against using one's teacher or *mashpia* to bypass the essential toil of figuring things out for oneself. The Rebbe reminded often that G-d gives each person the power to find the solution to his questions and doubts; they just need to put in the requisite work. As our Sages teach: "If you toil, you will succeed."[274]

Some years after moving with his family to Maryland to pursue a career in psychology, R. Tzvi Hirsh Weinreb found himself at a challenging crossroad in life and decided to call the Rebbe for guidance.

The Rebbe's secretary answered the phone and asked the caller to identify himself.

Not wanting to disclose his name due to the sensitive nature of his questions, R. Weinreb replied only, "A Jew from Maryland."

He went on to outline the questions for which he wanted the Rebbe's guidance—uncertainties regarding his life, career, and faith.

Suddenly, R. Weinreb heard the Rebbe's voice in the background: "Tell him there's a Jew in Maryland with whom he can speak. His name is Weinreb."

The secretary repeated the Rebbe's words. "Yes," he exclaimed to the secretary, "but...*my* name is Weinreb!"

R. Weinreb then heard the Rebbe saying gently: "If that's the case, he should know that sometimes one needs to speak to himself."[275]

Ultimately, when we embrace the role of mentorship and friendship in our lives, predicated on the Torah-based exhortation to do so, we open ourselves up to a providential and personalized conduit for Divine instruction. In this way, our mentor or friend becomes a touchpoint in our ongoing, unfolding conversation with G-d, Who speaks to us through the guides He places in our lives for this very purpose.

CHAPTER 22

Define Your Center:
The Importance of Crafting a Personal Mission Statement

A YOUNG MAN ONCE ASKED the Rebbe for advice regarding his future.

The Rebbe suggested that he remain in a *yeshivah* environment for the time being, where he could further his studies, develop his character, and explore his purpose in life.

Respectfully, the young man asked the Rebbe for the reasoning behind his advice.

The Rebbe responded by giving the young man a pencil and asking him to draw a perfect circle.

After attempting and failing to do so, the young man quipped that it simply wasn't possible.

"What would it take to draw a perfect circle?" the Rebbe asked.

The young man replied, "a drawing compass."

Opening his drawer, the Rebbe gave the young man a compass, which helped the young man complete the task.

The Rebbe asked, "How did the compass help you draw a perfect circle?"

The man replied, "The compass' needle provided the focal point and fixed center for the circle."

The Rebbe said: "The same is true with life. All the knowledge and experience we accumulate throughout our lifetime, all of our activities and endeavors are the circles we draw. We may draw many circles. But a person must have a center—a clear and cohesive purpose around which all of their knowledge and activities orbit. Without a focal point, without a mission, the circles in one's life will be jagged and incomplete."

The Rebbe concluded: "I see that at this point in your life, your center isn't yet defined, and I therefore suggest that you first stabilize your center before drawing your circles."[276]

As discussed in previous chapters, tangential distractions and conflicting opportunities are so abundant in the course of life that our own unique, Divine mission can get lost in the fray. Indeed, success in any area of life demands discipline, focus, commitment, and careful planning. But where do we begin? How do we ensure that our Divinely-entrusted hopes, dreams, ambitions, and aspirations manifest and come to fruition?

Whether for companies, organizations, or individuals, the first step is to craft a clear and compelling statement of purpose—in other words: a mission statement.

Know Your Role

You may have heard of, or even helped work on, a mission statement if you are involved in the world of business or social entrepreneurship. These brief statements serve to articulate the ultimate purpose of a company and to guide its executives, employees, and partners toward fulfilling its chosen ends.

For example, Disney's mission statement is: *To entertain, inform, and inspire people around the globe through the power of unparalleled storytelling.*

Disney's mission contains several essential components.

What they hope to accomplish: *Entertain, inform, and inspire.*

Who they aim to serve: *People around the globe.*

How they do it: *Through the power of unparalleled storytelling.*

This statement is the articulated purpose of Disney, its raison d'être, which helps guide every executive and more than two hundred thousand employees as they go about fulfilling the company's mission in their own unique way, using their particular set of skills, in their area of the workplace, at their level of influence. Though each individual contributes something unique to the effort, the ultimate goal and impact of those many efforts emerges from a single, carefully crafted statement of purpose.

Similarly, humanity as a whole has its own meta-mission in which we all play a critical and irreplaceable role. As elucidated in Chapter 2, Jewish tradition tells us that at the beginning of creation, sparks of G-d's essence were scattered and hidden throughout our world so they could be sought out, redeemed, and reunited by humankind. In this way, we become G-d's collaborative partners in the sacred work of unveiling the true, underlying oneness of creation and revealing G-d's unified presence on earth. And while this general mission is given to every human being, its implementation is unique for every individual. In other words: *You may share a common goal with all of humanity, but your role in this Divine drama, and the mission that defines it, is yours and yours alone.*

Mapping Your Mission

What follows is a brief guide to crafting your own mission statement in the hope that it will provide you with an anchor in the storm, something to refer back to as you navigate the transitions and complexities of life. In a few simple steps, you will crystallize your purpose in a statement that will become the axis from which all of your endeavors radiate, providing direction for all of the tools and resources you've been given to work toward the Divine purpose for which you were placed on this earth.

The following exercise will help you discern and distill the many options and opportunities on offer in today's world and identify those that are uniquely yours by Divine design. No one in all of creation can complete the tasks for which you were created, and your mission statement should be as unique as you are.

For example, it is common to reply to the question of "What is your mission in life?" with vague statements of sweeping ambition, such as, "I want to change the world," or "I want to inspire humanity."

However admirable and beautiful these ambitions may be, they leave out perhaps the most important aspect of any personal mission statement—the uniqueness of the person making it.

Anyone can aspire to make a difference in the world. But your true mission is one of a kind. If your general mission is to "change the world," for example, what follows will help you discover what makes *your* contribution to changing the world unique.

In the first portion of this exercise, you will explore through writing five providentially orchestrated aspects of your life: personality traits, talents, people, places, and opportunities. Clarifying and codifying these fundamental aspects will help you craft a mission statement as unique as you are.

You will need either pen and paper or a digital device.

1. Personality: You were created and blessed with a unique personality comprising specific characteristics, passions, quirks, and interests. Are you sensitive, smart, strong, and/or sagacious? Perhaps you are methodical and rational. Or maybe you are spontaneous and rely on your intuition. Perhaps you are adventurous and fiercely independent. You may be an introvert, extrovert, or ambivert. Are you passionate about the environment, education, art, spirituality, or human rights? Whatever the particulars, every aspect of your personality is a signal that can help point you toward your unique mission. An empathic and caring nature means you are uniquely empowered to provide comfort and healing to those around you. If you are born with an ambitious, industrious, and calculating nature, perhaps you are suited for business or organizational development. If you are ideological, charismatic, and inclined toward leadership, perhaps you are suited for public office or communal service. Take a moment to reflect and write down two or three fundamental aspects of your personality that might play a part in defining your mission.

2. Talent: Your natural gifts and talents can be mobilized and expressed as part of your sacred purpose. You may be a painter, a tech whiz, or an athlete, or you may have a talent for public speaking. Do you have a great memory and a gift for articulating complex ideas? You may be well suited for a life in academia. Are you a good listener? This might position you to thrive as a counselor, for example. Take time to assess and write down two or three natural talents that could be put to use in service of your mission.

3. People: The people in your life—whether they be family, friends, or strangers who cross your path— all carry sparks of G-dliness that relate to crucial aspects of your mission. They may need help that only you can provide, or vice versa. They may challenge you in ways that bring out your greatest strengths or help you grow. They may have a lesson or some critical information that will help you discover new aspects of your purpose. Think of the people in your life and write down a few individuals or groups of people whom you are positioned to influence for the good.

4. Place: The places you find yourself throughout life contain sparks that are waiting to be redeemed by you. Indeed, G-d directs you to those very places because the elevation of those specific sparks is essential to your mission. It may seem

counterintuitive to consider where you are right now while deciding where you want to go in the future. But your own unique place—your neighborhood, community, school, or place of employment, for example—contains fundamental indicators of your mission. These places each contain their own sparks, needs, and possibilities. Wherever you find yourself, you are there because there is a Divine purpose waiting for you. Take time to think about and write down two or three places that are central to your life.

5. Opportunities: The field of your life is seeded with myriad Divinely orchestrated opportunities for making a meaningful impact. Your work in the world preps the soil of your soul for all kinds of possibilities to elevate sparks awaiting activation in various projects or in the lives of the people with whom you work. Your neighborhood or community may present opportunities to build coalitions or improve the lives of your neighbors. Even a seemingly random trip to the corner grocer positions you to reveal G-dliness along the way—a kindness to bestow or an encounter with someone who needs your help. Every step and every circumstance that presents itself contains sparks waiting to be revealed and elevated. Take some time to identify and write down at least two significant

opportunities to serve that currently exist in your life.

At this point, you may discover that the rough contours of a mission have begun to emerge from the assembled sparks of your life. Give yourself time to reflect on these components and consider how they might coalesce into your sacred mission. You may want to pause and digest what you have learned about yourself so far. Take the time you need. When you are ready, move on to the final step of this exercise, which will guide you in weaving these elements together into a brief statement summarizing your mission.

A Powerful Statement

Working with the template below, plug in the different opportunities, personality traits, talents, places, and people that you wrote down in the previous stage. This will become the first draft of your personal mission statement. It may be helpful to first refer to the examples that follow as you construct your own mission statement.

My soul was selected by G-d and given a portion of the world that is mine to elevate and illuminate. I awake each morning knowing that my _____ [personality] and my _____ [talent] can bring benefit to _____ [place/s] _____ by achieving _____ [the desired impact] for

_____ [the people in your life],

thereby channeling my _____

[opportunity] for the greater good.

*Example: My soul was selected by G-d and given a portion of the world that is mine to elevate and illuminate. I awake each morning knowing that my love for people [personality] and my consensus building skills [talent] can bring benefit to my neighborhood [place] through building community solidarity. This empowers neighborhood improvement programs [impact], which enhance the lives of the people in my community [people], thereby channeling my influence as a community leader [opportunity] for the greater good.

*Example 2: My soul was selected by G-d and given a portion of the world that is mine to elevate and illuminate. I awake each morning knowing that my passion to care for those in need [personality] and my talents for cooking and community organizing [talents] will help me provide company, comfort, and sustenance [impact] by hosting cooking classes at the nearby community center [place], thereby channeling and elevating my connection with my elderly neighbors [opportunity].

Using the template above, fill in the fields with the corresponding words from the previous portion of the exercise. If something needs to be adjusted or changed, feel free to tinker with the statement until it feels right.

When you have finished writing out your draft mission statement, sit with it, read it out loud, and note how it feels when you have put it all together. If you have someone nearby and are so inclined, read it to them and note how it feels when you say it out loud and share it with someone else.

Once you have a statement that deeply resonates, write it down and place it somewhere conspicuous so you can regularly refer to it until it becomes second nature. If your mission is broad, as in the first example above, it may be useful to try applying the statement to the specific circumstances that arise throughout your day.

Testing your statement in the field, as it were, may help you discover ways that your statement requires adjustment or embellishment. That is to be expected. Mission statements and the missions they refer to are alive, and they often change over time, depending on the shifting course and circumstances of your life. As with life, mission statements are always open to revision, adjustment, and improvement.

That Reminds Me...

Once you have a mission statement and have begun to actualize it in your day-to-day life, it is essential to be reminded of it regularly. Knowing and being constantly conscious of your *why* will help shape and inform the *what* and *how* of your life's work, and it will help you remain focused amid the perpetual distractions and demands of daily life.

As Chief Rabbi Jonathan Sacks once observed:

"Timothy Ferris, compiler of the book *Tribe of Mentors*, once asked me an interesting question: 'When you feel overwhelmed or unfocused, what do you do?'

"I told him that just before I became chief rabbi…I realized that the sheer pressure of unexpected happenings, especially when you are in public life, can blow anyone off course…

"So it became clear to me that I had to set out my objectives in advance, in such a way as to ensure I would never forget or be distracted from them."

At the time, which was before the era of iPads and smartphones, Sacks decided to put a list of his greatest goals on the first page of his daily organizer/diary.

"This meant that I saw them every time I looked in my diary. I was reminded of them several times daily.

"I still have them, and they have not changed in all the intervening years. How far I was successful, I do not know. But this I know: I never forgot where I was traveling to. I never lost sight of the destination."[277]

We all need reminders, because, while the human brain

is wired to calculate and invent many incredible things, one thing our minds are not very good at is remembering. Our brains have a remarkable capacity for compiling millions of data points received from our senses to create a single image, and at lightning speeds. Yet, keeping our core principles and values at the forefront of our minds is often difficult, especially in a dynamic world that constantly pulls us in multiple directions and overwhelms us with distractions.

In the words of philosopher Alain De Botton while describing the existential function of the religious calendar: "In the secular world, we tend to believe that if you tell someone something once, they'll remember it...Religions [however] are cultures of repetition. They circle the great truths again and again and again. The religious calendar is a way of making sure that across the year you will bump into certain very important ideas. In Jewish chronology, Passover reminds us to reflect on the importance of liberty and freedom. Now, you won't typically do that by accident; you will do that because you are guided to do that. In the secular world, we think that 'If an idea is important, I'll bump into it. I'll just come across it.' Nonsense, says the religious worldview. We need calendars, we need to structure time, we need to synchronize encounters."[278]

Indeed, as the following study suggests, the key to acting on our values is how regularly we are reminded of them.

For instance, in a study conducted by UCLA Professor Dan Ariely, half the participants were asked to recall the Ten Commandments while the other half were asked to remember ten books they had read in high school before taking a quiz. The results overwhelmingly indicated that the mere fact of being reminded of the Ten Commandments reduced the tendency to cheat.[279]

Ultimately, it isn't *what* we believe but *how regularly we are reminded of our beliefs* that transforms our day-to-day behavior. Hence, the final step in our mission statement exercise asks you to identify specific times each day to return and rededicate yourself to your mission.

Purposeful prayers

Judaism itself is replete with such "reminders," regular practices that refocus our awareness on our deepest beliefs and commitments. Some examples of these ritual "reminders" include reciting the *Shema,* morning and evening, as a reminder of G-d's unity; observing Shabbat weekly as a reminder of creation and the exodus; and various Jewish festivals throughout the year that recall different providential events in Jewish history. Another example of Jewish tradition orchestrating rhythms of recalibration is the practice of reading from the Torah scroll every Monday, Thursday, and Shabbat. This regularly scheduled reading ensures that three days do not go by without Torah study, so that our connection to the core practices and principles of Judaism are never far from our minds. In fact, when you look closely, the entire regiment of the observant Jew seems to revolve around such prompts: prayer, study, ritual, dress—these are all experiential "reminders" designed to keep the religious practitioner focused on their mission.

Most relevant to our discussion, it is worth noting that Judaism liturgically bookends each day with the recitation of two particularly purpose-focused prayers to help frame our day and direct our consciousness from the moment we awake to the moment we go to bed. In this way, our every waking moment becomes imbued with a deep sense of our Divine mission and existential raison d'être.

The first meditation, titled *Modeh Ani*, is said immediately upon awakening, before one gets out of bed.

"I offer thanks to You, living and eternal King, for You have mercifully restored my soul within me. Endless is Your compassion; Your faithfulness is great."

Feel free to personalize the above in ways that resonate with you personally and include reference to your chosen mission after washing your hands. For example:

"Thank You, dear G-d, for another day to fulfill the mission for which I was created.

Thank You for making me Your partner in creation, and for giving me everything I need to

*play my part in Your Divine plan of healing and
redemption.*

[Your mission statement]"

If you have plans for the day, you may want to envision
yourself living out your mission statement while conducting this meditation or for a few moments afterward.

The second prayer is offered at the end of the day and
concludes the recital of the bedtime *Shema*. It is recited
after this verse from Psalms: *I entrust my spirit into Your
hand; [I have faith that] You will redeem me, L-rd, G-d of
truth.*

*"Master of the worlds! You have created Your world
in Your good will, as it has arisen in Your primordial thought, and You have created the heavens
and all their hosts, and the earth and everything
that is on it; You have created man upon it, and
You have blown into his nostrils a living soul, so
that he may recognize Your greatness and glory;
and You give life to them all, for You are the Soul
of all souls and the Life-force of all living things.*

*"And You, L-rd, my G-d—I entrust my nefesh,
ruach, and neshamah into Your pure and faithful
hand; and You, L-rd, my G-d, will cleanse them
of every impurity and malady that has become
attached to them through my wrongdoings, and
You will return them to me in peace, tranquility,
and security...*

"Blessed is He Who hears prayer."

Take some time to personalize the prayer above by including reference to your mission. For example:

"L-rd, my G-d, I return my soul to You knowing that today I did my best to [your mission statement].

Refresh and nurture my soul so that I may awaken revitalized and empowered to continue my mission tomorrow."

You may also find it helpful to spend some time reviewing some of the ways you lived out your mission statement throughout the previous day as part of this meditation. Did you take every opportunity to share your light with the world? In what ways were you successful? In what ways did you fall short? In what ways did you surprise yourself? Where is there room for growth?

No matter who you are, no matter where you are, there is a providentially arranged mission waiting for you to fulfill. Arming yourself with a succinct, personal, and meaningful mission statement is among the best ways to ensure that you don't miss a chance to maximize your unique contribution to creation. It doesn't matter if your mission and its impact is great or small, visible or unseen. It is yours, and no one before or after you in all of creation can bring that particular set of potentials to fruition. Your life is your garden. It is upon you to cultivate the gifts and opportunities you've been blessed to elevate and leave the world more beautiful than it was before you arrived.

CHAPTER 23

Happy Birthday to You

"The two most important days in your life are the
day you are born and the day you figure out why."
—Mark Twain

ONE MORNING IN THE early spring of 1988, a group of Chasidim gathered at the Rebbe's home in Brooklyn to pray. This was a day of particular sorrow because it marked what would have been the eighty-seventh birthday of the Rebbe's beloved wife, Rebbetzin Chaya Mushka Schneerson, who had passed away just a month prior.

The Rebbe had only recently returned from the traditional period of mourning to resume his communal responsibilities. At the conclusion of the day's *Shacharit*, the Rebbe surprised all who had gathered by delivering a spontaneous discourse.

With a voice both commanding and tender, the Rebbe

began to explicate the idea of *V'hachai yiten el libo—And the living shall take to heart*[280]—a verse that urges the living to take heart and take action in the face of great loss. The Rebbe then introduced a novel way to honor the Rebbetzin's memory and help elevate her precious soul. He announced that in honor of his wife's passing, he was proposing a new, life-affirming custom: From now on, each and every Jew would be encouraged to celebrate their birthday in a spiritually uplifting fashion.

The Birthday Campaign, as it became known, would bring full circle the Baal Shem Tov's foundational teaching that the birth of each individual is uniquely momentous and blessed with consecrated purpose.

Following in that spirit, the Rebbe offered a new way to think about and mark birthdays—not merely as a day of celebration, but also as a day of catalytic reflection and introspection.

> "This, then, is the suggestion: From now on, it would be most appropriate...on the occasion of one's birthday... [to] reflect on one's past year's accomplishment(s). This [inner reflection] should become the basis and foundation of new growth and continual ascent from one level to the next without any limits in all matters of goodness and holiness... [On one's birthday,] one must take time for sincere introspection that he has become a year older,

so that he must become a year wiser and a
year more connected to G-d."[281]

After his announcement and call for every Jew to honor
their birthdays, the Rebbe proceeded to introduce practical
steps that anyone can take to honor this personal mile-
stone in a way that optimizes their potential for growth
and refinement.[282]

Additionally, a short while later, the Rebbe was involved
in the publishing of a newspaper advertisement that called
for everyone to celebrate their birthdays with the profound
significance it deserves, with the headline: "Do not miss
out on observing the most important day of your life!"
The Rebbe also edited a special message that appeared in
a full-page ad in *The New York Times* with the headline
"Birthdays Matter." Taken altogether, it was clear that the
Rebbe was investing a great deal of attention and energy
into what seemed like the most secular of all holidays.

The question for many was "*Why?*"

Why Do Birthdays Matter?

Until the launch of the Birthday Campaign, the significance of birthdays was historically downplayed in Jewish
tradition, with widespread celebrations reserved for select
Jewish sages and luminaries. Indeed, birthdays were mentioned only a few times by Talmudic Sages.

In fact, the only mention of a birthday in the Torah
is a passage in which the Pharaoh uses his birthday to

display his own power by rewarding and punishing his many servants.[283]

The Rebbe saw birthdays differently.[284] In line with the teaching of the Baal Shem Tov cited above, he encouraged everyone to view their birthdays as the day on which they received their distinct, Divine calling and indispensable purpose.

From this perspective, rather than just being a day marking the passage of yet another year alive, the anniversary of your birth beckons you to celebrate your unique, Divine purpose and the tremendous power to impact the world that comes with it. Thus, your birthday is not just a day to simply sit back, relax, and receive your due; rather, it is a day to reflect on where you are at this moment of your journey of purpose and rededicate yourself to its ultimate fulfillment.

Indeed, the Rebbe went so far as to compare one's birthday to a personal Rosh Hashanah. In much the same way that Rosh Hashanah marks the birthday of humankind and the day humanity was given its unique purpose and cosmic importance, one's birthday is the day on which one receives their personally-tailored purpose, which is vital to the cosmic story of creation. Put differently, the day you were born is the day on which G-d decided that the world cannot exist *without you*.

A Celebration of Your Purpose

Nowadays, birthdays often mark little more than a fleeting celebration of the day you arrived in this world, or perhaps a notable moment on the march toward the end of life. There may be fanfare, indulgence, and festive celebration, but the deeper meaning and spiritual significance of the average birthday is often lacking.

With the launch of the Birthday Campaign, the Rebbe elevated birthdays, insisting that one's birthday resounds with the proclamation that you are not a product of mere chance or evolution. When it comes to the miracle of life, there are no mistakes. In a world with billions of people, G-d decided that your soul could make a difference that no one else could make. The mere fact of your birth means there is a unique gift that you have to offer the world that no one who has ever lived, or will ever live, can provide. Hence, your birthday marks the momentous day you received the mandate and power to transform the world for the good.

With that dynamic in mind, birthdays become less of a blind procession of years and more of a holy cycle wed to the sacred spiral of time.

Mazal Tov!

In Jewish cosmology, the anniversary of a momentous event allows us to tap into the same spiritual energy that catalyzed the original occurrence, mirroring a concept inherent in Jewish festivals, which consist of layer upon layer of cycles dedicated to infusing life with renewed permutations of a historic day's original power. Shabbat each week; Rosh Chodesh, the celebration of the new moon, each month; Rosh Hashanah and numerous Jewish festivals each year.

In this way, on the holy day of your birth, G-d endowed you with a soul replete with unique talents and qualities, all radiating through your *mazal*—a personalized channel of Divine energy that flows into your life and this world from G-d via the portion of His Divine essence that each of us receives at birth. The same potent energy present at our birth renews itself every year on our birthday, granting us the capacity to achieve more on that auspicious day than might be possible on other days.

In the Rebbe's words:

> "...On one's birthday, he receives greater strength, because his *mazal*, his 'fortune,' radiates with extra strength [*mazalo gover*]. It is called *mazal*, from the Hebrew word for flow. It is the conduit through which Divine vitality descends upon the person, and which he uses to accomplish his mission below."[285]

Based on the above, some have adopted the custom of offering blessings to family and friends on their birthday, thus harnessing their strengthened *mazal* in order to make optimum, sacred use of the extra spiritual potency present and available on their birthdays for the benefit of others.

This is just one example of the many ways we can celebrate and utilize the immense spiritual power of our birthdays. Below we will explore a number of other ways the Rebbe suggested we mark and elevate the anniversary of our birth.

How to Celebrate Birthdays

Along with proclaiming the general significance of birthdays, the Rebbe introduced a ten-point spiritual regimen to help infuse every birthday with spiritual significance. The Rebbe designed these powerful practices to help actualize the spiritual vitality of one's birthday. The components of the Rebbe's plan are briefly outlined below.

1. *Aliyah*: On the Shabbat preceding the birthdays of all males who are past bar mitzvah (older than thirteen), or on the actual birthday (if it is on a day when the Torah is read), they should be called to the Torah as a form of spiritual elevation.

2. *Tzedakah*: One is encouraged to give charity in an amount equal to the number of years they are celebrating, plus one.[286] When a birthday occurs on Shabbat or Yom Tov, which precludes the handling of money, a double portion should be given on Friday.

3. *Tefillah*: During prayer, one should deeply

contemplate the greatness of G-d and infuse each prayer with special heart and intention. Remember, one's spiritual strength is especially manifest on your birthday, so prayers should be chosen thoughtfully.

4. *Tehillim*: One should recite as much of the Book of Psalms as possible. In particular, in accordance with the instruction of the Baal Shem Tov, one should recite the chapter corresponding with their age plus one. One should learn the new chapter with special thoroughness and recite it with special emphasis throughout the year.

5. *Torah*: One should increase their Torah study by adding an extra lesson in addition to one's regular study schedule.

6. *Chazarat Dach*: One should study teachings of Chasidut and share it with a group of friends on one's birthday, or at the earliest opportunity.

7. *Hafatzah*: One should reach out and seek to spiritually inspire others, in the spirit of true *ahavat Yisrael*. Make a special effort to encourage others to do the same, exponentially amplifying the impact.[287]

8. *Hitbonenut*: Spend some time alone to reflect on the past, identify character flaws that need to be corrected, celebrate the ways you have lived up to your sacred purpose, and make special birthday resolutions for the coming year.

9. *Hiddur Mitzvah*: Make a special effort to enhance and vigorously perform a particular Divine commandment, as is customarily done on Rosh Hashanah.

10. *Farbrengen*: Host a *farbrengen* gathering with family and friends to give thanks to G-d for your special day and the gift of your life and your purpose. Part of this celebration can involve eating a new seasonal fruit so you can recite the traditional *Shehecheyanu* blessing and thank G-d for bringing you to this day.

Regardless of how you decide to honor the day of your birth, remember that all of your observances, blessings, prayers, and celebrations are supercharged with the spiritual energy that flows to and through you on your birthday. Every birthday is an auspicious opportunity to rededicate yourself to the unique and holy purpose for which you were born. When your birthday arrives, remember that there is nothing passing or frivolous about it. As the Rebbe often emphasized: Birth is G-d's way of saying *you matter.* The day of your birth marks an extraordinary opportunity to recognize and rededicate yourself anew to the singular, irreplaceable purpose for which you were created.

PART III

Reflections on Purpose

CHAPTER 24

Service over Self

E ACH YEAR ON SIMCHAT Torah from 1954 until 1964, the Lubavitcher Rebbe would teach an unknown Chasidic song. In addition to teaching the actual melody, the Rebbe would often explain its background and significance.

On one occasion, the Rebbe taught a song called *Anim Zemirot*, based on the devotional words of a liturgical poem attributed to R. Yehudah Hachasid:

"I shall sing sweet songs and poems I shall weave, because my soul longs for You.

My soul desires the shadow of your hand, to know every one of Your secrets."

After teaching the song, the Rebbe shared the following story:

Once, on the day after Yom Kippur, the community of a certain *shtetl* arrived at the synagogue for *Shacharit* and were surprised to find a Chasid dancing at the podium, singing *Anim Zemirot* with great fervor. It turned out that the man had been so engrossed in the melody that he danced the entire night, not even noticing that the fast had ended.

As the song became popular among the Chasidim, rumors began circulating that the pious individual in the story was the Rebbe himself.

When one of the Chasidim visited the Rebbe for a private audience, he decided to clarify the matter and asked if the rumors were true. The Rebbe replied that they weren't and then proceeded to recount the story in full:

"There once lived a rich man who made it his business to travel the region, locating and redeeming Jewish people who had been imprisoned by local barons after coming upon hard times. One day, he was passing by the local jail when he heard heartrending cries from a Jewish man who was being held there. He went to see the local baron in an effort to free the man from captivity, and he was told that the cost of the man's freedom was an exorbitant sum. The rich man was hesitant.

"Returning home, his conscience didn't let him rest. He proceeded to calculate the worth of his entire estate, which turned out to be approximately the amount it would take to free the Jewish man. He liquidated all of his assets and returned to the baron, handing him the necessary sum.

"With a wicked gleam in his eye, the baron burst out laughing as he opened the cell, calling out: 'Take your Jew, as promised.' To the wealthy man's shock and dismay, the poor man had already passed away.

"Feeling utterly devastated over selling his possessions to no avail, the now destitute man fell into a deep depression. No matter how much his family tried, the man's spirits could not be revived.

"One night, he fell into a deep sleep. As he slept, he had a dream, with a message from above: 'Your money was not wasted. On the contrary, your altruistic actions are worthy of reward.' The man was given two options. The first was to return to a life of extraordinary wealth. The second was to experience a taste of Gan Eden, heavenly bliss, while still in this world.

"The man chose the second option, and it was decided in heaven to bless him with spiritual rapture on Yom Kippur.

"Throughout that Yom Kippur, he experienced this sublime revelation, a taste of the World to Come. So caught up was he in ecstasy that he danced through the night, oblivious to his bodily needs."

When retelling this story, Chasidim would say: "From the man's choice, it is clear that he wasn't a student of Chabad Chasidut. For had he benefited from the teachings of Chabad Chasidut, he would have chosen the wealth. Just imagine how many more lives he could have saved then!"[288, 289]

The story above frames the difference between two fundamentally divergent approaches to seeking G-d: Is our purpose in this life to seek transcendence and spiritual enlightenment for ourselves, or are we here to dedicate our lives to acts of service and mending our broken world?

Me, Myself, and I

Regardless of particular tradition, most spiritual seekers in our day are in pursuit of transcendence and enlightenment. But the exclusive pursuit of the metaphysical and spiritual can also blind us to the everyday struggles of the people around us.

At the heart of this pitfall is the desire of the spiritual individual to feel—to perceive and sense—the intangible beyond. The operative words are "feel" and "sense," which ironically describe the gratification of selfhood rather than its transcendence. The seeker's departure and arrival points are all too often the same: an expanse called Me.

Counter to this propensity, the Rebbe repeatedly reinforced the perspective of Chasidism, which privileges compassion over communion, empathy over ecstasy, and other-centeredness over self-centeredness.[290]

For example, in conversation with a spiritual seeker who asked how he might live a more spiritual life, the Rebbe reinforced this point, saying: "Although it's important to work on self-refinement, the call of the hour is to better the lives of others."

The Rebbe proceeded to illustrate this revolutionary perspective with the following story:

> "A great Jewish sage was once asked for a substantial donation by a person in need. The rabbi went straight to his drawer, took out his savings, and gave the entire amount to the poor man. When the rabbi's wife realized what he had done, she was very upset, exclaiming, 'What have you done? You've given away all of our savings!'
>
> "The rabbi replied, 'My dear wife, last night I dreamed that I had passed away. When I arrived at the gates of heaven, a renowned Torah scholar was waiting to enter. After some time, it was confirmed by the heavenly court that he had spent his lifetime in the study of G-d's wisdom, but he was not admitted immediately.

"Then another soul came along. His passion in life had been giving charity. It was established that he had devoted most of his energies to helping others. The gates of heaven swung open immediately, and he was allowed into Gan Eden.

"Of all the worthy pursuits one can be involved in," the Rebbe concluded, "acts of giving have the most merit in the eyes of G-d."[291]

A Holy Yom Kippur Meal

This was the message at the heart of the Rebbe's very first address upon assuming the mantle of Chabad leadership in 1951.[292] As his first official act as Rebbe, he delivered a *maamar*, a Chasidic discourse, during which he broke down in tears as he recounted a story about each of the Chabad Rebbes, highlighting their legendary *ahavat Yisrael*—their love for a fellow Jew. He began with a story about the first Rebbe of Chabad, R. Schneur Zalman, known as the Alter Rebbe, which he would retell many times throughout his four decades of leadership, reinforcing its powerful message.

It was the day of Yom Kippur, the holiest time of the year. The entire community was gathered in the synagogue waiting for the most hallowed prayers of the year to commence, when suddenly the Alter Rebbe removed his *tallit* and walked out.

Unbeknownst to the townspeople, the Alter Rebbe left the small village. While his Chasidim waited worriedly for him to return, he had gone to the edge of the town and entered a dilapidated cottage, where a young mother was lying with her newborn child. He chopped wood, made a fire to warm the house, and prepared a soup for her.

He acted with the sacred awareness that saving a life is so important that chopping wood and creating fire—normally forbidden on the holy day—were permitted. No task was beneath this great Torah scholar as he cooked a meal and tenderly fed the woman before returning to the synagogue to commence Yom Kippur services.

When he was later asked why, on the holiest day of the year, he chose to help this woman and her family himself rather than send an emissary, he replied that according to Jewish law, one should never delegate the holy task of saving a life, even if it is Shabbat, a festival, or Yom Kippur.[293] [294] [295]

How poignant a story for the Rebbe to share that evening in Brooklyn, especially considering what had transpired just one night earlier in his office at 770 Eastern Parkway.[296]

Moshe Groner was a rabbinical student at 770 and was catching up on his studies on the eve before that historic *farbrengen,* when he heard the phone in the office at Chabad headquarters ring incessantly. After checking that none of the secretaries were around, he picked up the phone thinking it might be an emergency.

Imagine his surprise when he recognized the voice of the Rebbe on the line.

The Rebbe asked him whether he was available to assist with an urgent matter at home. Moshe ran over to the Rebbe's home, and the Rebbe explained that there was a Jew in poor health who had been admitted to a local hospital, and he was trying to reach the man's doctor in order to get permission to visit the patent. The Rebbe asked Moshe whether he could stay on the line until the doctor was contacted, as he needed to tend to something in the next room.

When the doctor was finally reached, Moshe called the Rebbe to take the phone and stepped into the other room to give him some privacy.

On the dining room table lay a number of *sefarim*, sacred books, and it appeared that the Rebbe had been preparing a lesson. After hanging up the phone, the Rebbe told Moshe that he needed to go see the patient in the hospital, and he asked Moshe whether he could look up certain sources in the materials laid out and place them on the table before he left for home.

Imagine Moshe's shock and amazement when the very next evening, during his very first address as Rebbe, the Rebbe referenced the holy books that had been spread out on his table the night before.

It was then that Moshe was struck by the profound *ahavat Yisrael* he had witnessed the previous evening.

While preparing the equivalent of his inaugural address, on the night before arguably the most important and transformative event of his life, the Rebbe had put everything on hold for a Jew in need.[297]

On his very last evening as a "private citizen," less than a day before being propelled into the unrelenting spotlight that would follow him for the next forty-three years until his passing, instead of dedicating those precious moments to his own spiritual passions, he did not think twice about rushing to a hospital ward to ensure that an overlooked Jew with no family was being cared for.

Like the Alter Rebbe before him who refused to delegate the holy task of caring for a Jew in need on the holiest day of the year, the Rebbe chose not to delegate the hospital visit on that most important night of his life.

This quiet act of altruism and kindness is deeply symbolic of the mission of outreach for which the Rebbe would become known, in which he charged his students and followers to forgo some of their own spiritual comforts in order to ensure the material and spiritual well-being of others.

With every opportunity, the Rebbe drove this point home—a single act of kindness rises above all acts and practices, no matter how presumably lofty.

Indeed, at its heart, Judaism is a religion of concrete action, of deeds in the here and now. We were not placed on this earth to merely enjoy and experience the fruits of spiritual transcendence. We were sent to this world with a holy purpose, a mission defined by service, sanctified by the impact of our deeds on the lives of the people we touch.

In the following chapter, titled A Reluctant Rebbe, we encounter the moving story of the Rebbe's personal struggle to assume the mantle of Chabad leadership, in which he sacrificed a life of private devotion to take on the unrelenting burden of public service. This heartfelt illustration is offered as a poignant portrait of the way in which the Rebbe himself resolved the universal tension between self and service, providing a powerful example for us all.

CHAPTER 25

A Reluctant Rebbe

T HE YEAR WAS 1950.

The date, January 28, 10 Shvat 5710.

The Jewish world awoke to the devastating news of the passing of the sixth Lubavitcher Rebbe, R. Yosef Yitzchak Schneersohn. His passing created a leadership vacuum in this tight-knit community of scholars, mystics, simple Jews, and survivors.

Those who had taken refuge in the United States were a meager remnant of a once glorious dynasty, which in the past had numbered in the hundreds of thousands, with centers and outposts active across much of Eastern Europe.

But now their future was uncertain—what would become of their way of life in this new land? What would be their marching orders into the future?

Numerous debates and deliberations ensued. Where would they turn for comfort, strength, and guidance in life and Torah? Who would lead them? Who would become the next Rebbe?

Some in the community considered the elder of R. Yosef Yitzchak's sons-in-law, R. Shmaryahu Gurary, a renowned Chasidic scholar and communal activist, to be the natural candidate to lead the movement. Most of the Chasidim, however, looked to the younger son-in-law, R. Menachem Mendel Schneerson, known then as Ramash,[298] to fill his father-in-law's place.

Unlike his brother-in-law the Rashag, who had been raised and incubated in the court of the fifth Lubavitcher Rebbe, R. Shalom DovBer, known as the Rebbe Rashab, and had worked closely with R. Yosef Yitzchak on many communal matters, the Rebbe grew up in isolation from the epicenter of Chasidic life, spent much of his early years studying alone with tutors, and later lived a relatively cloistered life at the Berlin and Sorbonne universities, where he studied.

For his part, R. Menachem Mendel, who was fiercely private, had vigorously rejected the persistent requests of the Chasidim that he become the new Rebbe.[299]

However, as Providence would have it, rather than continuing to live a life of quiet obscurity, the Rebbe would become one of this century's most public Jewish figures.

The Most Extroverted Introvert

Like Moses, whose initial response to the prospect of

leadership was, *"Who am I that I should go to Pharaoh, and that I should take the children of Israel out of Egypt?"*[300] the Rebbe initially responded to his communal charge with expressions of inadequacy.

"I received your letter [proposing my candidacy as Rebbe], and I was shocked to read it, demanding matters that are not [part of] me... I do not blame you, because you do not know me personally, but at least you should have checked before writing to me."[301]

When R. Dubov, a prominent Chabad Chasid, urged the Rebbe to assume the mantle of leadership, the Rebbe questioned the very assumption that he was fit for leadership by exclaiming, "What do you suppose? That Mendel Schneerson is a Rebbe?!"[302]

Indeed, so opposed was the Rebbe to assuming the mantle of leadership that, at one point, he even threatened to run away if the Chasidim did not stop pressuring him to accept the role!

As late as two weeks before he accepted the position of Rebbe, he was still vehemently objecting to the nomination.

On January 2, 1951, a group of Chasidim came to see him with a letter announcing their acceptance of him as Rebbe. After reading just the first sentence, the Rebbe folded the letter and put it on his table. With tears on his face, the Rebbe said, "Please leave. This letter has no relevance to me."[303]

So what changed the Rebbe's resolve, and consequently the history of Judaism in post-war America?

A pointed comment from his wife, who was the daughter of the Previous Rebbe, has been said to have made the difference: "If you don't become Rebbe, thirty years of my father's life will have gone to waste."[304]

Once it was put to him as an urgent call to preserve the community, the Rebbe assumed the public and all-consuming role of a Chasidic Rebbe.

Nevertheless, even after he accepted the demanding role and progressively expanded his responsibilities, the mantle of leadership still failed to grow on the Rebbe, as he once confided in a letter:

"I must emphasize that despite the aforementioned [urging you to be active in communal affairs], it remains now, just as it was when we met in person, that I myself take no pleasure in being involved with communal affairs..."[305, 306]

This personal disclosure echoes another statement made during a private audience in 1965 with R. Hillel Pevzner, a *shliach* in Paris whom the Rebbe was trying to encourage to increase in his communal activism.

R. Pevzner complained, "Rebbe, it is too much for my introverted personality!"

The Rebbe replied, "By nature, I, too, am introverted.

Nevertheless, I reluctantly accepted upon myself to be active in public life, because I knew how essential it was."

And it is here that we arrive at the profoundly human struggle and question at the heart of the Rebbe's story.

To live for myself or to live for others? *That* is the question.

From the moment he made his choice, this introspective scholar would spend day and night absorbing the pains, fears, anxieties, and aspirations of millions of people, at times responding to over four hundred letters a day, seeing people in private audience throughout the night three times a week, standing on his feet for seven to eight hours on Sundays to hand out dollars for *tzedakah*, giving out *kos shel brachah* (wine of blessing) to thousands of people on the night after Yom Tov, following a two- or three-day festival during which he would teach Torah to thousands of his Chasidim for many hours.

And to think that, by his own admission, the Rebbe's public role and persona still did not come naturally to him, even nearly fifteen years after becoming Rebbe.

A Life of Service

To live for myself or for others—*that* is the question we are all called to answer, as individuals, as communities, and as nations.

As individuals, will we live a life devoted exclusively to self-actualization and development, however noble and lofty, or will we devote significant time, energy, resources, and mind-space to the well-being and betterment of our communities, schools, and wider society?

Will we design home and family cultures that are self-centered or other-focused, that look out for others or only for our own?

When structuring our communal value systems, what will we elevate above all other aspirations: ambition and success or altruism and service?

These questions have become increasingly relevant and urgent to address in a world and for a generation that has replaced the collective priority of We with the singular pursuit of Me.[307]

It was in this milieu of twentieth-century American hyper-individualism and self-absorption that the Rebbe emerged as a humble yet towering role model of someone who gave his all for others.

The Rebbe took the first step onto the bridge between post-Holocaust devastation and global renewal with an inaugural speech given on 10 Shvat 5711 (1951), at a gathering honoring the first anniversary of the Previous Rebbe's passing. On the first night of his over forty-year quest to change the face of Judaism around the world, the Rebbe spoke with sober gravity, occasionally breaking into tears, choking on the poignancy and magnitude of the moment. Clearly outlining his intentions to help uplift all

Jews, the Rebbe took upon his shoulders the overwhelming task of leading the way, and he fervently implored those gathered before him to do their part.

If you read the following excerpt from his inaugural speech with your heart, you may see in these words not only an attempt to turn a historically inward and insular community into a global taskforce for spiritual outreach. You may also discern in them the faint but forceful echoes of an inner struggle and a painfully honest, soul-searching conversation that was more intrapersonal than interpersonal:

> "...It may not be by virtue of your own choice. It is not through your own achievements. Rather, it is handed to you. An individual cannot argue that this status is beyond him because of personal limitations. To the contrary, Chasidut explains in many places that every single Jew, without exception, must ask himself: When will my actions reach those of my fathers, Abraham, Isaac, and Jacob?...
>
> "What was the approach of the first, Abraham? He was not looking for sacrifice. All he knew was that he had a mission to bring others close to G-d, to go to a place where they don't know about G-dliness, [where] they don't know about Judaism, [where] they don't even know about *alef-bet*, and to place his own

needs aside and devote himself to them. And when someone argues, 'Look, the verse says only, *He called out,* it is enough if you yourself know G-d,' we say, 'No! Do not read it, *He called out.*' If you want G-dliness to affect you, then [you must] cause others to call out...even if he feels no spiritual strength within himself, even if he feels he has nothing, and he cries out, 'Who am I? What am I?' and he has proof of this. He is nevertheless told it is not by your own choice...and since the path has already been trodden, each of us is obligated to take up this mission... He must realize how cherished he is and how much has been invested in him. He will then be able to fulfill his part of the mission to draw G-d's essence back down into this material world."[308]

In the heartfelt words above, one can discern the Rebbe arguing the cause and making the case, addressing that most universal of struggles, and answering that most human of questions, in a way that would irrevocably change his life and so many others by extension.

Will I live only for myself or will I live for others?

To live a life of service—that was the Rebbe's answer on that historic evening. May his inspirational example help each of us answer the call when the same question inevitably comes our way.

CHAPTER 26

The Power of One Good Deed

————————

C ONTRARY TO POPULAR BELIEF, the roots of the underground spiritual movement that came to be known as Chasidism began nearly a century before R. Yisrael Baal Shem Tov was born on 18 Elul 5458 (1698).

Forgoing the complex palimpsestic histories of why, suffice it to say that this was a treacherous time to practice Jewish mysticism, especially within the communities in which the Baal Shem Tov had been raised and taught the intricacies of Kabbalah and Torah. Jewish mystics of the age were received with severe suspicion by some members of the Jewish community, so they went about their intense and devoted study in relative anonymity.[309]

For his part, the Baal Shem Tov was committed to

concealing his holy light, preferring a private life of Torah study, deep contemplation, and holy mystical practice, while resisting all efforts by his mentor, R. Adam Baal Shem, to bring him out of his self-imposed obscurity.[310]

But there was a truth that lingered in the corners of the great master's quiet life—an awareness about his soul's purpose on earth, embedded within a story revealed to him by his teacher when he was a teenager.

As told to the young Yisrael in a letter:

In the year 1573, there lived a simple Jew in the holy city of Safed, in the northern reaches of Israel. This man lived in a state of simple piety and was uniquely devoted to serving G-d, despite knowing almost nothing of Torah. At best, he was able to read well enough to manage his duties to prayer.

One night, while reciting *Tikkun Chatzot*—the midnight prayer of the pious lamenting the destruction of the Holy Temple—this man was surprised by a knock at his door.

After asking who was there, he heard the unbelievable reply, "It is Elijah the Prophet."

Without a moment's doubt, the young man quickly opened the door, welcoming Elijah as the room filled with Divine light and the joy of the prophet's holy presence.

The glowing figure looked at him briefly before saying, "I have come to divulge to you the wondrous secret of when Mashiach will come. But only if you first reveal to me the special meritorious act you performed on the day of your bar mitzvah, for that is what moved the heavenly court to rule that you are worthy of hearing this great revelation."

The truth of what the prophet said washed over him— that he had done something on the day of his bar mitzvah that had been so profoundly pure and holy that it had bypassed the sight of the loftiest souls and even the heavenly court, and as such was received and known only by G-d Himself. These lofty souls, in turn, were willing to bless him with one of the greatest secrets kept in the heavens, all to know what he had done that was so singularly meritorious.

Incredibly, the young man turned down the prophet's tremendous offer, saying, "I was raised to believe that the good deeds one does should be hidden from others to ensure they are done for the sake of G-d alone."

The great prophet then disappeared and returned to the heavenly court, where a significant tumult ensued over the man's rejection, which expressed his astounding devotion to G-d, even at the expense of an unfathomable reward. After consideration, the heavenly court ruled that the man should receive even greater holy rewards, including knowledge of all aspects and dimensions of Torah.

After receiving his spiritual boon, this previously simple man became a once-in-a-generation paragon of purity, scholarship, and G-dliness, but he never lost his hallmark modesty, choosing to preserve his knowledge, inspiring deeds, and holy achievements solely for the glory of G-d. He lived a life of solitude and inimitable piety, and when he passed, the man came before the heavenly court to be judged. Of course, he was widely pronounced worthy of the highest appointment in heaven.

After pondering the fate of the man's soul, it was decided that he would descend again to the physical world, except that this time he would be forced to reveal his greatness, and his soul would be tasked with initiating a new path in the service of G-d. His righteous mission would glorify G-d in an unprecedented way, infusing creation with Divine wisdom in a manner that would greatly hasten the arrival of Mashiach.[311]

R. Adam Baal Shem concluded his letter to the young Yisrael, saying, "You are this Divine soul, sent to this world once more in order to bring it a new light."

This soul, reborn as R. Yisrael Baal Shem Tov, delivered Chasidut—the path of loving-kindness—to humanity and gave birth to a tremendous revolution in Judaism. As a result, age-old Jewish conceptions of devotion and merit, practice and purpose were turned upside down and inside out.

How fitting that it was the Baal Shem Tov who would reveal the following stunning spiritual truth—one that the

Rebbe would repeat endlessly and emphatically in an effort to crystallize the importance of a single act of service and kindness:

"A soul can descend to this world for seventy or eighty years just to do one favor for another."[312]

Here was a soul who had risen to spiritual heights surpassing even those of the Patriarchs, who carried mastery of every dimension of the Torah and a life lived in perfect alignment with the Divine. And yet this soul, whose merit and holiness were beyond description, was sent back with a final commandment—you must share your wisdom with your fellow Jews.

The distillation of that wisdom, and its manifestation, is crystallized by each of us in *one act of kindness*, which the Baal Shem Tov privileged uniquely as justifying an entire lifetime.

One Good Deed

During a momentous Purim *farbrengen* in 1962, at a time when his vision of "outreach" had not yet fully taken hold, the Rebbe elaborated on the story of the Baal Shem Tov's singular purpose in an effort to inspire and reorient a community of inwardly-focused Chasidim toward a life of *shlichut* and service:

> "The descent of the soul 'from a high rooftop to a deep pit' is the greatest of descents, beyond comparison. As *Tanya* explains...[the

soul's state while embodied in this world is]
not comparable to the soul before it descended
to this world, and even less comparable to the
soul as it is within its Source.

"...That being so, an explanation is required:
What reason can there be to justify such a
descent?"

Here the Rebbe referenced the hallowed words of the
Baal Shem Tov:

"A soul can descend to this world for seventy or eighty
years just to do one favor for another."

Commenting on this revolutionary teaching, the Rebbe
observed:

"Now think about this. We are speaking of a
righteous Jew who studies Torah and fulfills
mitzvot throughout a seventy- or eighty-year
life span. Nonetheless, the descent of his soul
to this world is essentially for just one or
two actions! ...And since the main point of
the descent [of the soul] is for this action, it
is understood that this action matters more,
and by its means the soul reaches higher than
through all the other matters during its lifetime in this world.

"That is also the lesson for each and every
individual regarding their current service of
G-d...

"...Since none of us really knows with certainty [the reason their soul was sent to this world], it may just be that *this* action is that essential action for which his soul has descended for the span of seventy or eighty years.

"And when he argues that he has already lived many years, putting on *tefillin*, studying Torah, performing *mitzvot*, and doing much good for others, and that being so, how is it possible that all those things should be merely secondary to this one action of just doing a spiritual favor for a single Jew or even just a material favor? Is it possible that all his seventy years are merely a side note to this one action?

"The Torah teaches us: *Don't despise a day of small things.*[313] This is talking about an action that seems in your estimation to be the most trivial of things, but nonetheless, since it has fallen to you to do it, 'Don't delay it.'[314] ...It is possible that each and every action or matter that comes to hand *could be the one thing that is the whole reason for his soul coming down to this world...*

"And when one's approach to *every matter* of Torah and *mitzvot* rests on the premise that it may be just for this action that his soul came down for the seventy or eighty years of his life, and everything else was only secondary, then he does that action with an entirely different kind of animation, and then he will succeed incomparably."[315]

This is The One

As exemplified in the following story, it was precisely this urgent, mission-oriented consciousness that the Rebbe personally embodied and sought to impart to everyone he encountered.

Early one morning, as the Rebbe was leaving his home on his way to 770, a man who had traveled from afar in need of guidance approached him and began a conversation.

This was a breach of protocol, since meetings with the Rebbe were typically arranged through his secretariat many months in advance due to the extreme demands on the Rebbe's time.

Nonetheless, the Rebbe stopped and took the time to address the man's troubles, leaving him comforted and reinvigorated before heading off to the synagogue.

As the man turned to depart, he was confronted by a few *yeshivah* students who had witnessed his exchange with the Rebbe and wanted to chastise him for his audacity. They admonished him for considering himself above those who waited patiently to be seen at *yechidut* or who simply wrote the Rebbe a letter and waited for a reply.

The man was overcome with remorse and sent the

Rebbe a letter of regret, apologizing profusely for having taken his time in this way.

The Rebbe began his response by lightening the feelings left by his encounter with the *yeshivah* students, saying, "Firstly, the *yeshivah* students who accosted you did so during school hours, when they should have been studying in *yeshivah* rather than offering you rebuke."

The Rebbe then offered a soul-stirring response, radically reframing his interaction with the man:

"One of the cardinal teachings of the Baal Shem Tov was that 'a soul can descend to this world for an entire lifetime, all in order to do one favor for another.' Who knows? Perhaps the reason my soul came to this world was so that I could help you this morning!"[316]

Across thousands of stories about the Rebbe, we see this conviction in action—that every encounter with someone in need warrants our utmost loving focus, regardless of the mountain of demands that looms on the other side of the encounter. Even as his list of duties became astounding in length, he remained true to the Baal Shem Tov's edict that every encounter may be the most important opportunity in your life—the very act of kindness your soul was incarnated to complete. It may be a destitute stranger who reaches out in need as you rush to your next appointment, or a friend who calls you heartbroken after you've had a particularly exhausting day. It may be a child who interrupts to ask a question while you are working desperately to keep up with your workload.

It is in those very moments that we must remember that no opportunity to be there for another is trivial or dismissible, and that every encounter is pregnant with tremendous, unknown possibilities. In fact, that seemingly trivial opportunity, that single act of charity or goodwill, may embody the very purpose and potential your soul came to this world to fulfill.

CHAPTER 27

The Greatest Mitzvah of All

O N SUNDAY, 20 TEVET 5749 (1988), the Rebbe stood before a line of hundreds of people who had come from far and near to 770 Eastern Parkway in Brooklyn to receive their portion of Sunday Dollars. For more than two years, the Rebbe had received countless visitors like this each Sunday, handing out single dollar bills, and occasionally a few more, to everyone who arrived. They were expected, in turn, to give an equivalent dollar to someone in need, an act of *tzedakah* (charity), which the Rebbe was known to encourage in his followers with unique dedication.

On this particular Sunday, the Rebbe received a visit from international philanthropist, diplomat, and public servant Ronald Lauder. The Rebbe handed Lauder a single dollar bill, saying:

> "It is my idea that at the first encounter of two Jews, they should do something for a third Jew. And the first thing they can do for a third Jew is to give *tzedakah*. And that is the idea of giving: It is not much money, but it is an indication of what every one of us should do: When any one of us meets a Jew, start by looking to do something that will benefit a third Jew..."[317]

This idea adds an astounding additional dimension to our search for purpose. In the same way that each individual has their own unique Divine purpose, each generation receives its own overarching, collective purpose, representing a distinct area of focus for that generation.[318]

During the era of Talmudic Sages, for example, this arch-mitzvah was the all-consuming study of Torah.

But the Rebbe heralded a radical, new generational mission, first introduced by the Alter Rebbe, which was dictated by the needs of our precise time and place in the story of creation. This new meta-mitzvah would take the lofty, inward focus of past Sages and turn it outward, creating a new paradigm that emphasized action and service to others. This was not a call to deprioritize introspection and study.[319] It was simply a new, predominant priority that directs us to do the particular work of our time, and a call to be willing to shift focus when our portion of that work arrives.

Our generation's purpose, according to the Rebbe, was to become a charitable generation —a generation of givers.

Mitzvah of the Day

This revolutionary reorientation toward *tzedakah* was first noted in the *Tanya*, which declared that the time for a profound shift had arrived. The Rebbe often quoted the following passage in promoting this principle:

> "...Direct your hearts to these words, which are expressed very briefly, how in these times, when the approaching footsteps of Mashiach are close upon us, the principal service of G-d is the service of *tzedakah*. As our Sages, of blessed memory, said, 'Israel will be redeemed only through *tzedakah*.'

> "Our Sages, of blessed memory, did not say that '...The study of the Torah is equivalent to them all' [to all the *mitzvot* previously enumerated in the Mishnah], including acts of loving-kindness, except in their own days, for with them, the principal area of Divine service was the study of the Torah, which is why there were such great scholars at that time...

> "However, in a time when the approaching footsteps of Mashiach are close upon us, [the

main service of our generation pertains] to the level of *Asiyah* [action or deed, because] there is no way of truly cleaving unto it [G-d's presence in the world] and transforming the darkness of the world into its light except through...the act of *tzedakah*."[320]

Give It Your All

Understanding why *tzedakah* is the mitzvah of our time requires us to examine briefly its metaphysical nature as it relates to purpose, and the unique role that giving to others plays in fulfilling the mission of our time. According to Kabbalistic interpretations, *tzedakah* is singular in its power to elevate humanity and fulfill the ultimate purpose of creation. As with all *mitzvot*, the energy we invest in acts of giving elevates the animal soul, and, in so doing, brings the light of G-dliness into the world. When you fulfill a typical mitzvah, however, you are only putting a portion of yourself into the act—you use your arm and head to put on *tefillin*, for example. You may use your mouth to eat matzah, but your intellect isn't necessarily involved. But when you perform *tzedakah*, you're doing so much more.

As the Alter Rebbe summarized in *Tanya*:

"Now, you will find no other mitzvah in which the animating soul [of the body] is clothed to the same extent as in the mitzvah of charity. For in all other *mitzvot*, only one faculty of the [animating] soul is clothed (e.g., the faculty of action in the hand donning *tefillin* or holding an *etrog*), and even this one faculty is clothed in the mitzvah only while the mitzvah is being performed.

"In the case of charity, however, which one gives from the proceeds of the toil of his hands, surely all the strength of his [animating] soul is clothed in (i.e., applied to) the effort of his labor or in any other occupation by which he earned this money that he now distributes for charity. Thus, when he gives to charity this money to which he applied all the strength of his [animating] soul, his entire [animating] soul ascends to G-d. Hence the superiority of charity over other *mitzvot*.

"Even he who does not earn his livelihood from his labors, nevertheless, since he could have purchased with this money that he gave for charity sustenance for the life of his [animating] soul, he is giving his soul's life to G-d in the form of charity. Thus, charity comprises and therefore elevates more energy of the [animating] soul than any other mitzvah.

"This is why our Sages have said that charity hastens the redemption. For with one act of charity, one elevates a great deal of the [animating] soul, more of its faculties and powers, in fact, than he might elevate through many other active *mitzvot* [combined]... The Messianic Era is a result of our efforts in purifying and elevating the [animating] soul; charity, which effects this elevation in such great measure, thus hastens the redemption."[321, 322]

Out of the Box

As part of his effort to concretize and actualize the *tzedakah* consciousness he tirelessly endeavored to seed everywhere and in everyone he encountered, the Rebbe launched a worldwide *tzedakah* box campaign.[323] Typically a can or small box with an opening for receiving coins and cash, these containers, known colloquially as *pushkas*, represent far more than charitable piggy banks. The Rebbe encouraged Jews at every turn to place these boxes as permanent[324] fixtures in places of living, working, leisure, and elsewhere, because their presence would transform every context and location into a hub of giving[325] and blessing.[326]

"A *tzedakah* box," the Rebbe taught, "redefines an entire space, transforming it into a center of kindness and caring."[327]

His goal, as with Sunday Dollars, was to create a critical mass of giving, and to help transform our lives, our homes, and our entire generation into fonts of generosity.[328]

Over time, the Pushka Campaign's gravity expanded far beyond homes and Jewish families. The Rebbe labored to link all environments, institutions, professions, and endeavors in a sequential chain of charitable giving. He encouraged an Israeli naval officer, for example, to tell his superiors to place a *pushka* on every naval ship.[329] In the winter of 1990, the Rebbe asked one of the managing directors of El Al Airlines for a list of all the planes under his management so he could donate a dollar to jumpstart the placement of *pushkas* on every plane.[330] He told college students to put them in dorm rooms.[331] He even encouraged Avraham Fried, a famous Chasidic singer, to give *tzedakah* before and after a concert, which became a ritual of Fried's, who makes a point of giving charity onstage at every concert. Indeed, the Rebbe was always scanning for an opportunity to spread *tzedakah* consciousness.

Chanukah 5747 (1987), thirteen years after he launched the Pushka Campaign, the Rebbe announced a campaign to place one in the bedroom of every child. The next day, he emerged from his office in 770 Eastern Parkway with a bag of nickels, which he distributed to children for placement in their new *tzedakah* boxes.[332] Over time, his constant distribution of coins to children became one of the Rebbe's most visible innovations.

"We have recently been promoting the education of Jewish children in the mitzvah of *tzedakah* through giving them a coin to put into the *tzedakah pushka*. There are those who look for problems and argue: What's the point? These are children who are not obligated to fulfill *mitzvot*, and they don't even have their own money. What's the point of giving them a penny to put into the *pushka*?"

The Rebbe explained:

"The answer lies in an explicit verse: *Train a child according to his way, even in his old age he will not deviate from it*.[333] When you educate a child to put money into a *pushka*, he will certainly continue doing so when he grows up. This trains his hand to be "a hand that distributes *tzedakah*."[334]

From the Rebbe's perspective, each act of giving, no matter how small and regardless of the age of the giver, inoculates us against the pernicious modern trend that says life's satisfaction and fulfillment is predicated on maximum acquisition. In this way, we rise above the dictates of the animal soul, which views the world through a lens of scarcity and survival, leaving little room for generosity and charity, while strongly encouraging a life defined by accumulation, materialism, and excess. The charitable offering becomes the spiritual antithesis of the scarcity-driven dash for more and more, and it reorients us toward G-dliness, interconnectedness, and faith.

The message is clear: Don't defer giving. Start with something small. Put a *pushka* in your home. Create a special savings account dedicated to charitable giving. Begin working your way toward *maaser*—the mitzvah of tithing.[335] Make a five-year "*tzedakah* plan" and grow your giving capacity over time. Empty your pockets each day in a spirit of generosity.

The Rebbe insisted that anyone choosing to become a conduit of generosity and loving-kindness contributes to the grand effort that will hasten the arrival of Mashiach.

> "Through also ending this talk with making each person here an emissary to give *tzedekah* at the right time and with their own additional contribution, this will further bring closer and hasten the time [of Mashiach]... And [at that time] we will dance together with our *tzedakah* boxes and with our accumulated good deeds..."[336]

CHAPTER 28

The Path to Happiness

DURING A TIME OF unexpected financial hardship, one of the affluent Chasidim of R. Schneur Zalman of Liadi, known as the Alter Rebbe, approached him seeking blessings and insight into how to turn his life around.

Until very recently, the man explained, he had been fortunate in business, but his affairs had taken a downward turn, and he found himself in debt and unable to meet his many financial obligations.

The Alter Rebbe listened and then with one sentence changed the trajectory of this man's life and spiritual journey, saying, "Until now, you have spoken about what *you* need. But you have not given thought to *what you are needed for.*"[337]

How easy it is for each of us to confuse what we want from life with the purpose of life itself. Now, more than ever, in an age of unprecedented abundance, it is widely believed that the ideal life is dependent upon achieving the highest levels of happiness, pleasure, and personal satisfaction.

But the desperate pursuit of happiness rarely bears the fruit we hope it will. Rather than looking for fulfillment in pursuit of what we think we need, we are far more likely to find true satisfaction and joy by focusing on our Divinely imparted purpose—that is, what our Creator needs of us.

Here we find one of the great, revolutionary ideas inherent to Judaism. G-d created the world because He needs you. Reread the last sentence. Your Creator—G-d Himself, eternal, omnipotent, and without limitation—*needs you.* Not because He is inadequate or lacking anything. G-d is unlimited and complete by His very nature. Rather, metaphorically speaking, He chose to make Himself "vulnerable" for the sake of experiencing love and the singular, infinite joy of being chosen in return. Put simply, G-d doesn't love you because He needs you. He needs you because He loves you. Not for lack but for love. This yearning manifested in the creation of all things, so you could be, so you could reach for G-d by fulfilling your sacred purpose.

This was the clarifying message offered by the Rebbe to a struggling student who asked how he might find his mission in life:

"The Mishnah states that man was created in order to serve his Creator."[338]

Here, and in countless other exchanges with individuals seeking a path toward fulfillment, the Rebbe offered this text and teaching as the very mission statement—in fact, the very raison d'être—of humankind. This spiritual axiom defines service rather than happiness as the beating heart of our existence, and it serves as a clarion call to everyone who seeks true happiness.

More to Life

The consequences of bypassing our Divine purpose in pursuit of self-focused happiness is illustrated by a written exchange between the Rebbe and a student who reached out in a state of protracted depression. The student wrote to the Rebbe, "I would like the Rebbe's help. I wake up each day sad and apprehensive. I can't concentrate. I find it hard to pray. I keep the commandments, but I find no spiritual satisfaction. I go to the synagogue, but I feel alone. I begin to wonder what life is about. I need help."

The Rebbe sent an incisive response that clarified the source of the student's unhappiness without using a single word. He simply took his pen, circled the first word of every sentence in the letter, and sent it back. When the student opened the letter and saw the Rebbe's markings, he understood.

The Rebbe had diagnosed the perspectival root of his

malaise and set him on the path to recovery by circling every instance of the word "I."[339]

With delightful clarity and style, the Rebbe highlights the way in which many of us become trapped in the self-centered pursuit of experiences and accolades that we think will satisfy our ever-molting individual wants and needs, which typically leaves little room in the picture for serving our Divine purpose. At best, such an approach to life involves G-d and others as facilitators or contributors to our personal search for satisfaction and fulfillment. Any happiness found in this mad dash rarely satisfies for long, requiring us to seek ever-newer, bigger, and better experiences as the joy we gather and grasp for rapidly evaporates. In most cases, no matter how profound our so-called peak experiences, the happiness extracted leaves us paradoxically empty and hungry for more. In this way, over time, our appetites begin to consume us.

Indeed, according to modern researchers, the single-minded pursuit of happiness is leaving people less happy, and in many cases downright miserable. In fact, as observed in an *Atlantic* article titled, "There's More to Life Than Being Happy," author Emily Esfahani Smith points out that researchers and health experts are beginning to caution against the pursuit of happiness as an end unto itself.[340]

Their caution emerges from persistent findings that

a "meaningful" life and a "happy" life overlap in certain ways, but they are ultimately very different and derive from very different approaches to living. Most importantly, the pursuit of a happy life, researchers find increasingly, is predicated on being a "taker," while leading a meaningful life corresponds with being a "giver."

The article goes on to quote Kathleen Vohs, one of the authors of *Some Key Differences Between a Happy Life and a Meaningful Life*, a study published in *The Journal of Positive Psychology*. There she observes, "Happy people get joy from receiving benefits from others, while people leading meaningful lives get a lot of joy from giving to others."[341]

Paradoxically, it seems that it's precisely when we don't go looking for happiness and are willing to set it aside for the sake of others that we find it unexpectedly.

This truth is reflected more and more in the work of modern social scientists, who suggest that unlike the fleeting and fickle pleasures of a more self-centered approach to life, giving and service generate a particular quality of happiness that is both meaningful and long lasting.[342] Indeed, according to current research, the joy that you feel when you do a good deed has a tangible impact on your body. In much the same way that exercise releases endorphins into your brain that make you feel good naturally, acts of charity generate what scientists call the "helpers' high."[343]

In other words, human beings are hardwired to derive true happiness from service.

This was recently confirmed as part of a study that surveyed data from across one hundred thirty-six countries. According to Elizabeth Dunn, a psychologist at the University of British Columbia and member of the research team, "In contrast to traditional economic thought—which places self-interest as the guiding principle of human motivation—[our] findings suggest that the reward experienced from helping others may be deeply ingrained in human nature, emerging in diverse cultural and economic contexts."[344]

These conclusions echo what Jewish wisdom has been telling us for centuries—namely, that true happiness emerges from following our innate desire to serve and do good in the world rather than from the pursuit of pure self-satisfaction.

In the words of the Rebbe, written in the fall of 1961:

"There can be two approaches to life:

(a) To consider [one's aim in life] as a matter of pleasure—in which case every effort should be made toward getting the most [pleasure] out of life...

(b) To consider life as a challenge...to help make a better world to live in, especially since the society we live in is far from perfection. In this case, every effort must be made toward this end, even if it means the sacrifice of certain personal pleasures, and even if it requires a great deal of continuous physical and mental exertion. But, as a matter of fact, *it is this latter approach that offers the maximum pleasure—real pleasure and gratification.*"[345]

The Seeds of True Happiness

The inborn inclination to offer oneself in the service of something beyond the self is instilled in every one of us. According to the Kabbalists,[346] one of the reasons G-d created the world was to express loving-kindness. As the Sages teach, "*Teva Hatov l'heitiv*—it is in the nature of He Who is good to do good." Accordingly, our unique propensity for giving is a natural reflection of the Divine image in which we were created. In this way, our commitment to a life of service becomes the only true route to sustainable well-being and happiness.

As pioneering Austrian psychologist and neurologist Dr. Viktor Frankl so potently put it, "Happiness cannot be pursued; it must ensue, and it only does so as the unintended side-effect of one's dedication to a cause greater than oneself..."[347]

This radical realization, in turn, becomes a sacred antidote to the creeping, debilitating notion that tells you that happiness is to be found in the pursuit of personal pleasure above all, and it invites you to rise up and claim the path to happiness that G-d made just for you.

As we learned previously, there are tasks built into your

life, things only you can do because you are precisely who and what you are, living in your time, forged by your experiences, and aligned with circumstances that are built into the story of your Divine purpose. G-d needs you to answer the call to service He created you to fulfill—a kindness to deliver, charity to give, peace to sew, pain to heal, wrongs to right, or lives to mend. It is precisely in pursuit of this personalized holy purpose that meaning, and therefore happiness, is truly found.

As the Rebbe reminds us: It is not what you think you need but what *you are needed for* that brings true happiness.

CHAPTER 29

A Source of Healing and Resilience

—————

THE REBBE ONCE RECEIVED a letter from a man wrestling with feelings of worthlessness and intractable depression. He wrote to the Rebbe that he saw no value in his continued living, and that he was contemplating taking his own life. The Rebbe wrote back:

"Surely you know that one of the basics of our religion and our Torah is to have complete *bitachon* [trust] in Hashem, Whose benevolent *Hashgachah Pratit* [Divine Providence] extends to each and everyone individually, and Who is just and good…This certainly leaves no room for pessimism or despair, G-d forbid.

"As for your wondering how much your life may be worth as things now stand—this is quite incomprehensible, since you surely know the saying of our Sages, referring to every Jew, without exception, 'I was created to serve my Creator.'"

Could there be anything more important than such a special Divinely-given task and mission in life?"[348]

For the countless wounded souls he encountered, the Rebbe offered the strong and loving medicine of Divine responsibility, which, he insisted, could light the way out of even the deepest spiritual abyss. For those suffering from depression, trauma, despair, and even thoughts of suicide, the Rebbe taught that there was no need to *find* a reason to live. Rather, as in the story above, he taught that every person is *born* with the greatest reason of all to live—a Divinely-appointed, one-of-a-kind mission that their soul alone can fulfill.

He Needs You

This was the course of treatment offered by R. Manis Friedman to a despondent young man who had been hospitalized after attempting suicide. Having repeatedly failed to accomplish his goals, the young man concluded that he was altogether worthless and had become convinced that suicide was his only option. But even his attempt at that had failed. He was at rock bottom. While hospitalized, he received several visitors, none of whom had been able to help him out of the voracious darkness that threatened to consume him.

R. Friedman, a Chasid of the Rebbe, arrived to find the boy in bed listlessly watching television, a portrait of despair. The boy hardly acknowledged the rabbi, and before he could even say hello, the boy said quietly, "If you are here to tell me what the priest just told me, you can leave now."

Taken aback, the rabbi composed himself and asked, "What did the priest say?"

"He told me that G-d loves me, which is a load of garbage. Why would G-d love me?"

It was clear to R. Friedman that this boy had lost sight of his own value and purpose, and that he considered himself utterly unlovable in light of his own perceived failure.

"You may be right," he replied.

That was the last thing the boy expected to hear from a rabbi. Now he was paying attention. R. Friedman continued, "But one thing's for sure. He *needs* you... The very fact that you were created means that G-d needs you. He had plenty of people before you, but He added you to the world's population because there is something you can do that no one else can. And if you haven't done it yet that makes it even more crucial that you continue to live, so that you are able to fulfill your mission and give your unique gift to the world."[349]

Echoing the Rebbe's perspective, R. Friedman offered the only route out of a self-destructive bias that leads many into a pit of despair. It may be common to remind those who find themselves in such a state just how much they are loved. But the rabbi, based on the Rebbe's teachings, offered a different delivery system for G-d's healing and redeeming love—a life of purpose that is rooted in selfless service to G-d and humanity. This redemptive awareness was offered as medicine for what had become a near fatal disease—too much self-emphasis, which had left very little room for G-d and the uniquely uplifting holy purpose He had woven into the young man's life.

Time and again, rather than merely telling the legions of pained and broken souls who came to him for guidance and support that they were merely *loved*, the Rebbe insisted that *they must love*—just as they had been created to do in their own precious way.

From Self to Service

The Rebbe once shared this healing viewpoint with renowned clinical psychologist and author Dr. Ruth Benjamin. During a private audience, Benjamin had asked the Rebbe to share wisdom for people suffering like one of her patients who had attempted suicide only to be saved by Benjamin, who intervened and rushed him to the hospital in time to save his life. Later, during a visit amid his recovery, the patient had confounded the doctor by saying, "You are responsible for my being alive. Now give me something to live for."

Having been unable to produce a satisfying answer in the moment, Dr. Benjamin asked the Rebbe what he would recommend saying to someone with a similar request.

"Tell him that he is part of G-d's world," the Rebbe replied. "And that means that he has to answer to G-d."[350]

The Rebbe's answer resounds with one simple, monumental truth: *You matter!* You are an indispensable part of G-d's great plan, and you thus carry a duty to live up to His faith in you!

This point led them further into a discussion about remedies for suicidal despair, including some patients for whom Holocaust experiences had brought intolerable anguish. The Rebbe said that Dr. Benjamin should tell her Jewish patients that with so many Jews murdered, those alive today have a double duty. They must live not only for themselves but also for those who are no longer here.

"When they realize this, they will find that their own turmoil will pass," he said.

Again and again, the Rebbe emphasized this crucial point: For those suffering from soul-crushing despair, even to the point of self-destruction, the way out of the existential abyss is to shift our focus from self to service, whether that be to G-d or to someone who is waiting for us along the path of our Divine purpose.

Heart of Darkness

In the case of Dr. Benjamin's patients and consistently in his public teaching and private counsel to those in turmoil and need, the Rebbe shared this perspective, which is strikingly similar to one espoused by pioneering Austrian psychologist and neurologist Dr. Viktor Frankl. Indeed, the Rebbe wrote admiringly about Dr. Frankl's therapeutic approach: "It is obvious [that] some doctors have helped and healed their patients in straight ways, especially since one professor (Dr. Frankl) found the courage in his soul to declare and announce that, contrary to the opinion of the famous founder of psychoanalysis (Freud), faith in G-d, and a religious inclination in general, which gives meaning to life, etc., is one of the most effective ways of healing."[351]

Dr. Frankl's novel perspective on resilience and healing was deeply informed by his own devastating experiences in Nazi concentration camps, where he witnessed the power of purpose to help people endure unimaginable trauma and suffering.

Dr. Frankl himself was arrested and transported to a Nazi concentration camp with his wife and parents in September 1942. Three years later, when his camp was liberated, most of his family, including his pregnant wife, had perished. But he, prisoner number 119104, had survived.

In his bestselling book, *Man's Search for Meaning*, in which he chronicled his experiences in the camps, he concluded that the difference between those who had lived and those who had died often came down to two things: meaning and purpose. As he saw in the camps, those who found meaning and purpose, even in the most life-extinguishing circumstances, were far more resilient and likely to survive than those who did not.

In the three years he spent in Auschwitz, Dr. Frankl survived and helped others to survive by inspiring them to discover a purpose in life, even in the midst of hell on earth. In his book, he provides the example of two suicidal inmates he encountered there. Like many others in the camps, these two men were hopeless and thought that there was nothing left to live for.

"In both cases," he writes, "it was a question of getting them to realize that life was still expecting something from them; something in the future was expected of them."[352]

For one man, it was his young child, who was then living in a foreign country. For the other, a scientist, it was a series of books that he needed to finish. Each of these men, with Dr. Frankl's encouragement, found fuel to continue their journey in the sublime promise of service.

"A man who becomes conscious of the responsibility he bears toward a human being who affectionately waits for him, or to an unfinished work, will never be able to throw away his life," Dr. Frankl wrote. "He knows the 'why' for his existence and will [thus] be able to bear almost any 'how.'"[353]

Elsewhere he observed, "Life is never made unbearable by circumstances, but only by lack of meaning and purpose."

Poignantly, Dr. Frankl's view of the human psyche corresponds quite closely with the Chasidic understanding of our unique nature: We have a soul beneath the surface of the self, and this soul forms the foundation of our very being and purpose, which connects us intrinsically to others and to G-d. He believed that the activation of this inner axis is what allows us to heal, survive, and even thrive amid suffering.

Darkest Before Dawn

Over the years, Frankl's unorthodox and daring theory of human psychology brought constant derision of his life's work by his colleagues in the field. His view of human nature differed in certain key areas from the party-line views that dominated the discipline of psychology before the war, making him and his work a consistent target of scholarly derision.

It was this very demeaning of his deepest held beliefs regarding the inner makeup of the human being that led to his own breaking point in 1960. Though he had survived the attacks of the Nazis on his body, he could no longer bear the attacks of his peers on his soul. In an act of despair, Dr. Frankl decided to upend his entire life, close his practice, suspend his research, and take his family from Vienna to live in Australia.

It was at that moment when Marguerite Kozenn-Chajes, a well-known opera singer and descendant of Vizhnitz Chasidim, knocked on his door in Vienna. Dr. Frankl came to the door and found a sharply dressed woman whom he had never met before standing on his doorstep.[354, 355]

She announced herself as the bearer of a personal message addressed to him by a Chasidic Rebbe, R. Menachem Mendel Schneerson, from Brooklyn, New York. Upon hearing this startling explanation for her visit, and recognizing the name of the Rebbe, he promptly invited Mrs. Chajes inside to speak privately.

"The Rebbe asked me to tell you," she began, "that you must not give up. You must be strong. Do not be disturbed by those who ridicule you. You will succeed, and your work will achieve a major breakthrough."

Upon hearing the Rebbe's reassuring voice from afar, Dr. Frankl broke into tears. He had only just recently been filling out his immigration papers to Australia, and he had, tragically, finally given up. But the Rebbe's reaffirmation of his purpose brought Dr. Frankl back to life, just as the good doctor had done for so many others.

After regaining his composure, Dr. Frankl was ignited with renewed commitment to continue his life's work.

Following his fateful message from the Rebbe, Dr. Frankl redoubled his efforts to spread his unique insights and therapeutic approaches to mending the fractured human psyche. Not long afterward, his magnum opus, *Man's Search for Meaning*, was translated into English, sparking immediate popular interest in his work and worldview that has endured to this very day. That work alone has been translated into twenty-eight languages and sold more than ten million copies, giving birth to an entire genre of self-help literature as well as the field of logotherapy, Dr. Frankl's unique philosophy and practice of psychological health and healing.

Both the Rebbe's and Viktor Frankl's purpose-driven path to psychological healing and spiritual survival can be summed up in one of Frankl's most penetrating declarations, *"The way to find meaning is not to ask what we want from life. Instead, we should ask what life wants from us."*

Indeed, our Divine purpose is the answer to this most human prayer. Our every action is how we say amen.

This was the life-saving advice given by the Rebbe to a man who had survived the Holocaust. Having witnessed the murder of his family at the hands of the Nazis, he had decided he would never have a family of his own and had concluded he had nothing left to live for. On the advice of his rabbi, he traveled from his home in London to visit the Rebbe, hoping to receive guidance.

Arriving at 770 [Chabad headquarters in Brooklyn], the man was granted an audience and poured his heart out to the Rebbe, crying out: "The Holocaust ripped my whole life and my family from me. I cannot sleep at night because I'm reliving the horrors I've seen. I have decided never to get married and bring children into this dark world."

The Rebbe looked deeply into his eyes and said, "Given your terrible loss, I understand your feelings. Just know that your entire family is watching you, and they care deeply about you. If you live the life of a dead person, you are only continuing the tragedy of their death. If you live a life of love, you will bring them some comfort. The only thing you have left is the love you have for your family and the love you will give to other people...

"Otherwise, why did G-d leave you on Earth; for what reason?"

Here the Rebbe reminds the man that his survival was part of G-d's plan and was His way of saying, "I still need you!"

"Find a way to show love to the people around you, and that love will bring light back into your life. Even if you don't feel up to it, just do it."

Urged by the Rebbe's insistence, the man made a commitment that day to bring joy to the people at his synagogue by distributing sweets to others. He discovered that the joyful recipients of his gifts rekindled his heart one smile at a time.

Later, he said, "My life is far from easy, but I found a purpose...and the Rebbe taught me a way to bring light into my life, through the love that I give to others."[356]

With this critical, purpose-igniting message, the Rebbe helped heal a generation of displaced and broken survivors, transforming them into a taskforce of Divine light and love. In one encounter after another, he lifted people from the mire of their own suffering with the radical rejoinder—G-d needs you! In so doing, he turned people who had every reason to expect the worst from life and humanity into people who would devote their lives to finding and redeeming the best in humanity and the world.

CHAPTER 30

The Final Frontier

A WOMAN ONCE CAME BEFORE the Rebbe to ask for a singularly significant blessing.

"If you would bring Mashiach, all our prayers would be answered."

The Rebbe replied, "I am ready, but I require the cooperation of all the Jews around me."

Without pause, the woman revised her request, asking instead, "A blessing that we should work harder to bring him."

"Yes," the Rebbe replied with a smile. "And as soon as possible."[357]

If there is one thing that the Rebbe and Chabad in general are known for, it is their fervent belief in the imminent arrival of Mashiach. Sometimes implicit, but more often explicit,[358] in almost every one of his talks, teachings, and encounters, the Rebbe revealed this cherished, heartfelt aspiration: To see our imperfect world enter into an era of peace and wholeness, devoid of war and suffering, replete with revealed goodness and the pursuit of G-dly knowledge.

Without getting too deep into the finer points of Jewish philosophy and prophecy, Mashiach is the main meta-historical character, both perpetually absent and potentially present at all times, throughout our story of creation and redemption. His inevitable arrival will signal the ultimate redemption and end goal of history, when the world will be made right and the Divine presence will be clear for all to see, here, now, in our world.

According to the Rebbe, this greatest of goals is ours to bring about. From his very first discourse as Rebbe to the final moments of his leadership, he made one thing clear. *If we want Mashiach now, it is up to us.*

Dream On

For the Rebbe, the arrival of Mashiach was a childhood dream. From his earliest days, and despite the immensely challenging times he lived through, he never stopped nursing the dream of Mashiach's arrival. In a letter addressed to Yitzchak Ben-Zvi, the second president of Israel, the Rebbe wrote:

> "From the time when I was a child attending *cheder,* and even earlier than that, there began to take form in my mind a vision of the future

redemption—the redemption of Israel from its last exile, redemption such as would explain the suffering, the decrees, and the massacres of exile..."[359]

In many ways, this vision is what made the Rebbe unique among other towering Jewish figures of our time. Most leaders see their life and impact in terms of their specific generation, but the Rebbe viewed his role through the wider lens of Jewish and world history in its entirety. He saw his generation as a whole, while at the same time also as a small but critical part of a much larger process that would culminate in the ultimate redemption of creation itself, brought about by the cumulative efforts of each and every individual.

Indeed, on the very night he assumed the mantle of Chabad-Lubavitch leadership, 10 Shvat 5711 (1951), in his discourse entitled *Bati L'gani*, the Rebbe emphatically stated that after thousands of years of baby steps and quantum leaps, going all the way back to Adam and Eve in the Garden of Eden, at this very moment in history, "It is up to us to complete the job and usher in the final redemption."[360]

But what exactly does this mean for us, and how does it relate to our individual purpose?

Down and Out

To understand the profound, personal implications of the Rebbe's call to action and where each and every individual fits into the ultimate trajectory of Mashiach's story, we must first delve into two paradigmatic modalities that frame the world's journey from genesis to redemption: *mil'malah l'matah,* from above to below, and *mil'matah l'malah,* from below to above.

These two teleologies frame the story arc of creation and will help us understand the various movements and milestones that lead to the grand drama of the final chapter—and why each soul and the fulfillment of its Divine purpose plays such an essential part in Mashiach's arrival.

As discussed in Chapter 2, the purpose of creation is no less than the marriage of heaven and earth; that is, for G-d's unifying presence to permeate human consciousness.

As the Midrash tells us, "G-d desired to have a dwelling in the lower realms."[361] That is, from among all of the lofty realms, dimensions, and worlds described by the Sages and mystics, G-d chose this physical universe as his ultimate home.

The means to this ultimate end, according to Kabbalah and Chasidut, is the gathering and elevation of Divine sparks that are hidden throughout creation and the circumstances of our everyday lives, thereby revealing G-d's presence and Providence in the world everywhere, always, and to everyone.

According to the Sages, there are two ways for those

sparks to be rescued and redeemed: from the top-down or from the bottom-up.

The first, *mil'malah l'matah*, refers to a process that is initiated from heaven to earth, from G-d to creation and humanity.

In this top-down model, the Divine imposes its truth and will upon the earth and its inhabitants.

This mode can be seen in Torah stories of miracles, catastrophes, and other wondrous displays of Divine force that shaped the world and humanity in explicit and spectacular ways. The Great Flood, the exodus from Egypt, and the subsequent giving of the Torah on Mt. Sinai are three emblematic examples of this dynamic.

The founder of Chabad Chasidut, R. Schneur Zalman, known as the Alter Rebbe, offered an image to illustrate this paradigm of redemption, describing the process as analogous to lit candles drawn to a flaming torch.[362] According to this analogy, the flames are pulled toward a spiritual epicenter, which draws and incorporates them into itself by its sheer, overwhelming power and potency, asserting its truth and centrality rather than inspiring or evoking it from within its indigenous setting. According to this model, the source of holiness is singular and highly focused in one place.

Upside: This process is exceptionally efficient and unquestionably effective.

Downside: This process does not affect the natural environment or host of the flames whatsoever, who themselves remain unrefined as the flame contained within is plucked suddenly and forcefully from its mundane container. The spiritual transformation that emerges from this process is superimposed and therefore ultimately superficial.

Bottoms Up

The second approach to redemption, *mil'matah l'malah*, is initiated from earth to heaven, from creation to Creator. In this bottom-up model, awareness of Divinity in the world is meant to emerge organically from within the context of human perception, experience, striving, and struggle.

In this model, the source of spiritual power and elevation is decentralized and distributed widely throughout the entire world and all of humanity. Accordingly, every one of us becomes a Divine agent to elevate all sparks, in all people, places, times, situations, and objects.

Upside: The elevation process is organic, localized, indigenous, and holistic, thus facilitating a more comprehensive and thorough redemption of the "lower world," because the Divine truth is internally elicited and revealed rather than externally imposed. This approach results in a more authentic, all-encompassing process of whole system transformation.

Downside: This process is much slower and is dependent

on the gradual, emergent, grassroots effort of lamplighters and individuals around the world, committed to elevating the local sparks within every place, culture, and context. In comparison to the overwhelming efficiency of the top-down approach, the bottom-up approach to redemption is much more incremental, unpredictable, and laborious.

Now that we have introduced these two epistemological orientations, we can more productively explore how they relate to our personal lives in the context of the cosmic story of Mashiach, as understood by the Rebbe.

From Revolution to Evolution

Throughout history, according to the teachings of Chabad Chasidut, there has been a gradual shift from the top-down model of redemption and unification to a bottom-up model. This is a paradigmatic shift from revolution to evolution, and it can be seen in two critical contexts— the successive, diasporic movements of the Jewish people from a centralized hub to all corners of the globe,[363] and, as it pertains to individual purpose, in the progressive distribution of spiritual autonomy and free will.

From Adam to Abraham, Moses to Joshua, the judges to the prophets, the kohanim to the rabbis, and the rabbis to every individual, for a majority of human history, the top-down mode was predominant. G-d's presence and authority, when shown, was overwhelming and obvious. For example, when the nation of Israel was first "born," their existence and reality was infused and openly imbued with the supernatural, the miraculous, and the revelatory—from the ten plagues, to the parting of the Red Sea, to manna falling from heaven, to the many miracles that blessed the Jewish people on their formative, forty-year odyssey through the desert.

During these early days of Jewish history, the epistemological result of this overwhelming Divine presence was that, for the individual, the free will that infuses every action with meaning and redemptive potency was eclipsed by Divine fiat. So revealed and overwhelming was G-d's presence in Jewish life, in fact, that deviation from the Divine will had immediate, stark, physical consequences, such as *tzaraat*, the Biblical skin condition brought about by speaking gossip. Socially, religiously, and culturally, this manifested in the uniform and ubiquitous rule of religious law. Put simply, in Biblical times the Jewish people didn't really have much choice to keep the commandments when the consequences for various violations were so concrete, including corporal punishment, and, in more extreme cases of transgression, capital punishment.

That can hardly be called free will. Moreover, even as G-d's overt miracles receded from history, spiritual leaders, from prophets to *kohanim*, were designated as authoritative intermediaries or interpreters of Divine will. This hierarchical model reinforced a passive posture of deference and dependence in the lives of the vast majority of people. But the story does not end there. As history unfolds and humanity experiences progressively greater degrees of free will, there is a concurring realization of the Divine plan for the elevation of—*and from within*—the "lower worlds," through the more difficult but ultimately more meaningful and comprehensive vehicle of individual choice.

On average, this model of redemption may result in innumerably more poor decisions, mistakes, and diminished overall religious adherence. Nevertheless, despite these risks and downsides, the bottom-up approach was the Rebbe's prescription for our time—a time of radical, purpose-driven authenticity that would welcome Mashiach thanks to the cumulative, grassroots efforts of each individual.

Indeed, the Rebbe endorsed this approach precisely because the arrival of Mashiach, which depends on the redemption of the "lowest realms," *requires* the completion of the creation-spanning transition from *mil'malah l'matah* to *mil'matah l'malah*.

For this to happen, redemption must emerge organically from within the lowest, furthest, and most obscure corners of creation.

As the Rebbe said:

Then, when we [constructed a Temple in the Holy Land and thus] seemed to be near the fulfillment of our journey, G-d announced, in effect: This is not yet the final step. True, a G-dly light shines in the Temple in Jerusalem, and from there, it spreads to the entire world, but this is not the objective. The goal is even higher. The goal is not for a fire to glow in just one place and for the entire world to derive benefit from its light; rather, it is that the source of the light itself will reach every place. In every corner of the world, a Divine energy will emanate. As long as there remains one corner where the light does not shine on its own, this is proof that the light is limited. When the boundless light of truth shines, it will illuminate every place and every corner.[364]

Free Bird

Reflecting this final stage of history, the Rebbe insisted that there was one final missing piece of the puzzle called redemption—namely, the distribution and transfer of spiritual responsibility for the state of world redemption from the leader to every individual.

In his very first discourse, the Rebbe stated boldly and emphatically,

> "...We are now very near the approaching footsteps of Mashiach; indeed, we are at the conclusion of this period [of global redemption], and our spiritual task is to complete

the process of drawing down the *Shechinah* [G-d's Presence] within specifically our lowly world."[365]

After presenting his marching orders in this inaugural teaching, the Rebbe framed the aforementioned, final paradigm shift by sharing a colloquial Yiddish phrase: *"Leigt zich nit arayn kayn foigelach in buzem,"* lit., "Do not place birds in your bosom."

This curious phrase traces to antiquity and refers to one who places a bird in their pocket and walks off a cliff, erroneously believing that the wings of another will empower them to fly.[366] The reference was a clear declaration that the time had come for each individual to bear responsibility for their own elevation, as well as the world's. The time for passive dependence on the top-down guidance of spiritual leaders had passed. As the Rebbe elaborated, the traditional interpretation of the verse, *A tzaddik lives by his faith*, was that one's salvation depended on their faith *in the tzaddik*. However, it was now time for each of us to *become the tzaddik*, spread our own wings, and use the full power imparted to us by G-d to do our individual part in bringing Mashiach. Each and every one of us must embrace our role as a partner of G-d, imbued with our own piece of Providence and a sacred mission to become a source of light in our own corner of creation.

Passing the Baton

Nearly forty years after that first paradigm-shifting proclamation, and after countless campaigns and efforts dedicated to the realization of his childhood dream, Mashiach had not yet arrived. At the Purim *farbrengen* in 5747 (1987), the Rebbe sat surrounded by hundreds of Chasidim and began to speak in a low, even tone about the reasons for Mashiach's delay, and our precious role in his ultimate arrival.

> "Regarding the discussion on the subject of redemption, one may wonder: Why the sudden change of emphasis? The subject is not new, G-d forbid...but there has been a change in recent years...At *farbrengens* during the early years, as well as by all the previous Rebbes, this topic was mentioned. But never as a primary focus. Especially not in the same manner as of late, when we specifically select and highlight those Chasidic discourses that explain that the true and ultimate redemption is connected to the actions of every single Jew. In Rambam's words: 'young and old alike,' and as Rambam rules, 'one good deed, speech, or thought could bring salvation to oneself and the entire world.' ...The Talmud, already in its day, stated 'all "end times" for the redemption

> have passed; it now awaits only repentance [which is dependent on the individual].'"

The Rebbe cited numerous "end times" that had been predicted by scholars and Sages throughout Jewish history. Each "end time" had passed without realization, yet the subject of the end of history and the arrival of Mashiach persisted, with renewed permutations spoken as recently as 1906 by the fifth Lubavitcher Rebbe, R. Shalom DovBer, known as the Rebbe Rashab.

> "Now the Talmud states that 'all end times have passed,' yet still the Rebbe Rashab discussed an 'end time' [which did not come to pass].... After that gathering, the issue was not discussed for decades, until my father-in-law, the Rebbe, began his campaign: 'Immediate repentance, immediate redemption,' and he specifically instructed that it be published and disseminated...
>
> This makes our question even stronger: How long must we wait for Mashiach?! There was an end time predicted by the Rebbe, and since then decades have passed? So I searched for an answer. The only explanation I can find is this: The Torah states, 'The leader of the generation is the entire generation.' But this responsibility must now be transferred to 'the generation'—to every individual Jew.

"In the past, the average student relied on the Rebbe [to lead followers toward redemption]. They were a part of his efforts, but they relied on the Rebbe for the results; yet despite this, the redemption did not come. Now, the generation may be spiritually weaker, but at the same time, we are closer to the time of the redemption...This necessitates that we increase our efforts in this matter. What can each individual do? We must expand every effort to publicize to every Jew that by his single deed, by his single word, or by his single thought... his every action can truly bring deliverance to the entire world! So although in the past one relied on the Rebbes and on the end times predicted by them, now that decades have passed since the last 'end time' was predicted, it is obvious that the only thing left to do is to alert every Jew that it is now his personal responsibility, and he must weigh his actions to bring the redemption. There is no alternative...this depends on you, and on you...and on every single man woman and child—and everyone together....."[367]

According to the Rebbe, it is time for each of us to activate our innermost point of holiness and righteousness. No leader, no matter how exalted, can do it for us.[368]

It's All Up to You

Ultimately, the Rebbe saw Jewish history through the lens of a human life. Like a baby, whose first steps and development require constant hands-on attention and reassuring affection, the Jewish people in our national infancy required overt miracles and revealed G-dliness to help us learn to walk out of Egypt. This spiritual caretaking continued as Israel grew up through Divine revelations, and under the wing of *kohanim* and prophets, judges and kings. But as time passed, the Jewish people continued to mature spiritually; along with this maturation, the revealed Presence and Providence of G-d diminished correspondingly. This journey has created the conditions for us to grow into our own faith and develop a connection with G-d and a spiritual worldview that comes from within, without external pressure or even revelation. This has given us the exceptional opportunity to manifest the ultimate, deepest, and highest level of faith from the bottom up, within the context of our own daily lives. For all the struggle and strife it entails, this opportunity and its actualization is the ultimate expression of *mil'matah l'malah*, and the remaining, unrealized precondition of Mashiach's arrival.

"For so long as a Jew's compliance with the will of G-d is externally motivated—however commendable such motivation is in itself—it is not yet quite complete," wrote the Rebbe in a letter.[369]

Indeed, it is clear from many public talks and pro-
nouncements during this period that the Rebbe was
consciously preparing his followers to take the baton from
his hand.

Through it all, one radical message consistently rings
loud and clear: We cannot rely on "help" from without. We
must find the eternal light within our own souls and ignite
it, not once but over and over again, through good deeds,
the cultivation of a providential perspective, and purposeful, passionate expressions of holiness and faith. *If we want
Mashiach now, it is up to us.*

"What else can I do so that all Jewish people should
agitate, truthfully cry out, and effectively bring Mashiach
in actuality…. We are still in exile…and, more importantly,
in an internal exile with regards to serving G-d," cried out
the Rebbe in the spring of 1991. "The only thing I can do
is give it over to you: I have done my part. From now on,
you must do all that you can."[370]

It is precisely this fractal distribution of Divine responsibility that defines the paradigmatic shift the Rebbe
sought to inspire and strengthen within each individual,
the Jewish people, and humanity as a whole. It is now up
to each of us to redeem our corner of the world as part of a
providentially ordained bootstrap effort to bring history to
its glorious, final fruition. Each of us, one by one, step by
step, spark by spark, will do this our own way, in our own

place and time. But the goal is the same—by embracing our Divine purpose, we will ultimately, finally, welcome G-d home to His heavenly garden of earthly delights.

With this in mind, body, soul, and heart, throughout his life, every day, in every way, the Rebbe reminded us: We are no longer waiting for Mashiach. *Mashiach is waiting for us.*

Afterword

L ATE ONE NIGHT, TWO hours into an audience with the Rebbe, the Israeli diplomat Yehuda Avner asked, "Rebbe, what is it that you seek to accomplish?"

"Yehuda," said the Rebbe, "look there, on the shelf. What do you see?"

"A candle," he replied.

"No, it's not a candle; it's just a lump of wax with a string down the middle. When does this lump of wax become a candle? When you bring a flame to the wick."

His voice rising, the Rebbe continued in a Talmudic sing-song: "The wax is the body of the human being, and the wick is the soul. The flame is the fire of Torah.

"When the soul is ignited by the flame of Torah, that's when the person becomes a candle, achieving the purpose for which he was created.

"This is what I try to do—to help every man and woman achieve the purpose for which they were created."

An hour later, with the sun about to rise and the meeting drawing to a close, Avner asked, "So has the Rebbe lit my candle?"

"No," answered the Rebbe quietly.

"I have given you the match. *Only you can light your own candle.*"[371]

The Rebbe would often cite a teaching of the Mishnah,[372] "*Hamaaseh hu ha'ikar,*" which means that the essential thing is the deed, not abstract study. Otherwise, teachings and words, no matter how beautiful, wise, or aesthetic, are *devarim beteilim,* "empty talk," and their power to move and inspire action is wasted.

Spiritual teachings, no matter how inspiring or wise they are, must never be allowed to remain in the realm of thought alone. Truth seeks tangible expression in the world and in our lives.

Books, like candles, are exceptional and essential tools for illuminating our lives and our world, at least in potential. But every book needs a reader to open it and act on the ideas within for its light to enter the world. Similarly, words and ideas also contain great power to motivate and transform people—but only if they are internalized and taken seriously enough to be acted upon. If a word remains inert on a page or trapped inside our heads, it is as bright as an unlit candle. Its true illuminating potential is only fulfilled when it is taken deeply into the core of our very being.

Essentially, this collection of principles and practices on purpose is a book of matches.

But remember: *Only you can light your own candle.*

In the end, this book's success depends on how well you integrate its wisdom into your life, thereby shining your unique light into the world.

It is my sincere prayer that each of you, in your own way, is ignited by these teachings, bringing them into your lives and relationships through continued reflection, passionate conversation, and practical action. May we all merit to see the infinite light and Divine goodness radiating out from within ourselves, within each other, and within the world, always and forever!

Acknowledgments

I would like to acknowledge the following individuals:

Rabbi Zalman Shmotkin, the executive director and driving force behind the legendary Jewish website, Chabad.org, for his support for this book.

Rabbi Meir Simcha Kogan, director of Chabad.org, for his constant wisdom and patience.

The editorial team at Kehot Publication Society for their rigor and professionalism. In particular, Rabbis Yosef B. Friedman, Dovid Olidort, Avraham D. Vaisfiche, Yirmi Berkowitz and Mendel Laine.

Rabbi's Simon Jacobson, Yossi Paltiel, Yossi Jacobson, Moshe Genuth, Aaron Leib Raskin, Yanky Raskin, Levi Raskin, Naftali Silberberg, Mordechai Dinerman for their valuable insights and for directing me to relevant source material relating to the Rebbe's philosophy on finding one's purpose in life.

Shmuel Klatzkin for his expert translation of numerous

letters and talks of the Rebbe from the original, included in the book.

To the entire team at JLI (Jewish Learning Institute), for generously sharing valuable source material that contributed to the research of the book.

My supremely gifted editor, Paul Schrag, who is one of the kindest and gentlest collaborators I have had the privilege of working with.

My editor, R. Eden Perlstein, a man of many talents, whose unique ability to crystalize and contextualize has enriched this book immeasurably.

Chanie Kaminker of Hannabi Creative, for the creative cover design. This is our sixth book together and I look forward to future collaborations.

My dear and esteemed brother, Yekusiel, for co-sponsoring this book. His constant care and friendship are truly one of life's greatest gifts, for which I am profoundly grateful.

My dear and esteemed friend Sacha Gaydamak for co-sponsoring this book in honour of his beloved wife, Tanya, and their beautiful children. I am profoundly grateful for their unwavering friendship.

My dear and esteemed friends Helly and Tatiana Nahmad and their beautiful family for their enveloping love and friendship and for co-sponsoring this book in honor of a special man I was privileged to know and cherish dearly, Ezra Nahmad, of blessed memory.

My wife and life partner, Chana, whose unwavering support and clarifying insight helped facilitate and improve his book, and whose depth of character and companionship is one of life's greatest blessings.

I would like to express, as well, our gratitude to G-d for our beautiful children, Geula, Dov, Ester and Zelig, who bring unlimited joy to our lives.

My dear parents, Rabbi Yosef Yitzchak and Hindy Kalmenson, my beloved grandmother Sara Shanowitz, and my dear father- and mother-in-law, Rabbi Yosef and Tamara Katzman, for their constant counsel, love, and support.

My life and that of my family is greatly enriched by their living example of Jewish and Chasidic values.

A few years ago my maternal grandfather, Rabbi Sholom Ber Shanowitz, of blessed memory, returned his soul to its maker. His love and passion for Torah study and his zest for life were legendary and his memory serves as a constant source of inspiration to our entire family who aspire to emulate his example.

My dear brothers and sisters, Chanie, Nechama Dina, Menucha, Yekusiel, and Moishy. I feel so blessed to have you in my life.

Lastly, I would like to express a profound debt of gratitude to the Rebbe, of righteous memory, whose example, wisdom, and teachings continue to inspire and guide me daily.

Mendel Kalmenson

Endnotes

1 pubmed.ncbi.nlm.nih.gov/26630073

2 www.ncbi.nlm.nih.gov/pmc/articles/PMC2740716

3 sleep.biomedcentral.com/articles/10.1186/s41606-017-0015-6

4 www.forbes.com/sites/nelldebevoise/2023/10/06/
the-power-of-purpose-how-ikigai-can-help-us-live-longer

5 www.midus.wisc.edu/newsletter/purpose.pdf

6 journals.sagepub.com/doi/abs/10.1177/0956797614531799

7 www.washingtonpost.com/health/boosting-our-sense-of-meaning-in-
life-is-an-often-overlooked-longevity-ingredient/2020/12/31/84871d32-
29d4-11eb-8fa2-06e7cbb145c0_story.html

8 www.wbur.org/hereandnow/2019/08/06/
neil-pasricha-retirement-happiness-equation-work

9 www.ted.com/talks/dan_buettner_how_to_live_to_be_100

10 pubmed.ncbi.nlm.nih.gov/22811911

11 archive.nytimes.com/www.nytimes.com/books/first/s/shenk-data.html

12 www.nytimes.com/2018/01/01/upshot/finding-purpose-for-a-good-life-
but-also-a-healthy-one.html

13 *Tanya*, ch. 37.

14 As the Rebbe put it: Every person was born to a mission in life that is
distinctly, uniquely, and exclusively their own. No one—not even the
greatest of souls—can take his or her place. No person who ever lived
or ever will live can fulfill that particular aspect of G-d's purpose in
creation in his stead.

15 See *Torat Menachem – Hitvaaduyot* 5748, vol. 3, p. 41; *Likkutei Sichot*, vol.
2, p. 601ff. See also *Torat Menachem – Hitvaaduyot* 5743, vol. 4, p. 1974.

16   *Teshurah Kotlarsky-Hertz* 5774, p. 39; Chabad.org/133497

17   I heard this from R. Chaim Shalom Deitsch. See also: mishpacha.
      com/master-of-soul-speak During his inaugural discourse, the
      Rebbe made reference to this sentiment of inadequacy, as well—see
      here:Chabad.org/1102138

18   www.bretthall.org/an-anthropic-universe

19   Communal letter of 14 Kislev 5714, Chabad.org/4831371;
      Chabad.org/2187392

20   *Sanhedrin* 37a.

21   Chabad.org/2987770; see chabad.org/1692239.

22   Chabad.org/2987771

23   Genesis 1:28.

24   Chabad.org/1861674

25   *Gedulat Hatzadikim*, p. 21.

26   See beginning of *Bereishit Rabbah*; *Sefer Hasichot* 5748, vol. 2, p. 589.

27   Chabad.org/2188391

28   See *Zohar*, III:53b; *Gur Aryeh*, beginning of Genesis, citing Radak.

29   See, for example, *Likkutei Torah, Bechukotai* 43c.

30   *Keter Shem Tov* §194; Chabad.org/3432275

31   Psalms 107:5.

32   To be sure, there were certain texts and teachers throughout Jewish
      history who alluded to this approach, thus providing the seed for this
      path and paradigm of Torah interpretation, which was later brought
      to full fruition and elucidation by the Baal Shem Tov and the Chasidic
      masters.

33   Chabad.org/1107

34   Genesis 3:9.

35   *Likkutei Sichot*, vol. 1, p. 73.

36   *Sanhedrin* 37a.

37   Ibid.

38   *Mishneh Torah, Hilchot Teshuvah* 3:4.

39   From a letter of the Rebbe dated 20 Kislev 5745.

40   *From Day to Day: Young Scholar's Daily Calendar & Encyclopedia* (5704).

41   Chabad.org/1858362

42   See *A Chassidisher Derher*, Iyar 5775, interview with R. Itche Meir
      Gurary, p. 70.

43   This does not mean that we are made to rule over creation like
      appointed monarchs. Rather, we are all sacred custodians tasked with

elevating our corner of the world, and by extension the entirety of creation.

44   Chabad.org/1861674

45   Chabad.org/386812

46   Chabad.org/4372

47   *Avot* 4:2.

48   Chabad.org/71930

49   And a mission whose total costs exceeded twenty-four billion dollars!

50   An English edition of this *sichah*, with the Rebbe's edits, can be found in *Teshurah Kaplan 19 Shvat 5784*; Chabad.org/947466

51   *Midrash Rabbah, Bereishit* 87:7; *Midrash Tanchuma, Vayeishev* 8–9; *Zohar* I:222a; *Sotah* 36b, quoted in Rashi to Genesis 39:11.

52   The following rendering was inspired by an article written by R. Yosef Yitzchak Jacobson, accessible here: Chabad.org/ 339995. It is based on an address by the Lubavitcher Rebbe given on 19 Kislev 5721 (December 8, 1960) and published in *Sichot Kodesh*.

53   *Bava Metzia* 84a and *Bava Batra* 58a. Cf. *Tanya*, Iggeret Hakodesh 7.

54   *Igrot Kodesh by R. Yosef Yitzchak*, vol. 6, p. 295.

55   Ezekiel 8:12; see *Sefer Haarachim Chabad*, vol. 2, p. 277.

56   *Sefer Hamaamarim 5696*, p. 120.

57   Chabad.org/80721; see *Shomer Emunim* (R. A. Roth), ch. 17, on *Hashgachah Pratit*.

58   Soon after he undertook the leadership of the Chasidic community, the Alter Rebbe delivered the following teaching: [It is written:] *"A man's steps are made firm by G-d.* When a Jew arrives at a particular place, this is for the purpose of doing a mitzvah—be it a mitzvah between man and man or between man and G-d.

   A Jew is an agent of [G-d] above, and wherever an agent is, he derives his power from the Sender. The superiority of souls over angels [in this regard] lies in the fact that [G-d confers His agency to] the souls through the Torah [*Hayom Yom*, 10 Tamuz; Chabad.org/3316640].

59   *Hayom Yom*, 3 Elul; Chabad.org/3316880

60   *Likkutei Dibburim*, vol. 4, p. 1131 (2021); Chabad.org/377509

61   The Rebbe included this crucial lesson in his first published work, a compendium of daily meditations called *Hayom Yom*, and he noted at a *farbrengen* years later that he had repeated that particular lesson over a thousand times over the years. *Shabbat Parshat Shemor 5743 (Hashmatot)*.

62   *Igrot Kodesh*, vol. 15, p. 443.

63   The Rebbe's response from Iyar 5740 (1980) can be found at Lahak. org/2938448, p. 42.

64 www.statista.com/statistics/273016/
    number-of-mobile-broadband-subscriptions-worldwide-since-2007

65 www.nytimes.com/books/first/s/shenk-data.html

66 hbr.org/2012/10/biG-data-the-management-revolution

67 This paralysis was predicted and dubbed "future shock" by writer,
    futurist, and businessman Alvin Toffler, native of Brooklyn, NY, and
    son of Polish Jewish immigrants. Toffler coined this term while working
    as a researcher at IBM in the 1960s; he defined it as anxiety and
    paralysis brought on by "too much change in too short a period of time."
    Later, in a book titled after the syndrome he predicted, Toffler said he
    believed that global information systems, along with the acceleration
    and preponderance of knowledge, would dramatically disrupt our sense
    of the world and our place in it. The results, as he described, would be
    "shattering stress and disorientation."

    These predictions began to come true during the rise of the Internet in
    the 1990s, which coincided with a growing number of research reports
    emphasizing the resulting mental and physical illness allegedly caused
    by information overload.

    Today, future shock syndrome impacts nearly every person living on the
    planet.

    Source: *Future Shock*, Alvin Toffler

68 Today, we have many names for future shock. Researchers and theorists
    refer to it alternatively as information overabundance, infobesity,
    infoglut, data smog, information pollution, information fatigue, social
    media overload, information anxiety, infostress, infoxication, and
    communication overload.

69 This was the Rebbe's message to a couple working in the army:

    "...Every person is an emissary of G-d to do good and increase good
    in the world. This is typically not accomplished through revolutions
    or roaring self-sacrifice, but, rather, through...activism to help those
    in *your surroundings,* even if most of these activities are labeled by the
    world as..."insignificant." May G-d grant you and your husband success
    in bringing the potential given to you to actuality." (*Heichal Menachem*,
    vol. 3, p. 44.)

70 In the words of *Tanya* (ch. 37): "...Each [soul] is related [to] the vitality
    of [a certain] part of the entire world. This [part of the world] depends
    on their soul for its elevation... [By using the objects of this world that
    one's body and vital soul need for the sake of serving G-d, one elevates
    his portion of the world.]"

71 Chabad.org/4449212; see also *Seeds of Wisdom*, vol. 1, p. 156.

72 *Baba Metzia* 71a.

73 But how can these sorts of efforts—immediate, personal, and local—heal the entire world?

Former British Prime Minister Margaret Thatcher helped answer this daunting question when describing her decades as Conservative Member of Parliament for Finchley, a predominantly Jewish neighborhood in North London. Thatcher shared that in thirty years of serving this neighborhood and community, not once was she approached by a person in need, thanks to the Jewish community's many and varied welfare programs geared at supporting those in need.

If only every neighborhood and community operated in the same way, the well-being and stability of the greater whole would be overwhelmingly improved.

74 Chabad.org/3177278

75 www.5tjt.com/shliach-from-montana-the-power-of-one

76 Derher.org/wp-content/uploads/2020/10/94-sivan-5780-interveiw-with-rabbi-berel-lipsker.pdf.

77 *Seeds of Wisdom*, vol. 2, p. 46.

78 A similar perspective was offered to a new chaplain on a university campus who was feeling overwhelmed by the magnitude of his role there. "Rebbe," he asked during *yechidut*, "How am I, one individual, supposed to reach the seven thousand Jewish students who attend my university?!"

The Rebbe replied, "Your job is not to work with seven thousand. Your job is to work with seven. Those seven will reach another seven, who in turn will reach another seven, and so on." Chabad.org/4449212; *Seeds of Wisdom*, vol. 1, p. 139.

79 Genesis 40:7.

80 Exodus 2:11-12.

81 Chabad.org/4167368.

82 Jemcentral.org/wp-content/uploads/2023/08/551.-Eikev-5783.pdf.

83 Chabad.org/3358107

84 From an article about Mr. Eli Lipsker, published in Kikar Shabbat; see also: www.jewishpress.com/news/breaking-news/farewell-to-chabad-lubavitch-chassidic-master-of-melodies-eli-lipsker-zl-76/2017/02/28/

85 myencounterblog.com/?p=2462;Chabad.org/3570929

86 rabbisacks.org/videos/rabbi-sacks-on-finding-purpose-jinsider

87 Chabad.org/375092

88 Chabad.org/395099

89 Chabad.org/115228

90 Proverbs 3:9.

91 Rashi, ad loc.; Chabad.org/16374

92 The full quote from the Midrash reads as follows: "It states: *Honor the L-rd with all of your possessions.* [This means] with whatever He has graced you. [For example], if you have a beautiful voice, lead the communal prayers. Chiya, the nephew of R. Elazar Hakappar, had a beautiful voice. R. Elazar would tell him, 'Chiya, my son, rise and honor the L-rd with what He has graced you" [*Yalkut Shimoni, Melachim* I §221].

93 Chabad.org/4778545

94 *Kos shel brachah* (lit., cup of blessing) refers to the Rebbe's custom of distributing to thousands of people small portions of the wine he used to make *Havdalah.*

95 www.meaningfullife.com/natan-yellin-mur Chabad.org/3046548; Chabad.org/3046553

96 *Tanya,* ch. 27.

97 Chabad.org/60468

98 *Likkutei Sichot,* vol. 3, pp. 747-750.

99 To learn more about the Tefillin Campaign, see Chabad.org/k1643

100 jemcentral.org/wp-content/uploads/2023/02/528.-Terumah-5783.pdf

101 jemcentral.org/wp-content/uploads/2023/01/521.-Vayechi-5783.pdf.

102 Chabad.org/3240787

103 Chabad.org/1872939

104 *Shabbat* 77b.

105 Chabad.org/ 3316117

106 Moreover, an individual can learn to identify his main personal mission in life by noting which of his tasks encounters the most challenging obstacles. The explanation is that since this particular task is his unique mission, the evil inclination works overtime to obstruct its successful fulfillment. See *Likkutei Sichot,* vol. 2, p. 347.

107 However, the Rebbe did also point out that "once the power of the animal soul has been used for good, the 'unusable' aspects of the person—the selfish motivations, etc.—must be jettisoned." See *Teshurah Kaplan 19 Shvat 5784,* p. 42.

108 As told to me by R. Levi Avtzon; he heard it from the protagonist, who is now a renowned Talmudic scholar. For more examples, see *Positivity Bias,* ch. 17.

109 As told to me by R. Naftali Loewenthal.

110 You can hear R. Lipskar telling this story at Chabad.org/930194 (Sensitivity (JEM)).

111 The Rebbe elaborated on the uniquely compromising conditions of

prison, wherein a person is stripped of their most basic human gift and capacity: their sense of agency and free will. It is for this reason that, as a rule, the Torah does not include prison as part of its varied options to achieve penitence and rehabilitation in the case of sin. Given the aforementioned diminishing conditions of prison, those who find themselves there are seen to possess great reservoirs of inner strength in order to help them overcome their severe external limitations. Hence, if the current era is considered one of exile in relation to the ultimate redemption, a prisoner is considered to be in an "exile within an exile."

112   In an interview regarding this momentous encounter, R. Lipskar shared some moving details about the Rebbe's extraordinary care and sensitivity to the visiting inmates. In his words: "When I brought the group of prisoners to the Rebbe for Shabbat, I had arranged for a group of *yeshivah* students to reserve a table for the group at the *farbrengen*, but R. Groner [the Rebbe's secretary] came looking for me before the *farbrengen* began and said that the Rebbe instructed that they shouldn't sit together, and he would also not give us a bottle of spirits [as was the custom for groups of guests], 'although they were more worthy than anyone else,' so as not to draw attention to them [and cause them to feel uncomfortable, G-d forbid]." Beyond the Rebbe's sensitivity to a group of individuals who many in society look down on, the Rebbe's words, "Although they were more worthy than anyone else," conveys his belief that those who are given the greatest challenges are the ones who possess the greatest spiritual potential and powers to help overcome their challenges.

113   *Yoma* 86b; Chabad.org/5446501

114   *Megillah* 6b.

115   As told to me by this woman.

116   myencounterblog.com/?p=2538.

117   During his talk on *Shabbat Parshat Naso* 5745, the Rebbe shared the same message with the group of inmates mentioned above. In the Rebbe's words: "Having spent time in prison himself, upon his release, he is empowered to fulfil his mission in life to an even greater degree than before (for 'all descents are designed to bring us to greater heights'). [This is the case] in a number of ways...the second way is that he is now best positioned to influence others [who are contemplating a life of crime] not to make the same mistakes he made, since he is speaking from experience..."

118   *Seeds of Wisdom*, vol. 2, p. 93; Chabad.org/2627353.

119   See Chabad.org/5559665

120   To be sure, the Rebbe did not take an exclusionary approach to converts or conversion, G-d forbid. To the contrary, once someone chose to convert and went through the proper process, the Rebbe welcomed

them with tremendous warmth and respect. As he once said to a convert during Sunday Dollars: "G-d loves you [the convert] more than he does me [the Rebbe]." Perhaps the Rebbe was alluding to the fact that the Torah commands us to *love our fellow* only once but instructs us to *love the convert* no less than thirty-two times. Chabad.org/1317511

121　As heard from this woman.

122　See *Derher*, Iyar 5778, p. 13, "Not Your Calling,"

123　From an unsent letter of the Rebbe, dated 12 Adar II 5741 (1981).

124　This was the truth shared by R. Akiva during a time when being Jewish had become dangerous under the oppressive Roman Empire. Despite the decree that Jewish people were forbidden to study Torah, R. Akiva had been seen convening gatherings in public and studying Torah with those who arrived.

　　　Fearing for himself and his fellow Jews, one man approached and asked, "Akiva, are you not afraid of the government?"

　　　R. Akiva replied with a parable:

　　　A fox was walking along a river and saw fish rushing about as if in danger.

　　　He asked the fish, "What are you fleeing?"

　　　"The nets that the humans spread for us," they replied.

　　　"Why don't you come out onto the dry land? We'll live together, as my ancestors lived with your ancestors," the fox proposed.

　　　"Are you the one of whom it is said that you are the wisest of animals?" the fish asked coldly. "You are not wise but foolish! If we have cause for fear in our environment of life, how much more so in the environment of our death?!"

　　　"The same applies to us," R. Akiva summarized. "If now, when we sit and study the Torah, of which it is said, *For it is your life and the lengthening of your days*, such is our situation, how much more so if we neglect it?"

　　　Brachot 61b; Chabad.org/5299950

125　From a letter the Rebbe sent in 1975. An excerpt can be found at Chabad.org/4405203

126　*Hitkashrut*, Issue 1235.

127　Chabad.org/4597984

128　Years later, after his father had come to accept his gravitation toward Chabad and its customs, the Rebbe encouraged him to adopt the Chabad customs that called to him.

129　Chabad.org/2858781

130　collive.com/the-rabbi-was-asked-to-remain-behind/

131 *Likkutei Sichot*, vol. 24, pp. 143-144.

132 *Shabbat Parshat Tzav* 5733 (1973); Chabad.org/5989479

133 *Likkutei Dibburim*, vol. 2, p. 551; Chabad.org/2716881

134 *Igros Kodesh*, vol. 28, p. 18.

135 As heard from R. Shlomo Zarchi.

136 *Igrot Kodesh by R. Yosef Yitzchak*, vol 6, p. 295.

137 While R. Yosef Yitzchak does not specify siblings, it stands to reason that the same principle of specific Divine Providence applies in relation to them, as well.

138 Exodus 20:12; Deuteronomy 5:16.

139 See Zohar III:91b.

140 Chabad.org/4783733

141 It is important to note that if a parent, sibling, or spouse is abusive, we are not obligated to maintain that connection. To the contrary, there is an obligation to end the relationship if it compromises our safety and well-being. In fact, the Torah not only allows for divorce, but it mandates it under certain circumstances.

142 *Likkutei Torah*, Emor 38d. See also *Yonat Eilem*, ch. 5, and *Likkutei Sichot*, vol. 30, p. 286.

143 R. David Aaron, *Endless Light: The Ancient Path of the Kabbalah to Love, Growth, and Spiritual Power* (Simon and Schuster, 1997), pp. 37-38.

144 This is the deeper meaning behind the veiling ritual that occurs just prior to a Jewish wedding ceremony, in which the groom places a veil over the face of his bride. When he does so, he is declaring, "I will love and respect all of you, including those aspects I have yet to discover."

145 This is reflected later, when it is Leah, not Rachel, who gives birth to the lion's share of Jacob's children, who would become the fathers of Jewish people. Poignantly, it would also be Leah, not Rachel, who would be buried at Jacob's side in Hebron.

146 Chabad.org/392392

147 *The Letter and the Spirit*, vol. 3, p. 378.

148 uh.edu/news-events/stories/2023/january-2023/011123.php.

149 www.theatlantic.com/ideas/archive/2019/02/religion-workism-making-americans-miserable/583441

150 This new paradigm dominates especially among so-called millennials, the world's dominant age category at 1.8 billion people, who grew up during the rise of workism in the 1980s and '90s. This massive age group, characterized by a predilection for delaying marriage and other major life decisions, indicated strongly in a recent survey that while purpose was their priority in life, it was foremost to be found in work and personal achievement, not family. Among this group and others,

family is increasingly characterized as a so-called "capstone," with family and children being reserved until after a person has achieved sufficient career success.

Source: www.deseret.com/2023/2/2/23574501/ money-marriage-careers-parenting-pew-research.

151 *Bava Metzia* 71a.

152 *Petakim Mishulchano Shel Harabi*, vol. 2, p. 168.

153 Chabad.org/395795

154 *Teshurah Telzner*, Adar II 5774.

155 Truly, he earned the title applied uniquely to Chabad-Lubavitch Rebbes, Nasi, a word that combines leader and king. The title is not merely honorary; it denotes the true complexity and magnitude of their roles.

156 Chabad.org/2676615 from 16:20.

157 As recounted in Genesis 16, when Sarah saw that she could not bear children, she offered her handmaiden Hagar to Abraham, who would then provide him with a child.

158 See Rashi, Genesis 21:10.

159 Ibid. v. 14.

160 This rendering is inspired by a talk given by the Rebbe on *Shabbat Parshat Chayei Sarah* 5738 (1977).

161 Today, approximately four thousand years after his passing, more than half of the planet's population still attribute their spiritual heritage to this man!

162 Genesis 18:19.

163 jemcentral.org/wp-content/uploads/2022/09/504.-Ki-Seitzei-5782-2.pdf.

164 The term "foreign thoughts," *machashavah zarah* in Hebrew, typically refers to inappropriate or unholy thoughts. Notably, in this story and on other occasions, the Rebbe applied this term to what might be considered noble or spiritual desires in instances where they serve to detract or distract from one's essential purpose in life.

165 "Sometimes, a person can be discontent with the place he is in and look for another, "better" place. Remember that G-d put you there with a special mission.

"There is no running away from G-d (a lesson we learn from the story of Jonah)... You will have to fulfill the *shlichut* anyway; there is no need to look for a better place..."

Simchat Torah 5715.

166 Igrot Kodesh, vol. 26, p. 76.

167 "They should dedicate themselves to the community's good, [because] it is most likely that their chances for success in this are greater when

the educator is a child of the country of the students who require his guidance and influence, as he knows the dispositions of their soul, having grown and having been educated among them. None of this is present in an educator sent from another country and community."

168   Chabad.org/5707391

169   The Rebbe offered similar clarity to a young man from Melbourne, Australia, whose role in the local *yeshivah* had proven critically beneficial for the students there, and yet he desired to relocate to a yeshivah in New York, where he felt he would receive a superior education. The Rebbe wrote to this young man's superior at the *yeshivah*, who had supported this young man's relocation and was in a position of influence over him:

"...He explains in his letter what a good and upright thing it would be for him to leave behind his good portion [in life], which Providence from above has orchestrated for him to [merit to] help strengthen and develop the [local] *yeshivah*. Instead, he wishes to seek 'great and wondrous' things overseas, etc.

"His further point that [relocating] will lead to an increased knowledge of Chasidut—even were it true that it would only be possible to do so by going overseas, I am still doubtful (and this is a doubt that is a near-certainty) as to what would be better for *him*: fulfilling the mission of Supernal Providence in the service of Yeshivat Ohalei Yosef Yitzchak [the local *yeshivah*], or to become a more knowledgeable expert in the revealed Torah and Chasidut than he is now.

"And in particular, since at the beginning of his letter to me, he cited the Alter Rebbe's teaching that through charity (which includes spiritual charity as well) one's mind and heart become refined a thousandfold, then the one hour that he studies in Australia, whether in the revealed Torah or in Chasidut, combined with his involvement with the matters above, will bring the success of a thousand hours in another place, since there he would not have the merit of that involvement." Igrot Kodesh, vol. 11, p. 33.

170   Chabad.org/2387581; collive.com/weekly-moment-with-the-rebbe-218

171   myencounterblog.com/wp-content/uploads/2018/05/279.-Behar-Bechukosai-5778.pdf.

172   Chabad.org/2861908

173   Years later, while studying at a seminary in Crown Heights, Adeena had a chance to meet the Rebbe while accompanying her father for yechidut. After greeting her father, the Rebbe turned to Adeena and asked, "Are you still angry with me?"

Deeply embarrassed, she replied, "Well, I didn't know that I was angry with you."

"Weren't you angry about the letter?" the Rebbe asked, concerned that Adeena had held a grudge over the Rebbe's letter explaining why he forbade her family from moving to Israel.

Adeena replied that she was not angry, of course, but that she was deeply touched that he cared so much about her feelings all those years later.

174   This message of the Rebbe helped change the trajectory of another great Rebbe who sought the Rebbe's blessing, R. Avraham Friedman, the Rebbe of Sadigur.

As recounted by Gedalya Schreiber in an interview:

"During the summer of 1980, I took the opportunity to visit the Lubavitcher Rebbe as part of the entourage of R. Avraham Friedman, the Sadigura Rebbe. The conversation that followed was conducted in Yiddish with phrases of Hebrew being interjected from time to time. The Rebbe began by inquiring about the Sadigura Rebbe's institutions and his plans for the future. The Sadigura Rebbe replied that most of his schools were in Bnei Brak while his synagogue was in Tel Aviv, so he was planning to move to Bnei Brak in order to be closer to his institutions.

"But if you move to Bnei Brak, what will become of the Jews of Tel Aviv?" the Rebbe asked. "If all the Rebbes move away, they will be abandoned."

This argument touched the Sadigura Rebbe, who ended up remaining in Tel Aviv until he reached his twilight years. And even then, he made a point of returning regularly to help the community there. Chabad.org/4445925

175   Col.org.il/news/123070.

176   *Igrot Kodesh*, vol. 4, p. 480.

177   Chabad.org/4435339

178   Exodus 2:11-12.

179   Meaningfullife.com/shemot-care/

180   As our Sages teach: *"B'makom she'ein ish hishtadel lihyot ish*—In a place where there are no men, strive to be a man" *Avot* 2:25.

181   *Moed Katan* 9b (Chabad.org/5448186); Shulchan Aruch Admor Hazaken, Hilchot Talmud Torah 4:3.

182   *Seeds of Wisdom*, vol. 1, p. 160.

183   Torat Menachem, vol. 52, p. 138ff. (Chabad.org/5989039).

184   *Sippurim Meichadar Harabbi*, p. 48.

185   When the chief rabbi of Romania came to meet with the Rebbe, he noticed many people waiting for a private audience. After a few minutes with the Rebbe, he started to draw their conversation to a close.

"I don't want to take up too much of your time," he said.

The Rebbe replied with a question: "How many Jews are there in Romania?"

"Sixty thousand," the rabbi answered.

"Then we have as much time as is necessary for sixty thousand Jews."

186   *Torat Menachem – Hitvaaduyot* 5744, vol. 2, p. 1254.

187   *Mishneh Torah, Hilchot Teshuvah* 3:4.

188   jemedia.org/email/newsletter/My_Encounter/4-5-14.pdf; the full letter can be accessed at Chabad.org/2456771

189   This same principle was shared by the Rebbe with R. Nison Gordon, a writer, who was reconsidering his vocation because of the burden of his responsibilities.

"...since Divine Providence has given you opportunities to influence many people, by which I mean those who read your articles, and every opportunity given to a person requires him to utilize it completely as a part of the fulfillment of his role in the world. As the Mishnah teaches: "I was created to serve my Maker." In assigning that role, G-d does not come to vex His creatures with impossible burdens, but, rather, gives them the powers necessary to fulfill the task."

190   Deuteronomy 8:17.

191   Ibid. v. 18.

192   Psalms 37:23.

193   Deuteronomy 30:15.

194   Ibid. v. 19.

195   *Torat Menachem – Hitvaaduyot* 5744, vol. 3, p. 1439.

196   Chabad.org/924216

197   Chabad.org/79954

198   Myencounterblog.com/?p=4155.

199   *The Letter and the Spirit*, vol. 3.

200   The Rebbe further elaborated on another aspect of this point, saying:

"In this sense, I trust that your election as a Yale trustee will be meaningful also in that it will show that one could be a believing and practicing Jew and at the same time hold the highest honors in the society at large; that not only is the one not incompatible with the other, but to the contrary, for the Torah way, in addition to being the Jewish way of life, and a must for its own sake, is also the channel to receive G-d's blessings in every aspect of daily life.

"As one who is active in education, it is superficial to emphasize to you that instruction by example is much more effective than by sermon or precept. May G-d grant that you should be a living and inspiring example to others."

201 Similarly, the Rebbe helped guide R. Dr. Naftali Berg, who had enjoyed great success in his scientific career, working for prestigious organizations such as the famed Harry Diamond Laboratory, also known as Army Research Labs, a government research and development hub at the Pentagon. His prestige being what it was, R. Dr. Berg was continually beckoned to work in the private sector and had been offered opportunities to work on US government projects in Israel.

Berg, however, would always ask the Rebbe before making any decision large or small, and he was told repeatedly that he should remain in the public sector. He once explained that as a religious Jew holding a prestigious government position in America, he would have a greater influence—both on Jews who were making their way to Judaism as well as non-Jews—than in any other place.

Years later, a fellow Jewish professor overheard a pair of Jewish teenagers talking excitedly about a great Jewish scientist who wore a full beard and *tzitzit* at the Pentagon. "If he can do it at the Pentagon," they concluded, "then no Jew should be ashamed of being different anywhere."

202 Chabad.org/1899569

203 Later, after he read an article elaborating on how the professor had achieved a new, privileged position, the Rebbe wrote to him and his wife, saying:

"Supreme Providence has chosen you to be special messengers to bring the word of G-d to those circles where others could not have had access to, or at any rate, could not have had the same effectiveness and success. I am referring to the academic and scientific circles which wield considerable influence on Jewish youth, particularly in this day and age. More specifically, on young men and women going into scientific careers, who are yet to establish families of their own. In other words, they represent not individuals but family units, and the beneficiaries will become the benefactors, in the way of a chain reaction." Chabad.org/1899571

204 In the following letter, thanking a Jew for a donation, the Rebbe adds yet another dimension to the demand that every Jew use their influence to its utmost.

"In the present days, approaching Shavuot, the Festival of Mattan Torah, I take this opportunity of sharing a timely thought with you in connection with an area which is sometimes overlooked. I refer to the requirement of the Torah that Jews should not only observe all its Commandments in their own life but should also promote the so-called

Seven Noahide Laws among the Gentiles for the betterment of human society and human life in general.

"Those well-known seven laws, with all their ramifications, are the basic moral laws upon which every decent society must be founded, if it is not to become a jungle of inhumanity and lawlessness.

"Needless to say that a Jew who occupies a special position in society has even a greater obligation to spread the light of the Torah and *mitzvot*, not only among fellow Jews but also promote the above mentioned basic laws of the society at large. While the adherence to the Torah and *mitzvot* is a must for its own sake, it is well to remember that this is also the channel to receive G-d's blessings in all means, and every increased effort in this direction widens these channels."

205   In another case, the Rebbe offered similar counsel to veteran Israeli opinion journalist Moshe Ishon, who was having trouble deciding between two prestigious jobs: to become editor-in-chief of the Israeli daily newspaper *Hatzofeh* or to serve on the board of the Jewish Agency.

The Rebbe's answer was swift and direct—he should continue in journalism, which he saw as a role privileged with greater influence.

"A journalist who knows his role and mission has the power to influence, change, and guide public opinion." Chabad.org/1367241

206   myencounterblog.com/?p=4246.

207   *Turning Judaism Outward*, p. 355; Chabad.org/878369

208   *Torat Menachem – Hitvaaduyot* 5743, vol. 3, p. 1208ff. (Chabad. org/6011409, *se'if* 9), and p. 1335ff. (Chabad.org/6011413, *se'if* 43).

209   *Seeds of Wisdom*, vol. 1, p. 31.

210   *Torat Menachem*, vol. 27, pp. 214-216 (Chabad.org/4280442, *se'if* 48-9).

211   Esther 1:6 (Chabad.org/16474).

212   Ibid.

213   Ibid. v. 5.

214   Chabad.org/1451460; Chabad.org/5989478, *se'if* 25.

215   So important was this duty that the Rebbe once suggested it was to be found in the Ten Commandments! Once, in conversation, he revealed that the third commandment, *You shall not take the name of the L-rd, your G-d, in vain*, conceals a deep meaning relevant to the sacred duty of maximizing one's potential. "Each Jew carries G-d's name in their name. Each Jew carries an utterly unique mission. Each Jew carries a purpose. Do not forget that! Do not carry that spark of G-dliness in vain. You're too precious to not take advantage of the G-dliness that you carry within."

216   *Torat Menachem – Hitvaaduyot*, vol. 3, p. 1661 (Chabad.org/5996592); jemtv.page.link/guj8.

217 Elsewhere, in a letter written to man who felt his life was meaningless, the Rebbe wrote:

"The purpose of life on this earth is to make it a fitting abode for the Divine Presence, which requires that it be a world where justice, decency, and benevolence reign supreme. Everyone is expected to work for the realization of these ideals to the maximum degree—first and foremost in one's personal life, and through influencing the environment in this direction."

218 Chabad.org/1878120

219 Per the Rebbe's oft-repeated blessing, "May you go from strength to strength."

220 From a letter written by the Rebbe to Mrs. Groner, dated 11 Cheshvan 5722 [1961].

221 Jemcentral.org/wp-content/uploads/2022/03/479.-Tzav-5782.pdf.

222 This exchange took place between the Rebbe and Mr. Binyomin Specter on September 17, 1989, as seen in a video published by JEM titled *Never Enough* (Chabad.org/2243630).

223 11 Nissan 5732 (1972); Chabad.org/5989373

224 Chabad.org/4425430

225 Chabad.org/4098684; Jemtv.page.link/6Y39.

226 Chabad.org/1043183

227 This idea would become a dominant theme in *Hayom Yom* and would surface again and again throughout the book. For example:

"A person who believes in Divine Providence knows that *the steps of man are made firm by G-d.* [A person goes to] a particular place because his soul must refine and perfect something there. For hundreds of years, or even from the very beginning of creation, the object that must be refined or rectified waits for that soul to come and do that task.

Similarly, this soul itself, from the moment of its emanation and creation, awaits the time that it will descend [to the physical world] to refine and perfect that which has been assigned to it" [*Hayom Yom*, 3 Elul; Chabad.org/3316880].

228 *It was told to Laban...that Jacob had fled...He pursued after him a seven days' journey, and he overtook him on the mountain of Gilead* (Genesis 31:22-23).

Jacob had left behind holy letters that he had not yet extracted from Laban. This is why Laban pursued him—to give him the letters that remained with him. An entire chapter was added to the Torah for these letters (The Maggid of Mezeritch (*Maggid Devarav L'Yaakov*, p. 303 (Kehot, 2009)).

229 Chabad.org/2855443

230 When a Jew finds themselves in an undesirable situation, it isn't just by

happenstance, G-d forbid. And it is not intended simply to cause pain or grief, G-d forbid. You have to think of it as a Divine mission.

231 Every Jew has to know that wherever you find yourself, and in whatever circumstance you find yourself, you have a mission to do there. And while it might be cloaked in a situation where G-d seems concealed, you could certainly accomplish it, because as G-d's emissary, you have been empowered by G-d himself to carry it out.

232 myencounterblog.com/?p=4131.

233 Chabad.org/3752414

234 www.theyeshiva.net/jewish/item/7192 .

235 In the discourse *Vayachalom*. It was first delivered privately to his son, the sixth Lubavitcher Rebbe, R. Yosef Yitzchak, who later published it in his *Sefer Hamaamarim* 5708 [1948]. See p. 88ff. there; see also the entry for 5 Adar I; Chabad.org/3316640

236 From a talk the Rebbe gave on December 26, 1986. Audio of the talk can be accessed at videos.jem.tv/video-player?produced=3231&utm_source=email&utm_medium=social%20 media&utm_campaign=1032.

237 myencounterblog.com/wp-content/uploads/2017/05/228.-Behar-Bechukosai-5777.pdf.

238 A similar story was told by R. Marvin Tokayer, who spent thirty years as a rabbi in the Far East. You can access his interview at Chabad.org/1565878

239 Chabad.org/5355428; myencounterblog.com/wp-content/ uploads/2017/05/228.-Behar-Bechukosai-5777.pdf.

240 Jemcentral.org/wp-content/uploads/2022/05/488.-Behar-5782.pdf.

241 From a talk of the Rebbe given on 14 Tamuz 5746 (July 21, 1986). Audio of the talk can be accessed at videos.jem.tv/video-player?produced=3231&utm_source=email&utm_medium=social%20 media&utm_campaign=1032.

242 Genesis 28:16-17.

243 During Communist rule in Ukraine and elsewhere, Torah study was forbidden by the government authorities. Jewish schools were established in hiding, "underground," because of the grave danger and risk for both the organizers and the participants. This boy had attended one such school.

244 portraitofaleader.blogspot.com/2011_06_19_archive.html.

245 "When I spoke with my uncle about his wedding, I thought about what the Rebbe had said to my grandfather, and I put the following information together:

"When my grandfather went for his visa to the US for the first time, he was refused. The people at the American Embassy in Israel saw that he was a former Russian citizen, and in light of the tension between the United States and Russia at the time, that was reason enough to be refused a visa. The Americans were afraid to allow possible Russian spies into the country.

"My grandfather was turned down again and again, and he despaired of being able to attend his son's wedding. The groom went to America by himself, and the family made peace with the fact that his father would not be attending. A few days before the wedding, the American Embassy contacted him and said he could submit another request. He did so, and this time the visa was granted.

"When the family reviewed what the Rebbe had said to my grandfather, they realized that Divine Providence had orchestrated matters so he could travel to the United States in order to save that Jew and not necessarily because of the wedding of his son" https://portraitofaleader. blogspot.com/2011_06_19_archive.html.

246 *Pitgamin Kadishin*, p. 16; valleybeitmidrash.org/wp-content/ uploads/2016/07/VBM-COURSE-WHAT-IS-THE-SOUL_.pdf.

247 As the Rebbe once observed: "First and foremost, a Jew is G-d's emissary, wherever they find themselves, to fulfill the mission given to them by G-d. Like the teaching of the Baal Shem Tov, which my father-in-law, the Rebbe, repeated, [on the verse] *Man's steps are determined by G-d*—wherever you go, and in whatever situation you find yourself, you must bring G-dliness with you" videos.jem.tv/ video-player?produced=2187.

248 Based on *Avot* 6:6.

249 Chabad.org/5036770

250 In the words of the sixth Lubavitcher Rebbe, R. Yosef Yitzchak, and referenced by the Rebbe: "...In the realm of souls, one cannot draw a line [of distinction] between a Torah scholar's soul and other souls... Likewise, in their manifest [and embodied] state, the Alter Rebbe revealed, there is no difference between one soul and another...Every soul has its *shlichut*, its unique mission, and as far as the empowering input of the One Who dispatches them is concerned, all souls are equal, each soul having been sent down to fulfill its own distinctive mission." For a beautiful story that illustrates this point, see Chabad.org /4743

251 myencounterblog.com/wp-content/uploads/2020/02/369.- Beshalach-5780.pdf; *Igrot Kodesh*, vol. 16, p. 338 (Chabad.org/5071136).

252 *Hamashpia, R. Shlomo Chaim Kesselman*, vol. 2, p. 727.

253 A beautiful illustration of this powerful idea is the story of a young *yeshivah* student who, despite his best efforts, was only academically average. He felt badly about not achieving the level of scholastic excellence he aspired to based on the expectations of his family and

community, which caused him to fall into a depression. When one of his peers asked him what happened, he explained that he had gone to the dean to discuss his gnawing feelings of inadequacy, failure, and fear that he would never achieve the Torah renown he so desperately hoped for.

Trying to comfort him, the dean explained that even if he never became a Torah scholar or teacher himself, he could always go into business and use his success to support other Torah scholars and institutions.

Although well intentioned, these "comforting words" caused the young student to fall even deeper into despair. He had been raised with the belief that the highest achievement attainable was to be a great Torah scholar. Now he was being told that this childhood dream and aspiration was beyond his abilities, and at most he could support the achievements of others.

The friend to whom he had unburdened himself advised him to write a letter to the Rebbe to express his bitter feelings, which he did.

The Rebbe wrote back the following:

"There is a Mishnah that clearly articulates the mission statement of human existence: 'I was created to serve my Creator (Kiddushin 82a).'

"According to this simple but profound teaching, the goal of all human existence, our raison d'être, is to serve Gd. There are numerous pathways to do so. One of them is the study of Torah, but another, just as important, is the support of Torah study.

"Some personalities and abilities are well suited for one particular path, and others are better suited for another path, but the end goal for all human beings is the same, no matter the path.

"Our unique abilities are Gd's way of teaching us which pathway toward that universal goal is right for us."

The Rebbe's letter completely reframed the young student's understanding of his life's purpose and redirected his aspirations and ambitions.

254 *Hayom Yom*, 25 Nisan; Chabad.org/3316193.

255 R. Alter B. Metzger once shared the story of a scholar who asked the Rebbe, "It is said in certain sources that the great Kabbalist R. Shlomo Molcho (who was burned at the stake for maintaining his Jewish faith) reached the loftiest levels of holiness, yet in other texts it says that he did not fulfil his life's purpose?"

The Rebbe replied softly, "What is the contradiction...?"

256 From a talk given by the sixth Lubavitcher Rebbe, R. Yosef Yitzchak, on 12 Tamuz 5704 (*Sefer Hasichot* 5704, p. 154; Eng: Chabad.org/5175341, ch. 4).

257 12 Tamuz 5724 (Chabad.org/4304533, se'if 10); 12 Tamuz 5704

(*Sefer Hasichot* 5704, p. 154, Eng: Chabad.org/5175341 ch. 4); Chabad.org/114127.

258 Excerpt from an unsent letter, which can be found in *Moreh L'dor Navuch*, vol. 3, p. 196.

259 *Torat Menachem – Hitvaaduyot* 5742, vol. 2, p. 793; Chabad.org/3256477 (Living Torah (JEM), volume 151, episode 601).

260 *Avot* 4:1 (Chabad.org/2032).

261 From the *amidah* for *Shacharit* on Shabbat.

262 *Avot* 1:6 (Chabad.org/2165); see here Chabad.org/4928867

263 Jewish Educational Media, My Encounter interview with Mr. Charles Roth, March 2, 2010.

264 *Torat Menachem – Hitvaaduyot* 5747, vol. 2, p. 339; *Teshurah Hecht* 5776 p. 45.

265 *Torat Menachem* ibid., p. 631.

266 Ibid., vol. 1, p. 562.

267 "And if the rabbi says, 'I don't know,' that is a sign that in this matter, he is not a rabbi. What is this like? A doctor, whose job is to heal; as our Sages say: '*He shall certainly heal him*—we learn from this that a doctor is given permission (together with the ability) to heal.' Implicit is that if he says, 'I don't know how to heal this disease,' it is an indication that, in connection to this matter, he is not considered a doctor, and one must therefore seek another one. So, too, in our matter: You must search for another rabbi who will instruct you what to do in this matter. In the language of the Mishnah: 'Make for yourself a rabbi.' And since G-d tells us, 'I only request of you what is within your capabilities,' it is certain that you will succeed in finding a rabbi who will instruct you what to do.

268 Chabad.org/471223

269 Chabad.org/524749

270 *Teshurah Hecht* 5758, p. 13 (English side).

271 Chabad.org/ 1100022

272 Myencounterblog.com/?p=4353#more-4353.

273 R. Nachman of Breslov said that if someone does *hitbodedut*—deep meditative and introspective contemplation—for an hour every day, they are guaranteed to discover the reason why G-d brought them into the world (*Likkutei Moharan* §28).

274 We are told to appoint a *rav* for ourselves—but that is only after we work on it ourselves. Once we've found all the answers that we can, we should not convince ourselves that we know the answer to everything; rather, we should go to the *rav* for further guidance.

275 *Seeds of Wisdom*, vol. 2, p. 13.

276 www.meaningfullife.com/wp-content/uploads/woocommerce_
uploads/2016/02/E07_2016-Terumah_Center.doc.

277 rabbisacks.org/covenant-conversation/bamidbar/two-journeys

278 vialogue.wordpress.com/2012/01/22/
ted-alain-debotton-atheism-2-0-notes-review/

279 Another researcher, Deepak Malhotra of Harvard Business School,
found that Christians were three hundred percent more likely to give
charitable donations if the appeal was made on a Sunday than on any
other day of the week. Obviously, the participants did not change their
minds about the importance of charitable giving between one day and
the next. They were simply more likely to have attended church and
thought about G-d on Sunday. He referred to this phenomenon as "The
Sunday Effect."

280 Ecclesiastes 7:2.

281 Chabad.org/ 481233

282 See *Sefer Hasichot* 5748, vol. 2, p. 406.

283 Genesis 40:20.

284 As the Rebbe commented, "Even though in previous generations, this
was observed only by certain individuals and in a discreet manner, as
related by my father-in-law, the Rebbe. There will be those who will
object that until now this was never done. Nevertheless, it is obvious
that there are more negative influences and events, so that we must
increase in holiness on our part."

285 Chabad.org/ 481233

286 *Sichot Kodesh* 5724, p. 563. Kfar Chabad Magazine #1543 and #1712.
Teshura Slonim-Stein 5768.

287 The Rebbe once told R. Shmuel Lew that when he spoke on his birthday,
it would have a special impact because of his strong *mazal*.

288 ascentofsafed.com/Stories/Stories/5781/pdf/s1191RebbeAnimZemirot.
pdf

289 This conclusion may have been based on the following story: In the late
thirteenth century, it was forbidden for Jews to leave Germany without
express permission from the crown (which was usually not granted, as
Jews were considered property of the emperor). R. Meir of Rothenburg,
known as the Maharam, was the leading rabbi of the country, and in
his old age he decided to leave the rampant persecution of Europe for
the Holy Land. He fled in secret, but he was recognized by an apostate
Jew and was imprisoned by Emperor Rudolph I, who demanded an
exorbitant ransom for R. Meir's release.

Although his student, R. Asher, known as the Rosh, succeeded in raising
the vast sum, R. Meir decreed that he not be ransomed for fear that this

would lead to the kidnapping of other leading rabbis in order to extort large sums of money from the already destitute Jewish community.

After seven years in prison, R. Meir passed away in his jail cell, but the authorities would not allow him to be taken for burial until the ransom was paid. It was only fourteen years later that a wealthy Jew named Alexander Wimpen redeemed R. Meir and had his body buried in the Jewish cemetery in Worms, Germany.

The great Chasid R. Hillel of Paritch related that a short time later, R. Meir appeared to Alexander in a dream and offered him two options. The first was that he and his descendants for all time would live lives of wealth and honor. The second was that he would pass from this world very soon and merit life in the World to Come right next to the holy abode of R. Meir.

Alexander chose the latter option.

R. Hillel concluded that Alexander only made that choice because this took place before the revelation of Chasidut. However, according to the path of Chasidut, he should have chosen the first option, for the Baal Shem Tov teaches us that actionable *mitzvot* done in this world are greater than the World to Come. As our Sages say, "One hour of repentance and good deeds in this world are greater than the entire life of the World to Come." (*Reshimot Devarim*, p. 248.)

290 Indeed, the Rebbe rooted this perspective in the example of Abraham, the father of Judaism, who, according to our Sages, daringly asked G-d to stand by while he attended to the needs of three strangers who arrived at his tent amid a Divine revelation. This act of holy chutzpah led our Sages to articulate one of Judaism's most radical axioms regarding spiritual prioritization: "This teaches us that receiving guests is greater than receiving the Divine Presence."

291 *Seeds of Wisdom*, vol. 1, p. 140.

292 *Bati L'gani* 5711, ch. 6 (Chabad.org/3797996).

293 See *Yoma* 84b (Chabad.org/5446486); *Shulchan Aruch Admor Hazaken* 328:13 (Chabad.org/4050903).

294 *Reshimat Hayoman*, p. 361 and fn. 1 (can be found at Chabad.org/2988496, p. 9).

295 The Rebbe himself demonstrated a similar, emphatic drive to serve the simplest needs of those around him, elevating the call to serve above all other duties, and he took every opportunity to remind others to do the same.

For example, he once asked a businessman visiting 770 how his livelihood was faring. The man, out of concern and respect for the Rebbe's time and holy workload, was reluctant to take the Rebbe's time for such matters. Sensing his hesitation and intuiting its source, the

Rebbe shared a story that happened during the intermediate days of Sukkot, during which Jewish law discourages worldly actions such as writing in order to protect the joy and sanctity of the festival.

"One Chol Hamoed day, I entered the office of my father-in-law, the [Previous] Rebbe, and was surprised to see him writing a letter. Glimpsing the letter more closely, I was even more surprised to see that it was about the recipient's employment.

"I asked him how he allowed himself to write a letter on Chol Hamoed on so mundane a matter. My father-in-law replied: "His material concern is my spiritual concern." See *Seeds of Wisdom*, vol. 2, p. 144.

296   Stories like this would become a cornerstone of the Rebbe's motivational theology as he doggedly pursued his quest to redirect a historically inward-looking and spiritually-focused religious community into an outward-focused global network of lamplighters and emissaries.

297   Chabad.org/3317509, fn. 3.

298   An acronym of **R. M**enachem **M**endel **Sch**neerson.

299   The Rebbe was so reluctant to take on a public role that at first he was even hesitant to immigrate to America! In the winter of 1940, R. Yosef Yitzchak's secretary, R. Yechezkel Feigin, wrote a letter to R. Yisrael Jacobson, the leading Chabad representative in America at the time, explaining that the Rebbe was reluctant to immigrate for fear of being asked to take on a leadership role and asking that R. Jacobson carefully try to convince the Rebbe that he was needed in America out of honor for his father-in-law, R. Yosef Yitzchak. See *Harif*, p. 17.

300   Exodus 3:11.

301   *Igrot Kodesh*, vol. 3, p. 260 ; ibid., p. 308.

302   *Yemei Bereishit*, p. 84.

303   See *My Rebbe*, p. 64, note 18, where the story is quoted in the name of the Rebbe's secretary, R. Leibel Groner, whose father was a member of the group.

304   From an interview with R. Yosef Wineberg, June 24, 2008, conducted by Jewish Educational Media.

305   *Rebbe: An Appreciation*, p. 21.

306   A further window into the inner world of the Rebbe is a fascinating response he wrote to his father-in-law, who had gently admonished him for not writing more often:

The Rebbe wrote, "The reason I have not written is due to the lack of interesting events to report. There are people for whom the central, overwhelming focus of their lives is in the world of thought, the world of ideas, and their main activities are focused inward and not to the outside world surrounding them.

"After this introduction, I must say that, while I do not consider it to be a particular virtue, it seems that—whether as a result of my natural disposition or outside influences—I am such a person." See *Turning Judaism Outward*, p. 99. *Igrot Kodesh by R. Yosef Yitzchak*, vol. 15, p. 78.

307 Indeed, for many, that pursuit is motivated by instincts of survival, not selfishness. And yet, somewhere along the journey, many who have come to internalize Hillel's first teaching, *"Im ein ani li, mi li?—*If I am not for myself, who will be for me?"—have lost sight of the profound wisdom in Hillel's second teaching: *"U'ch'she'ani l'atzmi, mah ani?"—*But if I am only for myself, what am I?"

308 Chabad.org/1102138; Chabad.org/3797996.

309 See, for example, *Lubavitcher Rebbe's Memoirs*, vol. 3, chs. 42-43; Chabad.org/6214323

310 See *Hatamim*, vol. 1, p. 13; Chabad.org/2529.

311 ascentofsafed.com/cgi-bin/ascent.cgi?Name=431-21. To read the letter in the original Yiddish, see *Hatamim*, p. 14.

312 *Hayom Yom*, 5 Iyar; Chabad.org/3316270

313 Zechariah 4:10.

314 See *Mechilta* and Rashi, Exodus 12:17.

315 *Torat Menachem*, vol. 33, pp. 199-205; Chabad.org/2987969

316 crownheights.info/something-jewish/596540

317 Chabad.org/247481

318 As the Alter Rebbe describes, your purpose, on an individual level, is defined in part by the assignment of particular commandments, which become a sort of spiritual specialty. This is the area where you become most "luminous"—where you are empowered to bring the most Divine light into creation. This principle also applies to the great commandment of our age, which, as we learned in previous chapters, is the age in which the Rebbe declared we would bring creation to its ultimate fulfillment. To that end, in our time, *tzedakah* becomes the ideal channel for G-d's light to flow into the world [*Tanya; Shabbat* 118b].

319 In fact, according to his secretaries, every moment of the Rebbe's spare time outside of his communal obligations was dedicated to Torah study. In his lifetime, the Rebbe taught Torah publicly for thousands of hours and produced dozens of written volumes and commentaries on the Torah, with hundreds more published posthumously based on his teachings.

320 *Tanya, Iggeret Hakodesh*, Epistle 9 (Chabad.org/7954).

321 Chabad.org/2025

322 Chabad.org/7916

323 19 Kislev 5734; Chabad.org/6131861, ch. 36.

324 *Sefer Hasichot* 5749, vol. 1, p. 2.

325 Chabad.org/4263864

326 *Igrot Kodesh*, vol. 32, p. 34; *Sefer Hasichot* 5751, vol. 1, p. 31; Chabad.org/2497564

327 See *Sefer Hasichot* 5747, vol. 1, p. 326; Chabad.org/2507272; Chabad.org/ 142437

328 Ibid., p. 239ff.

329 Chabad.org/839504 (Living Torah (JEM), volume 59, episode 234).

330 This encounter took place during Sunday Dollars on the morning of December 23, 1990.

331 As an example, the Rebbe's suggested this to the major benefactor of a new dormitory being built by Rabbi Yitzchok Dovid Grossman, when they came together to the Rebbe at "Sunday Dollars."

332 Chabad.org/ 363040

333 Proverbs 22:6.

334 *Shabbat Parshat Nitzavim-Vayelech* 5743, ch. 13; Chabad.org/6011442

335 Maasar or tithing is the term describing the Biblical commandment to give ten percent of one's income to charity.

336 Talk of the Rebbe on 7 Adar, 5748 (February 25, 1988).

337 *Sefer Hamaamarim* 5708, p. 191; Chabad.org/78968

338 Mishnah and *Beraita*, end of *Kiddushin*.

339 R. Jonathan Sacks, *On Celebrating Life*, p. 47-48.

340 www.theatlantic.com/health/archive/2013/01/ theres-more-to-life-than-being-happy/266805

341 www.gsb.stanford.edu/faculty-research/publications/ some-key-differences-between-happy-life-meaningful-life

342 *Science* magazine, for example, states that when individuals dole out money for gifts to friends or charitable donations, they get a measurable and notable boost to happiness, while those who spend on themselves get only a short-lived boost.

In another recent study, researchers discovered that those who spent more of their income on others, rather than themselves, enjoyed significantly greater and longer lasting happiness. In fact, as little as a five-dollar gift to someone else was enough to produce measurable increases in one's happiness. Overall, the self-reported happiness of those who regularly give charity is 43% higher than those who don't.

Other findings include lower depression rates among those who donate more than ten percent of their incomes. And giving away money isn't the only way to enjoy the benefits of generosity. People who are very giving in relationships—being emotionally available and hospitable—are much more likely to be in excellent health than those who are not.

343   greatergood.berkeley.edu/article/item/the_helpers_high

344   greatergood.berkeley.edu/article/item/how_to_make_giving_feel_good

345   From a letter dated 12 Cheshvan 5722.

346   See *"Marei Mekomos, Hagahos V'he'aros Ketzaros"* to *Tanya, Shaar Hayichud V'ha'emunah*, ch. 4.

347   Viktor E. Frankl, *Man's Search for Meaning*, p. 37.

348   A photocopy of this letter was published in *Kovetz Hashamayim Hachadashim* (Yeshivas Dovid Shlomo) - New Haven, 3 Tamuz 5783, p. 145.

349   Chabad.org/1853663

350   myencounterblog.com/?p=4246

351   See *Igrot Kodesh*, vol. 22, p. 227.

352   Chabad.org/ 4405202

353   *Derashah*, Yom Kippur: *Towards a Meaningful Life*, Mendel Kalmenson.

354   As told by R. Yaakov Biderman, accessible at Chabad.org/2243631

355   www.theyeshiva.net/jewish/item/896

356   *Seeds of Wisdom*, vol. 1, p. 177.

357   Chabad.org/412664 (Living Torah (JEM), volume 26, episode 101).

358   *Sefer Hasichot* 5748, vol. 2, p. 629.

359   11 Nissan 5716, the Rebbe's fifty-forth birthday—*Igrot Kodesh*, vol. 12, p. 414.

360   Conclusion of *Bati L'gani* 5711.

361   *Midrash Tanchuma, Bechukotai*, sec. 3; *Tanya*, chs. 33 and 36.

362   See *Torah Ohr* 5d.

363   The first can be seen in the story of the exile of the Jewish people in Egypt, which serves as the prototype for the many exiles and dispersions of the Jewish people. For all the suffering and sorrow they entailed, these disruptions and redistributions also served as catalysts and accelerators for the transition from a top-down to bottom-up model of redemption. Through this lens, what appears to be a series of trials becomes a set of necessary triggers for our transition from *mil'malah l'matah* to *mil'matah l'malah*.

From the perspective of Divine Providence, these exiles represented a journey consistent with a higher spiritual plan and trajectory.

In the following letter, the Rebbe elaborates on this notion, spelling out how this and each subsequent exile becomes an ultimately benevolent instrument dedicated to the redemption of creation:

"To be sure, we recognize the *galut* (exile) as a punishment and rectification for failures to live up to our obligations in the past as, indeed, we acknowledge in our prayers: 'For our sins we were banished from our land.' But punishment, according to our Torah, called *Torat Chesed* (a Torah of loving-kindness), must also essentially be *chesed*. Since G-d has ordained a certain group, or people, namely the Jewish people, to carry the difficult and challenging task of spreading—in all parts and remotest corners of the world—the Unity of G-d (true monotheism) through living and spreading the light of *Torah* and *mitzvot*, a task that no other group was willing or capable of carrying out—the greatest reward is the fulfillment of this destiny, or, as our Sages put it, "The reward of a mitzvah is the mitzvah itself." Thus, the ultimate purpose of *galut* is linked with our destiny to help bring humanity to a state of universal recognition of G-d" [crownheights. info/letter-and-spirit/505622].

364 *V'atah Tetzaveh* 5741, as paraphrased by Professor Herman Branover

365 *Torat Menachem*, vol. 2, p. 195.

366 Heard from R. Yaakov Shwei, of blessed memory. See also: blogs. timesofisrael.com/if-birds-can-fly-why-cant-we

367 *Torat Menachem – Hitvaaduyot*, vol. 2, p. 613ff.; Chabad.org/ 2506389

368 In the Rebbe's words: "Mashiach's coming is connected to the changes in the world, and we have now witnessed great changes, but Mashiach still has not come. This is proof that it now depends on every individual... Not knowing which deed, word, or thought will be the final one, start with one good deed, followed by another, and then another and another...And eventually you will merit that G-d will lead you to the precise action, word, or thought that will bring deliverance to yourself and the entire world—the true complete redemption through our righteous Mashiach! *L'chaim!*"

369 Chabad.org/ 4380025.

"Helping to Bring Mashiach," 5751 (1991). A free translation of this talk was published in *Sichos in English*, vol. 48 (Chabad.org/ 2487406).

370 *Torat Menachem – Hitvaduyot* 5751, vol. 3, pp. 115-119.

371 *Seeds of Wisdom*, vol. 1, p. 10.

372 *Avot* 1:17.

About the Author

RABBI MENDEL KALMENSON is the author of several best-selling books including Seeds of Wisdom, Time to Heal, Positivity Bias and People of the Word. Mendel was an editor at Chabad.org, has published hundreds of articles on Jewish thought, and his writings have been translated into nine languages.

Mendel and his wife Chana established Chabad Belgravia in London, where they live with their children.